Supreme Court Economic Review

VOLUME 27

Supreme Court

THE UNIVERSITY OF CHICAGO PRESS
Chicago and London

Economic Review

Supreme Court Economic Review, Number 27, 2019

Published annually by The University of Chicago Press.
www.journals.uchicago.edu/SCER/

Subscriptions: Individual subscription rates are $63 print + electronic and $41 e-only. Institutional print + electronic and e-only rates are tiered according to an institution's type and research output: $78 to $164 (print + electronic), $68–$143 (e-only). For additional information, including back-issue sales, classroom use, rates for single copies, and prices for institutional full-run access, please visit www.journals.uchicago.edu/SCER/. Free or deeply discounted access is available in most developing nations through the Chicago Emerging Nations Initiative (www.journals.uchicago.edu/ceni/).

Please direct subscription inquiries to Subscription Fulfillment, 1427 E. 60th Street, Chicago, IL 60637-2902. Telephone: (773) 753-3347 or toll free in the United States and Canada (877) 705-1878. Fax: (773) 753-0811 or toll-free (877) 705-1879. E-mail: subscriptions@press.uchicago.edu.

Standing orders: To place a standing order for this book series, please address your request to The University of Chicago Press, Chicago Distribution Center, Attn. Standing Orders/Customer Service, 11030 S. Langley Avenue, Chicago, IL 60628. Telephone toll free in the U.S. and Canada: 1-800-621-2736; or 1-773-702-7000. Fax toll free in the U.S. and Canada: 1-800-621-8476; or 1-773-702-7212.

Single-copy orders: In the U.S., Canada, and the rest of the world, order from your local bookseller or direct from The University of Chicago Press, Chicago Distribution Center, 11030 S. Langley Avenue, Chicago, IL 60628. Telephone toll free in the U.S. and Canada: 1-800-621-2736; or 1-773-702-7000. Fax toll free in the U.S. and Canada: 1-800-621-8476; or 1-773-702-7212. In the U.K. and Europe, order from your local bookseller or direct from The University of Chicago Press, c/o John Wiley Ltd. Distribution Center, 1 Oldlands Way, Bognor Regis, West Sussex PO22 9SA, UK. Telephone 01243 779777 or Fax 01243 820250. E-mail: cs-books@wiley.co.uk.

The University of Chicago Press offers bulk discounts on individual titles to Corporate, Premium and Gift accounts. For information, please write to Sales Department—Special Sales, The University of Chicago Press, 1427 E. 60th Street, Chicago, IL 60637 USA or telephone 1-773-702-7723.

This book was printed and bound in the United States of America.

ISSN: 0736-9921
E-ISSN: 2156-6208
ISBN-13: 978-0-226-70985-7 (hc.:alk.paper)
ISBN-13: 978-0-226-70999-4 (e-book)

Supreme Court Economic Review

The *Supreme Court Economic Review* (SCER) is an international peer-reviewed academic journal specializing in law and economics. The journal has frequently published work focusing on economic and social science analyses of judicial decision-making, institutional analyses of law and legal structures, political economy and public choice issues regarding courts and other decision-makers, and the relationship between legal and political institutions and the institutions of a free society governed by constitutions and the rule of law. The series also publishes special symposium issues that build on SCER's traditional focus on the intersection between law and economics. Contributors include renowned legal scholars, economists, and policy-makers.

Please direct any correspondence to:

Editor, Supreme Court Economic Review
George Mason University Antonin Scalia Law School
3301 North Fairfax Drive
Arlington, Virginia 22201-4498

Supreme Court Economic Review

Table of Contents

The Independence of Prosecutors and Government Accountability

*Jerg Gutmann**
Stefan Voigt

Prosecutors are immensely influential in every judicial system, yet very little is known about the impact of their organization. Here we ask two questions: (1) whether crimes committed by public officials are more likely to be prosecuted when prosecutors are independent and (2) whether this effect depends on the integrity of the prosecutors themselves. We use a novel indicator for prosecutorial independence based on data from the World Justice Project to answer these questions. We find that prosecutorial independence favors the prosecution of different types of public officials and that this effect appears to be conditional on the level of prosecutorial accountability.

"The economics of prosecutors is largely underdeveloped."

(Garoupa 2012, 239)

1. INTRODUCTION

It is generally agreed that prosecutors possess sweeping powers and abundant discretion regarding the use of these powers (e.g., Tonry 2012; Weigend 2012). If anything, their powers have increased in recent years, as governments have attempted to reduce the workload of judges by shifting additional competencies to prosecutors.

* Both authors are affiliated with the Institute of Law and Economics, University of Hamburg and CESifo. The authors thank an anonymous referee, Murat Mungan, Giovanni Ramello, Eric Talley, and the participants of the 4th Workshop on the Economic Analysis of Litigation for constructive feedback.

Electronically published: October 11, 2019
 978-0-226-64653-4/2019/0027-0001$10.00

Given how powerful prosecutors are, research devoted to them is unusually scare. Whereas research on both the efficiency of court systems and the economic effects of independent judges has made substantial progress over the past 10 years (Voigt [2016] is a survey of the former; Voigt, Gutmann, and Feld [2015] is a recent contribution to the latter), progress regarding the efficiency of prosecutorial agencies or the effects of prosecutorial independence (PI) has been significantly slower (Gordon and Huber [2009] is a survey on the political economy of prosecution).

There has been some research on the efficiency of prosecutorial offices, which demonstrates that prosecutors in areas with higher income, less minorities, and more economic freedom tend to be more efficient (Gorman and Ruggiero 2009; Detotto and McCannon 2017). Quite a number of studies have demonstrated that prosecutors rationally respond to incentives and, thus, care about elections (Dyke 2007; McCannon 2013; Bandyopadhyay and McCannon 2014, 2015; Nadel, Scaggs, and Bales 2017) and other career concerns (Boylan 2004, 2005; Boylan and Long 2005; Daughety and Reinganum 2016, 2018). None of these studies, however, have focused on questions of PI.

This article aims to make some progress in understanding the consequences of PI. Specifically, we use a novel indicator of PI to evaluate its effects on the accountability of government officials in terms of being prosecuted when suspected of a crime. PI is a crucial precondition for realizing the rule of law. That everybody, regardless of their position in society, is treated equally under the law can be considered the most important single trait of the rule of law. If, however, prosecutors are not independent from the government, then the rule of individuals will prevail over the rule of law, because the government can influence who is and who is not prosecuted.

It has even been argued that for politicians who are interested in reaching political goals via the judiciary, putting pressure on prosecutors—and, thus, tinkering with their independence—could be more attractive than trying to influence judges, simply because the latter would arouse a lot more opposition (Voigt and Wulf 2019). It has further been argued that the prosecution of political figures may depend critically on the independence of prosecutors (van Aaken, Salzberger, and Voigt 2004). However, Voigt and Gutmann (2015) provide empirical evidence for their argument that the independence of judicial actors only takes effect if they are also insulated from private economic interests. In other words, it is the combination of freedom from government influence and accountability that implies the integrity of judicial actors, which in turn is expected to have important economic effects.

Here we are interested in two questions. First, is PI an important determinant of the actual prosecution of public officials in case of detected misconduct? Whenever public officials are suspected of having committed a crime, such as having accepted bribes, we would expect a higher propensity of this case being prosecuted in a country where prosecutors are independent. Second, what happens if prosecutors are independent from government but lack accountability? If prosecutors accept bribes, for instance, for not prosecuting specific cases or for recommending inappropriate indictments, then the prosecution of cases against public officials might suffer even when there are high levels of PI. Thus, we inquire into whether the effect of PI on the prosecution of public officials is conditional on the level of prosecutorial accountability (PA).

It should be noted that our empirical analysis, although targeting a novel research question, has clear limitations. Our regression results are conditional correlations and their causal interpretation should be treated with caution. Moreover, the novel data by the World Justice Project (WJP), which we are analyzing here, still cover only a limited set of countries, raising concerns regarding degrees of freedom in our interaction analysis and regarding the external validity of our results.

What follows in section 2 is a brief summary of the available literature that deals with PI and its effects. In section 3,we introduce two new indicators based on data from the WJP, one for PI and the other one for PA. In section 4, these new indicators are used to answer our research questions. Section 5 concludes and sketches possible follow-up projects that could help improve our understanding of a powerful, yet under-researched, part of the justice system.

2. SURVEY OF THE LITERATURE

Following van Aaken, Feld, and Voigt (2010), we speak of prosecutors if they have the following competencies: (1) to gather information on the behavior of criminal suspects or to instruct the police to gather information, (2) to indict a suspect, and (3) to represent the interests of the public during a trial.

Next, we propose to think of PI as a state in which prosecutors have no reason to expect that their lawful professional activities will result in negative consequences for themselves, such as being expelled, being transferred to another position or location, or being paid less. PI, thus, refers to the relationship between prosecutors and the government and is logically distinct from the presence or absence of PA.[1] Clearly, prosecutors could be independent from governmental

[1] PA describes the expectation of a considerable loss in utility for a prosecutor if his or her behavior deviates too much from a generally recognized standard, that is, the letter of the law (see also Voigt 2008).

interference and still lack impartiality if they are willing to accept bribes or behave in other corrupt ways.

The only cross-country study of the effects of PI on public-sector corruption in the extant literature is van Aaken et al. (2010).[2] They argue that crimes committed by government officials are more likely to be prosecuted if the prosecutors enjoy independence from influence by the government. The nonprosecution of crimes increases the attractiveness of committing them, which is why van Aaken et al. (2010) expect a clear association between high levels of PI and low levels of public-sector corruption. They construct two measures of PI, one de jure and the other one de facto, and show that only higher levels of de facto PI are robustly associated with lower levels of perceived public-sector corruption.

Here we add to the literature in various ways. First, we use a new indicator of PI that is based on data from the WJP. Second, we explain the likelihood that corrupt public officials will be successfully prosecuted, once they have been detected, based on characteristics of prosecution agencies. As argued in the introductory section, the nonprosecution of corrupt officials is not necessarily a consequence of a lack of PI; it could also be the result of limited PA. In our analysis, we distinguish five types of officials and their respective likelihoods of being prosecuted if they are suspected of having committed a crime.

3. MEASURING PI AND PA

The two indicators used in our empirical analysis to represent the characteristics of prosecutors come from the WJP. This project was founded in 2006 and since 2008 produces an annual rule of law index. As the WJP began only recently to collect data for a large sample of countries and individual countries are only surveyed every 3 years, we cannot exploit longitudinal variation in the data. The index is made up of eight categories, such as "absence of corruption" or "criminal justice," and the underlying data come from surveys that are drawn from both the general population and legal country experts (see Botero, Nelson, and Pratt 2011). The Econometrics and Applied Statistics Unit of the European Commission's Joint Research Centre has evaluated and confirmed the statistical reliability of the data in multiple years. One important caveat is that like almost all available data on de facto institutional quality, such as the World Bank's Worldwide Governance Indicators or Transparency International's Corruption Perceptions Index, the WJP data used here are based on

[2] Gordon (2009) studies evidence for biased public prosecutors under different US presidents.

assessments by experts. Thus, it is not possible to completely rule out that the assessments are affected by subjective biases (see Gutmann, Padovano, and Voigt 2015).

The two indicators used here make PI and PA comparable across countries. Each of them is based on a specific question in one of the WJP's surveys.[3] These questions aim at identifying to what extent the "lack of independence of prosecutors" and the "corruption of prosecutors" constitute a problem for the criminal investigation system in the city in which the respondent lives. We use corruption of prosecutors as a proxy for PA, as we consider these concepts to be two sides of the same coin (see also Voigt 2008). However, we prefer to speak of PA here, because this aligns well with the coding of the indicator by the WJP (higher values reflect more accountability but less corruption), making it easier to interpret our results. To indicate the significance of the problem, the respondent can choose an integer value between 1 and 10 on a scale. The WJP then aggregates all responses to a continuous indicator at the country level, such that 0 indicates the absence of PI or PA, respectively, whereas 1 indicates a very high level of PI or PA. In other words, higher values on WJP indicators reflect a better quality of governance. All indicator values for the 99 countries in the sample are documented in table A1.

The bivariate correlation between PI and PA of 0.89 suggests that the accountability and independence of prosecutors are relatively closely aligned. Nevertheless, there are several countries whose performance in one of the two dimensions is more troublesome than that in the other dimension. This is visualized in figure 1. Some countries do a lot better regarding the independence of their prosecutors than regarding their integrity. Kyrgyzstan, Panama, Tanzania, and Uganda are the most obvious examples covered by WJP data. Prime examples of the opposite case are Georgia, Iran, Sri Lanka, and Turkey. These countries perform better in terms of accountability than regarding the independence of their prosecutors.

4. EFFECTS OF PI ON THE PROSECUTION OF PUBLIC OFFICIALS

Next, the two indicators that we introduced in the last section are used to answer the two main questions of this article. Namely, can PI explain the actual prosecution of public officials deemed corrupt or criminal, and is this effect conditional on PA? Equation (1) depicts the expected payoff from accepting bribes based on Becker's (1968) seminal economic model of crime. If $(1 - p)$ is the likelihood that criminal

[3] We thank Alejandro Ponce and the WJP for making the data available to us.

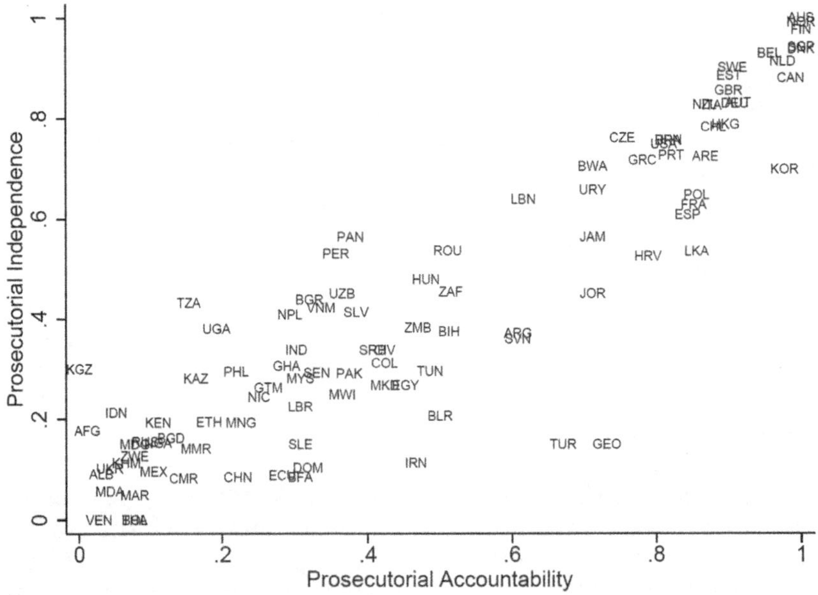

Figure 1. Prosecutorial independence and prosecutorial accountability across countries.

behavior is not detected, then the first term depicts the expected gain from being corrupt, whereas the second term describes the size of the threatened sanction if the corrupt practice is detected, which occurs with probability *p*:

$$\pi = (1 - p) \times \text{benefit} - p \times q \times \text{sanction}. \tag{1}$$

To date, studies working within this framework frequently calculate the expected cost of criminal behavior by multiplying the likelihood of being detected with the size of the sanction. Implicitly, it is assumed that detected crime is always punished, which shifts the focus of attention to issues of policing. But criminal justice systems are not perfect, and to make this explicit we add the probability q to the equation. This variable expresses the probability of a discovered criminal being prosecuted, sentenced, and punished. Because our focus is on both the independence as well as the accountability of prosecutors, q is interpreted here as the conditional probability that criminal behavior will be successfully prosecuted after it has been discovered. Our empirical analysis aims at measuring the importance of PI for the level of q. Thus, what distinguishes our model from many others in the literature is that we do not consider q to be purely stochastic, but we are proposing to endogenize it. It can then be expected that q is larger where prosecutors are more independent, at least if PA is sufficiently high. This would imply that increasing the independence and accountability of prosecutors is important as both are complementary instruments in deterring crime.

The WJP also produces indicators for the probability that criminal acts of various government officials are prosecuted in cases where they have been detected. These indicators reflect the prosecution of (1) high government officials, (2) legislators, (3) police officers, (4) local government officials, and (5) mayors. This means that we have five different continuous indicators for q. The WJP survey questions underlying these indicators are listed in table A2. In cases where more than one variable is available per category, for example, to measure the propensity that police officers are prosecuted, we simply take the mean value of these variables.

To inquire into the relevance of PI and PA for the level of q, we estimate the following model, once for each category of public officials:

$$q_i = \alpha + \beta \times \mathrm{PI}_i + \gamma \times \mathrm{PA}_i + \delta \times \mathrm{PI}_i \times \mathrm{PA}_i + \theta \times X_i + \varepsilon_i . \qquad (2)$$

Our vector of control variables X follows van Aaken et al. (2010) and includes a country's log-income per capita, trade openness, log-population size, share of Protestants in the population, and a dummy variable indicating whether the country was a British colony. Table 1 shows a correlation matrix based on these control variables and our two indicators of interest. As one would expect, countries with higher income per capita, more trade, and a larger share of Protestants in the population show higher levels of PI and PA. However, former British colonies do not perform better than other countries in terms of higher PI or PA.

Table 1. Correlation Matrix

	PI	PA	Income	Openness	Population	Protestants	Colony
PI	1	...					
PA	.89*	1	...				
Income	.27*	.28*	1	...			
Openness	.24*	.21*	−.24*	1	...		
Population	−.19	−.20*	.78*	−.47*	1	...	
Protestants	.50*	.42*	−.02	.04	−.21*	1	...
British colony	−.11	−.12	−.09	.00	.13	.04	1

Note: $n = 97$. PI = prosecutorial independence; PA = prosecutorial accountability.
$^*p < .05$.

Aside from the main effects of PI and PA, we also include an interaction term in equation (2). This allows us to estimate the conditional effect of PI on the prosecution of public officials, depending on the level of PA. As explained earlier, we expect that PI will only display an effect when PA is sufficiently high. However, before we test our conditional hypothesis, table 2 shows the regression results when controlling only for the level of PI and our vector of control variables *X*.

The results in table 2 are clear. In four out of five models, PI is statistically significantly correlated with a higher probability that government officials suspected of a crime are prosecuted and punished. Only for high-ranking government officers do we not find a statistically significant effect. Next, we try to ascertain whether the effect of PI is conditional on the level of PA.

The regression results including PA and an interaction term between PI and PA are displayed in table 3. Only in case of small-town mayors and local government officers do we find a significant interaction term, indicating that PI and PA function as complements in these cases. As it is well known that the interpretation of coefficient estimates for conditional effects can be complicated (see Brambor, Clark, and Golder 2006), we plot in figure 2 the marginal effects of PI on the propensity that public officials are being prosecuted, conditional on the level of PA and including 95% confidence intervals. The

Table 2. Propensity to Prosecute Public Officials

	(1)	(2)	(3)	(4)	(5)
PI	.067	.383***	.474***	.319***	.466***
	(.073)	(.075)	(.073)	(.073)	(.111)
Constant	.019	.210	−.148	−.051	−.029
	(.165)	(.150)	(.179)	(.146)	(.275)
Control variables	Yes	Yes	Yes	Yes	Yes
n	96	97	96	97	97
R^2	.349	.599	.708	.555	.527

Note: PI = prosecutorial independence. Ordinary least squares regression coefficients with robust standard errors in parentheses based on the sandwich estimator of variance, coefficient estimates for included control variables are omitted, dependent variables reflect the propensity that (1) high-ranking government officers, (2) members of the legislature, (3) police officers, (4) local government officers, and (5) small-town mayors are successfully prosecuted and punished.
***$p < .001$.

Table 3. Propensity to Prosecute Public Officials, Interaction Analysis

	(1)	(2)	(3)	(4)	(5)
PI	−.320	.120	.199	−.150	−.120
	(.194)	(.196)	(.163)	(.146)	(.230)
PA	.022	.059	.356**	.108	.017
	(.117)	(.138)	(.119)	(.128)	(.210)
PI × PA	.430	.250	−.020	.442*	.666*
	(.226)	(.230)	(.184)	(.175)	(.294)
Constant	.270	.375*	.012	.243	.346
	(.197)	(.184)	(.208)	(.168)	(.304)
Control variables	Yes	Yes	Yes	Yes	Yes
n	96	97	96	97	97
R^2	.388	.614	.752	.605	.563

Note: PI = prosecutorial independence; PA = prosecutorial accountability. Ordinary least squares regression coefficients with robust standard errors in parentheses based on the sandwich estimator of variance, coefficient estimates for included control variables are omitted, dependent variables reflect the propensity that (1) high-ranking government officers, (2) members of the legislature, (3) police officers, (4) local government officers, and (5) small-town mayors are successfully prosecuted and punished.
$^{*}p < .05$.
$^{**}p < .01$.

effects portrayed in these diagrams are statistically significant whenever zero is not enclosed in the confidence interval.

The results for members of parliament, local government officers, and mayors are in line with our theoretical predictions. PI increases the likelihood that these public officials are prosecuted in case they are suspected of criminal behavior, but only if prosecutors are sufficiently accountable. In other words, where prosecutors are corrupt, the accountability of government officials cannot be increased by merely enhancing the independence of prosecutors.

However, we find no statistically significant effect of PI on the prosecution of high-ranking government officers. Moreover, our empirical model has far less explanatory power for this indicator than for any of the other dependent variables. A possible interpretation is that the prosecution of such high-ranking government officers depends on factors other than the general level of PI.

We also find no statistically significant effect of PI on the prosecution of police officers, although our model can explain a large share

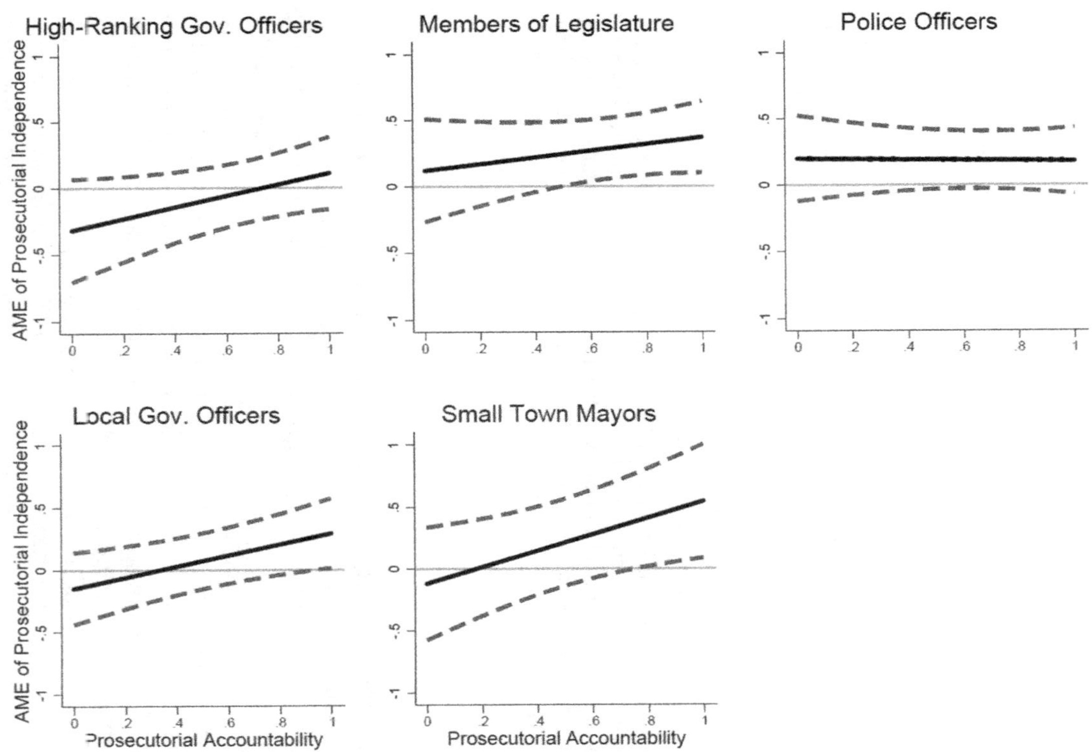

Figure 2. Average marginal effects (AME) of prosecutorial independence on the prosecution of government officials. Gov. = government. Color version available as an online enhancement.

of the variation in this indicator. We find that it is only PA that matters for the prosecution of police officers, independent of the level of PI (see model 3 in table 2). This means that police officers are prosecuted equally by dependent and independent public prosecutors, but they are less likely to be prosecuted when prosecutors are corrupt. This result makes intuitive sense, as police officers typically lack the necessary political influence to benefit from the nonindependence of prosecutors.

In table 4, we show the results of estimating our full model without the control variables in vector *X*. What speaks in favor of estimating this model specification is the high level of collinearity between PI and PA and our relatively small sample size. It is not surprising that our results are robust when omitting the control variables, and the interaction term is also statistically significant when high-ranking government officials or members of the legislature are suspected of a crime. Thus, table 4 suggests that for all categories of government officials except police officers does the effectiveness of PI presuppose

Table 4. Propensity to Prosecute Public Officials, No Control Variables

	(1)	(2)	(3)	(4)	(5)
PI	−.386	.102	.196	−.193	−.207
	(.205)	(.204)	(.153)	(.163)	(.221)
PA	−.081	−.051	.442***	.037	.011
	(.110)	(.130)	(.100)	(.121)	(.204)
PI × PA	.717**	.438*	−.008	.606***	.820***
	(.216)	(.217)	(.153)	(.169)	(.239)
Constant	.553***	.398***	.263***	.377***	.417***
	(.046)	(.050)	(.035)	(.041)	(.063)
Control variables	No	No	No	No	No
n	98	99	98	99	99
R^2	.310	.567	.742	.582	.553

Note: PI = prosecutorial independence; PA = prosecutorial accountability. Ordinary least squares regression coefficients with robust standard errors in parentheses based on the sandwich estimator of variance, coefficient estimates for included control variables are omitted, dependent variables reflect the propensity that (1) high-ranking government officers, (2) members of the legislature, (3) police officers, (4) local government officers, and (5) small-town mayors are successfully prosecuted and punished.
$^*p < .05$.
$^{**}p < .01$.
$^{***}p < .001$.

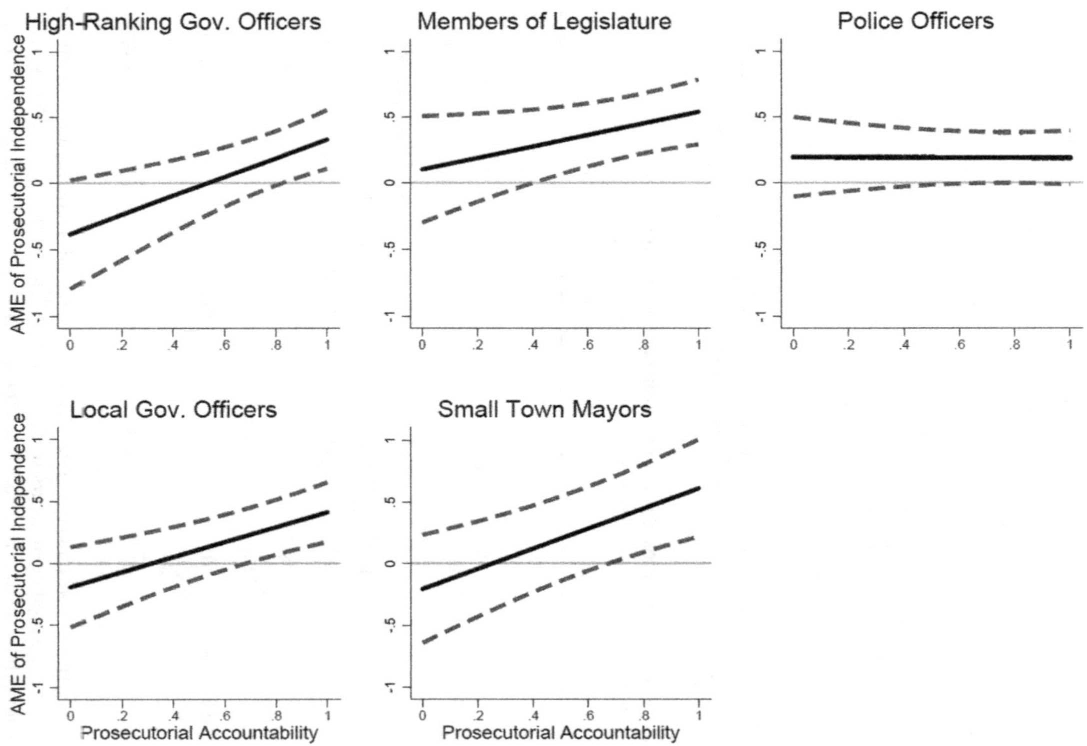

Figure 3. Average marginal effects (AME) of prosecutorial independence on the prosecution of government officials, no control variables. Gov. = government. Color version available as an online enhancement.

the existence of PA. The corresponding marginal effects are displayed in figure 3. Our results are also robust to other modifications. We have replaced the income and population data from the Penn World Tables with data from the World Bank. Instead of controlling for former British colonies, we have included a dummy variable based on La Porta et al. (1999) for common law legal systems.

Overall, our results suggest that PI is important for the successful prosecution of public officials suspected of criminal behavior and, hence, for the accountability of the government. Yet some high-ranking public employees might be sufficiently influential to get away with criminal behavior, even if prosecutors are formally independent. Our simple empirical model largely fails to predict the likelihood that these high-ranking government officers are prosecuted.

5. CONCLUSIONS AND NEXT STEPS

A few years back, Garoupa (2012) claimed that the economics of prosecutors is underdeveloped. It is about time to change this, because prosecutors enjoy a large degree of discretion and play an important part in establishing the rule of law. This study contributes to a new strand of literature that examines prosecutorial behavior under different organizational structures. As our analysis suffers from limitations in terms of sample size and causal identification, we are optimistic that future studies will be able to significantly enhance our understanding of the trade-offs involved in the organization of prosecutorial offices.

One interesting question that directly follows from our analysis concerns the determinants of PA. What factors cause the substantial differences in PA among countries such as Kyrgyzstan, Afghanistan, or Venezuela, on the one hand, and Australia, Denmark, Finland, Norway, or Singapore, on the other hand?

In terms of theory, the relationship between prosecutors and police can be analyzed as a principal-agent relationship. What are some possible solutions if the agent (the police) is corrupt? Perhaps setting up competing police organizations would have a positive impact on levels of corruption. If so, should they be based on geographical and/or functional criteria? What are possible solutions if prosecutors lack accountability? And so on.

PI is no panacea. Prosecutors might misuse their independence to prosecute crimes that have never been committed or not prosecute crimes that have been committed. They might do so to pursue their own political agenda. For example, prosecutors might choose the timing of their prosecutorial action strategically, as some have claimed regarding the announcement of FBI Director Comey shortly before the US presidential elections of 2016 that he would look into Hillary Clinton's past behavior (Silver 2017). Hence, research should pay more attention to instruments that hold independent prosecutors accountable without undermining their independence (see, e.g., Di Federico 1998; Rios-Fígueroa 2012; Michel 2017).

APPENDIX

Table A1. PI and PA Indicator Values

Country	PI	PA	Country	PI	PA	Country	PI	PA
Afghanistan	.177	.011	Germany	.830	.909	Norway	.992	1.000
Albania	.090	.031	Ghana	.306	.288	Pakistan	.291	.375
Argentina	.372	.608	Greece	.717	.781	Panama	.563	.377
Australia	1.000	1.000	Guatemala	.263	.263	Peru	.531	.357
Austria	.831	.913	Hong Kong	.789	.896	Philippines	.295	.219
Bangladesh	.163	.128	Hungary	.479	.481	Poland	.648	.856
Belarus	.207	.500	India	.338	.302	Portugal	.726	.821
Belgium	.930	.957	Indonesia	.213	.051	Romania	.537	.511
Bolivia	.000	.077	Iran	.113	.466	Russia	.155	.091
B-H	.376	.513	Italy	.826	.877	Senegal	.293	.331
Botswana	.704	.712	Jamaica	.563	.712	Serbia	.338	.407
Brazil	.756	.817	Japan	.757	.819	Sierra Leone	.150	.308
Bulgaria	.438	.321	Jordan	.451	.712	Singapore	.942	1.000
Burkina Faso	.085	.308	Kazakhstan	.282	.163	Slovenia	.361	.608
Cambodia	.113	.065	Kenya	.193	.110	South Africa	.454	.515
Cameroon	.082	.146	Korea, South	.699	.977	Spain	.608	.843
Canada	.880	.986	Kyrgyzstan	.300	.000	Sri Lanka	.535	.856
Chile	.783	.879	Lebanon	.638	.615	Sweden	.901	.906
China	.085	.221	Liberia	.225	.308	Tanzania	.432	.154
Colombia	.313	.423	Macedonia	.268	.423	Thailand	.000	.077
Cote d'Ivoire	.338	.423	Madagascar	.150	.077	Tunisia	.297	.486
Croatia	.526	.788	Malawi	.249	.365	Turkey	.150	.670
CR	.761	.753	Malaysia	.282	.308	Uganda	.380	.192
Denmark	.939	1.000	Mexico	.095	.104	Ukraine	.101	.042
DR	.102	.318	Moldova	.056	.042	UAE	.724	.868

Table A1. *(continued)*

Country	PI	PA	Country	PI	PA	Country	PI	PA
Ecuador	.088	.282	Mongolia	.193	.225	UK	.856	.900
Egypt	.268	.452	Morocco	.048	.077	United States	.748	.810
El Salvador	.413	.385	Myanmar	.141	.163	Uruguay	.657	.712
Estonia	.885	.901	Nepal	.408	.293	Uzbekistan	.451	.365
Ethiopia	.195	.182	Netherlands	.914	.974	Venezuela	.000	.027
Finland	.977	1.000	New Zealand	.827	.867	Vietnam	.423	.337
France	.628	.852	Nicaragua	.244	.250	Zambia	.383	.469
Georgia	.150	.731	Nigeria	.153	.110	Zimbabwe	.127	.077

Note: PI = prosecutorial independence; PA = prosecutorial accountability (higher values indicate higher governance quality); B-H = Bosnia and Herzegovina; CR = Czech Republic; DR = Dominican Republic; UAE = United Arab Emirates; UK = United Kingdom.

Table A2. Description of Variables

Variable	Description
PI	WJP-expert survey: The following question aims at identifying the main problems faced by the criminal investigation system in your country. Please tell us how significant are the following problems for the criminal investigative services in the city where you live: Lack of independence of prosecutors.
PA	WJP-expert survey: The following question aims at identifying the main problems faced by the criminal investigation system in your country. Please tell us how significant are the following problems for the criminal investigative services in the city where you live: Corruption of prosecutors.
Prosecution: high-ranking government officer	WJP-population survey: Please assume that a high-ranking government officer is taking government money for personal benefit. Please also assume that one of his employees witnesses this conduct, reports it to the relevant authority, and provides sufficient evidence to prove it. Please assume that the press obtains the information and publishes the story. Which one of the following outcomes is most likely? (*a*) The accusation is completely ignored by the authorities; (*b*) an investigation is opened, but it never reaches any conclusions; or (*c*) the high-ranking government officer is prosecuted and punished.

Table A2. *(continued)*

Variable	Description
Prosecution: member of legislature	WJP-expert survey: In practice, members of the legislature who commit crimes are prosecuted and punished.
Prosecution: police officer (I)	WJP-expert survey: Assume that a high-ranking police officer is found by a newspaper reporter to be taking money from a criminal organization. Assume that there is enough evidence to prosecute and convict. Which of the following outcomes is most likely? (*a*) The accusation is completely ignored by the authorities; (*b*) an investigation is opened, but it never reaches any conclusions; (*c*) the high-ranking police officer is prosecuted and punished; or (*d*) don't know.
Prosecution: police officer (II)	WJP-expert survey: Assume that a police officer inflicts severe physical harm on a criminal suspect to obtain a confession. Assume that the criminal suspect files a formal complaint with the competent authority (prosecutor, judge, ombudsman, etc.), and provides sufficient evidence to prove the case. Which one of the following outcomes is most likely? (*a*) The accusation is completely ignored by the authorities; (*b*) an investigation is opened, but it never reaches any conclusions; (*c*) the police officer is prosecuted and punished; or (*d*) don't know.
Prosecution: police officer (III)	WJP-expert survey: In practice, police officers who commit crimes are prosecuted and punished.
Prosecution: local government officer (I + II)	WJP-expert survey and WJP-population survey: Assume that, as a result of an audit, a local government officer is found to be unlawfully issuing a government license for personal benefit, for example, to a construction company owned by a family member. Which one of the following outcomes is most likely? (*a*) The accusation is completely ignored by the authorities; (*b*) an investigation is opened, but it never reaches any conclusions; (*c*) the local government officer is prosecuted and punished; or (*d*) don't know.
Prosecution: small-town mayor	WJP-expert survey: Assume that the mayor of a small town in your country is taking government money for personal benefit. Please also assume that one of the mayor's employees witnesses this conduct, reports it to the relevant authority, and provides sufficient evidence to prove it. Assume that the press obtains the information and publishes the story. Which one of the following outcomes is most likely? (*a*) The accusation is completely ignored by the authorities; (*b*) an investigation is opened, but it never reaches any conclusions; (*c*) the mayor is prosecuted and punished; or (*d*) don't know.
Income	Log-income per capita (Feenstra, Inklaar, and Timmer 2015)

Table A2. (*continued*)

Variable	Description
Openness	Sum of exports and imports of goods and services measured as a share of GDP (World Bank 2019)
Population	Log-population size (Feenstra et al. 2015)
Protestants	Protestants as share of the population in 1980 (La Porta et al. 1999)
British colony	British colonial origin. In cases of several colonial powers, the last one is counted, if it lasted for 10 years or longer (Hadenius and Teorell 2007)

Note: PI = prosecutorial independence; WJP = World Justice Project; PA = prosecutorial accountability.

REFERENCES

Bandyopadhyay, Siddhartha, and Bryan C. McCannon. 2014. "The Effect of the Election of Prosecutors on Criminal Trials." *Public Choice* 161 (1/2): 141–56.

———. 2015. "Prosecutorial Retention: Signaling by Trial." *Journal of Public Economic Theory* 17 (2): 219–56.

Becker, Gary S. 1968. "Crime and Punishment: An Economic Approach." *Journal of Political Economy* 76 (2): 169–217.

Botero, Juan C., Robert L. Nelson, and Christine Pratt. 2011. "Indices and Indicators of Justice, Governance, and the Rule of Law: An Overview." *Hague Journal on the Rule of Law* 3 (2): 153–69.

Boylan, Richard T. 2004. "Salaries, Turnover, and Performance in the Federal Criminal Justice System." *Journal of Law and Economics* 47 (1): 75–92.

———. 2005. "What Do Prosecutors Maximize? Evidence from the Careers of US Attorneys." *American Law and Economics Review* 7 (2): 379–402.

Boylan, Richard T., and Cheryl X. Long. 2005. "Salaries, Plea Rates, and the Career Objectives of Federal Prosecutors." *Journal of Law and Economics* 48 (2): 627–51.

Brambor, Thomas, William R. Clark, and Matt Golder. 2006. "Understanding Interaction Models: Improving Empirical Analyses." *Political Analysis* 14 (1): 63–82.

Daughety, Andrew F., and Jennifer F. Reinganum. 2016. "Informal Sanctions on Prosecutors and Defendants and the Disposition of Criminal Cases." *Journal of Law, Economics, and Organization* 32 (2): 359–94.

———. 2018. "Evidence Suppression by Prosecutors: Violations of the Brady Rule." *Journal of Law, Economics, and Organization* 34 (3): 475–510.

Detotto, Claudio, and Bryan C. McCannon. 2017. "Economic Freedom and Public, Non-Market Institutions: Evidence from Criminal Prosecution." *Economics of Governance* 18 (2): 107–28.

Di Federico, Giuseppe. 1998. "Prosecutorial Independence and the Democratic Requirement of Accountability in Italy: Analysis of a Deviant Case in a Comparative Perspective." *British Journal of Criminology* 38 (3): 371–87.

Dyke, Andrew. 2007. "Electoral Cycles in the Administration of Criminal Justice." *Public Choice* 133 (3–4): 417–37.

Feenstra, Robert C., Robert Inklaar, and Marcel P. Timmer. 2015. "The Next Generation of the Penn World Table." *American Economic Review* 105 (10): 3150–82.

Garoupa, Nuno. 2012. "The Economics of Prosecutors." In *Research Handbook on the Economics of Criminal Law*, edited by Alon Harel and Keith N. Hylton, 231–42. Cheltenham: Edward Elgar.

Gordon, Sanford C. 2009. "Assessing Partisan Bias in Federal Public Corruption Prosecutions." *American Political Science Review* 103 (4): 534–54.

Gordon, Sanford C., and Gregory A. Huber. 2009. "The Political Economy of Prosecution." *Annual Review of Law and Social Science* 5:135–56.

Gorman, Michael F., and John Ruggiero. 2009. "Evaluating US Judicial District Prosecutor Performance Using DEA: Are Disadvantaged Counties More Inefficient?" *European Journal of Law and Economics* 27 (3): 275–83.

Gutmann, Jerg, Fabio Padovano, and Stefan Voigt. 2015. *Perception vs. Experience: Explaining Differences in Corruption Measures Using Microdata*. https://doi.org/10.2139/ssrn.2659349.

Hadenius, Axel, and Jan Teorell. 2007. "Pathways from Authoritarianism." *Journal of Democracy* 18 (1): 143–57.

La Porta, Rafael, Florencio Lopez-de-Silanes, Andrei Shleifer, and Robert Vishny. 1999. "The Quality of Government." *Journal of Law, Economics, and Organization* 15 (1): 222–79.

McCannon, Bryan C. 2013. "Prosecutor Elections, Mistakes, and Appeals." *Journal of Empirical Legal Studies* 10 (4): 696–714.

Michel, Verónica. 2017. "The Role of Prosecutorial Independence and Prosecutorial Accountability in Domestic Human Rights Trials." *Journal of Human Rights* 16 (2): 193–219.

Nadel, Melissa R., Samuel J. A. Scaggs, and William D. Bales. 2017. "Politics in Punishment: The Effect of the State Attorney Election

Cycle on Conviction and Sentencing Outcomes in Florida." *American Journal of Criminal Justice* 42 (4): 845–62.

Rios-Fígueroa, Julio. 2012. "Justice System Institutions and Corruption Control: Evidence from Latin America." *Justice System Journal* 33 (2): 195–214.

Silver, Nate. 2017. "The Comey Letter Probably Cost Clinton the Election—So Why Won't the Media Admit as Much?" *FiveThirtyEight*, May 3.

Tonry, Michael. 2012. "Prosecutors and Politics in Comparative Perspective." *Crime and Justice* 41 (1): 1–33.

van Aaken, Anne, Lars P. Feld, and Stefan Voigt. 2010. "Do Independent Prosecutors Deter Political Corruption? An Empirical Evaluation across Seventy-Eight Countries." *American Law and Economics Review* 12 (1): 204–44.

van Aaken, Anne, Eli Salzberger, and Stefan Voigt. 2004. "The Prosecution of Public Figures and the Separation of Powers. Confusion within the Executive Branch: A Conceptual Framework." *Constitutional Political Economy* 15 (3): 261–80.

Voigt, Stefan. 2008. "The Economic Effects of Judicial Accountability: Cross-Country Evidence." *European Journal of Law and Economics* 25 (2): 95–123.

———. 2016. "Determinants of Judicial Efficiency: A Survey." *European Journal of Law and Economics* 42 (2): 183–208.

Voigt, Stefan, and Jerg Gutmann. 2015. "On the Wrong Side of the Law—Causes and Consequences of a Corrupt Judiciary." *International Review of Law and Economics* 43:156–66.

Voigt, Stefan, Jerg Gutmann, and Lars P. Feld. 2015. "Economic Growth and Judicial Independence, a Dozen Years On: Cross-Country Evidence Using an Updated Set of Indicators." *European Journal of Political Economy* 38:197–211.

Voigt, Stefan, and Alexander J. Wulf. 2019. "What Makes Prosecutors Independent? Analysing the Institutional Determinants of Prosecutorial Independence." *Journal of Institutional Economics* 15 (1): 99–120.

Weigend, Thomas. 2012. "A Judge by Another Name? Comparative Perspectives on the Role of the Public Prosecutor." In *The Prosecutor in Transnational Perspective*, edited by Erik Luna and Marianne L. Wade, 377–91. New York: Oxford University Press.

World Bank. 2019. *World Development Indicators*. Washington, DC: World Bank.

Comment on "The Independence of Prosecutors and Government Accountability"

*Alexander Lundberg**

My goal in this comment is merely to provide context for the contribution of this work. Gutmann and Voigt lead with a quote by Garoupa (2012): "The economics of prosecutors is largely underdeveloped" (239). I agree. Game-theoretic models of the plea bargain are the only well-developed knowledge of prosecutor behavior, and even there, work remains to be done.

Fortunately, economists do understand the importance of the prosecutor in modern society. Prosecutors wield tremendous discretion. They choose whether to file charges, what charges to file, and, with the power to negotiate guilty pleas for lesser sanctions, they largely determine what sentences citizens will receive. In a recent sample of 90 countries, 66 have instituted a trial waiver system in which defendants can waive their right to trial in exchange for lesser sanctions (Fair Trials 2017).

In the international context, Gutmann and Voigt focus on two understudied features of prosecutor behavior. The first is prosecutor independence (similar to the independence of the judiciary from other government actors). The other is prosecutor accountability, as measured by the absence of prosecutor corruption. They find the latter mediates the impact of the former on the likelihood of formal charges against government officials who engage in misconduct. This finding is the key contribution over the only other empirical study on the relationship between prosecutor independence and charges against

* Department of Economics, West Virginia University, Morgantown. Email: alexander.lundberg@mail.wvu.edu.

Electronically published: December 3, 2019
 978-0-226-64653-4/2019/0027-0002$10.00

government officials (van Aaken, Feld, and Voigt 2010). Independence only increases the likelihood of charges when accountability is high.

On a minor point, I might employ a different terminology for accountability here. The idea is that prosecutors may accept bribes to decline to file charges against powerful officials. Law enforcement can deter such bribes by holding prosecutors accountable. The empirical measure of "accountability," which is based on a low perception of prosecutor corruption, should then go up. This line of thought is perfectly reasonable, but I might choose a term like "integrity" over accountability, even if only as a nod to the US system.

To the best of my knowledge, the United States is unique in its predominant reliance on general elections for prosecutors, who are therefore accountable to voters. (Naturally, the strength of the accountability mechanism is debatable [e.g., Gordon and Huber 2009].) For better or worse, however, economic research on prosecutors has focused heavily on the United States. If the economics of prosecutors is largely underdeveloped, the economics of prosecutors in the international context is woefully underdeveloped. Gutmann and Voigt contribute to the literature by exploring the role of independence on prosecutor behavior, an already understudied topic, in an understudied global arena.

In cross-country regressions, Gutmann and Voigt find independence only predicts the probability that a government official will be prosecuted for misconduct when perceptions of prosecutor corruption are low. The data come from surveys of legal experts in each country conducted by the World Justice Project. Respondents state whether they believe government officials would be prosecuted in cases of known misconduct. Separate questions address high government officials, legislators, police officers, local government officials, and mayors. For all but police officers, the conclusion is roughly consistent. As long as prosecutors are not too corrupt, the more independence they have, the more likely they are expected to prosecute government officials. Conveniently, the survey posits cases of misconduct with perfect evidence to convict, so any decision not to pursue charges must depend on extralegal considerations.

For police officers, prosecutor independence has no effect on the decision to file charges, but accountability does. Loosely, this result is a reversal of those for other government officials. One explanation for the departure lies in the additional questions asked on police officers in the survey. For the other types of government officials, the hypothetical misconduct is financial in nature, as in bribery. For police, one scenario is financial, but another concerns severe physical harm inflicted on a suspect to obtain a confession, and a third asks respondents whether they believe police officers are generally prosecuted for any crimes they commit. For physical harm on a suspect and the general perception of police accountability, prosecutor corruption may carry more weight than independence in the decision to file charges. At least, if respondents believe so, then any effect of accountability in the regressions would likely outweigh any effect of independence because (1) the dependent variable is a mean average over all responses and (2) accountability and independence are highly correlated with each other.

A more interesting possibility, as noted by the authors, is how the relationship between prosecutors and police differs from that of other government officials. I tend not to view prosecutors and police as members of a principal-agent relationship, however. I see the relationship as more cooperative. Unlike with other government officials, prosecutors have regular interactions with the police by necessity. According to the American Bar Association (2019), prosecutors should seek justice, not convictions. I believe most prosecutors and police do seek the goal of justice. They also have no choice but to rely on each other. Prosecutors rely on police to identify and apprehend offenders, and police rely on prosecutors to convict those offenders. For one illustration of the collaboration, a number of jurisdictions are experimenting with police involvement in the plea bargain process (Abel 2017). In addition, in low-level offenses, prosecutors rarely decline to charge individuals arrested by police, suggesting substantial agreement between the two parties (Natapoff 2015).

Although the nature of the police-prosecutor relationship may vary by country, I suspect the respondents in the survey rightly distinguish the relationship from those of prosecutors with other government officials in general. Independence is simply not a big factor in determining whether prosecutors file charges against police officers. Rather, a sense of integrity, which overcomes the risk of alienating those in a close working relationship, determines whether prosecutors file charges against police officers. At the very least, the empirical results are consistent with such a story. This is another reason I think prosecutor "integrity" rather than "accountability" might be a better term here.

Returning to a broader perspective on prosecutor independence, I think Gutmann and Voigt take a step forward in demonstrating the topic is worthy of study. Data limitations in any cross-country regression are clear, but the results here do suggest independence shapes prosecutor decision making. Of course, the conclusion is inferred from perceptions of prosecutor behavior in surveys of legal experts. The next step forward would be a test of how actual prosecutor behavior responds to independence.

To achieve that next step, the definitions of independence and accountability will require more precision. A conceptual model may be helpful. To me, the two concepts overlap, and their boundaries are vague. In some cases, a prosecutor may be accountable to a specific government official, as with US attorneys and the president, who retains the discretion to appoint and dismiss them. A conceptual model would help identify when and where independence and accountability can be distinguished from each other and, as with US attorneys, where they cannot be. Even if "accountability" is narrowly defined to mean prosecutors face criminal repercussions for bribery, an absence of accountability may not guarantee corruption in jurisdictions with cultures of high integrity.

Despite their ambiguity, I have no doubt that independence and accountability do influence prosecutors. If they can be defined more precisely, future research will be able to better identify the extent of their influence. The question is clearly relevant, even urgent, as calls for criminal justice reform spread across the United States and the world. Again, I commend Gutmann and Voigt for addressing prosecutors in the international context. Independence is an even greater topic of importance for many countries with less stable political institutions where corruption is relatively widespread. I look forward to future research on the subject.

REFERENCES

Abel, Jonathan. 2017. "Cops and Pleas: Police Officers' Influence on Plea Bargaining." *Yale Law Journal* 126 (6): 1730–87.

American Bar Association. 2019. "ABA Criminal Justice Section." https://www.americanbar.org/groups/criminal_justice/#1.4.

Fair Trials. 2017. "The Disappearing Trial." https://www.fairtrials.org/sites/default/files/publication_pdf/Report-The-Disappearing-Trial.pdf.

Garoupa, Nuno. 2012. "The Economics of Prosecutors." In *Research Handbook on the Economics of Criminal Law*, edited by Alon Harel and Keith N. Hylton, 231–42. Cheltenham: Edward Elgar.

Gordon, Sanford C., and Gregory A. Huber. 2009. "The Political Economy of Prosecution." *Annual Review of Law and Social Science* 5:135–56.

Natapoff, Alexandra. 2015. "Misdemeanors." *Annual Review of Law and Social Science* 11:255–67.

van Aaken, Anne, Lars P. Feld, and Stefan Voigt. 2010. "Do Independent Prosecutors Deter Political Corruption? An Empirical Evaluation across Seventy-Eight Countries." *American Law and Economics Review* 12 (1): 204–44.

A Stream That Rises above Its Source: Judicial Review from a Public Choice Perspective

*Michael C. Munger**

A typical discussion of judicial review pits the view of Alexander Hamilton in Federalist no. 78 (protection from the "cabals of a representative body") against the much more circumscribed view of Justice Owen Roberts ("lay the article of the Constitution which is invoked beside the statute which is challenged and decide whether the latter squares with the former"). This tension between two views informs much of the current debate over judicial review. But the "tension" is illusory; the real problem can be analyzed as a two-dimensional spatial problem, with participants having preferences over both the substantive issue being litigated and the principle of judicial review in the abstract. This article presents a set of results based on such a spatial analysis and considers an answer to the apparent paradox that judicial review may prevail

* Department of Political Science, and Department of Economics, Duke University. This paper was presented, over a period of years, at two meetings of the American Political Science Association and two meetings of the Public Choice Society. It was originally presented at the Judicial Review UNC Workshop in Law and Philosophy, October 18–22, 2002, National Humanities Center, Durham, NC. The author acknowledges the advice of John Aldrich, Stuart Benjamin, Erwin Chemerinsky, Scott de Marchi, Peter Fish, Thomas Husted, Kenneth Koford, Kristin Renberg, Christopher Schroeder, Edward Schwartz, Nicholas Tideman, Mark Tushnet, Georg Vanberg, Jonathan Weiner, and Steven Wilkinson. Particular thanks go to Dhammika Dharmapala and Jaclyn Moyer, who each made many different and helpful suggestions. It should be pointed out, however, that several of these people (particularly Messrs. Chemerinsky and Tushnet) really hated the paper a lot and are even less responsible for the result than the usual disclaimer implies. Still, the usual disclaimer applies.

Electronically published: October 11, 2019
 978-0-226-64653-4/2019/0027-0003$10.00

against political majorities for long periods. Furthermore, the results from the model indicate that any purely issue-oriented "median voter" approach to court voting is misspecified and will lead to incorrect predictions.

1. INTRODUCTION

> [The Supreme Court] has no *general power* of declaring acts of Congress unconstitutional, and . . . the source of that power lies in . . . *the necessity of doing justice to individuals and of securing to them their rights* against the tyrannical acts of Congress and other legislatures. But the stream cannot rise above its source; the power cannot extend beyond the necessity which creates it. That much the Supreme Court . . . [must] vehemently assert. As they must, in order to escape the charge of usurpation.
>
> (Boudin 1932, 21; emphasis in original)

Courts check the elected branches of government. This check is often called the power, or obligation, of "judicial review." The degree to which such a check is effective varies considerably in different constitutional systems (for historical reviews, see Tanenhaus 1968; Ramseyer 1994; Vanberg 2011). In the US system, where no check is absolute, judicial review is in some ways weakened by powers possessed by the other branches. Still, there is a difference in the check available to the courts, as identified by John Hart Ely (1980): "When a court invalidates an act of the political branches on constitutional grounds, however, it is overruling judgment [of the Congress], and normally doing so in a way that is not subject to 'correction' by the ordinary law-making process. Thus, the central function, and the central problem, of judicial review: a body that is not elected or otherwise politically responsible in any significant way is telling the people's elected representatives that they cannot govern as they'd like" (cited in Riker and Weingast 1988, 378).

If unelected judges can prevent elected representatives from governing "as they'd like," then doesn't that empower judges to rule as they like? Just what is "judicial review," and how does it apply to a constitutional system of checks and balances when all actors are acting in a self-interested fashion? In this article I present a theoretical representation of preference, equilibrium, and outcomes in judicial oversight of the legislative and executive branches. Justices are motivated by two considerations: their own political views and a desire to preserve the power and prestige of the Court. The "public choice" approach is well suited for using a spatial model to represent trade-offs between these two considerations.

My conclusion is not very controversial or insightful, but it is hoped that the clear means of representing the argument for that conclusion is of some value. It is likely that there are many people who have similar overall views of the value of policy and the value of stable institutions. What will vary is the attitude individuals have about the trade-off with some favoring ideological victories and some favoring preservation of tradition and precedent. Those who favor preserving precedent and prestige—what one might call the "legacy" of the Court—possess what is commonly called "the judicial temperament." My article argues that the judicial temperament is far more important than ideological conviction and offers an explanation for why many judges surprise those who appoint them. The policy implication is clear: Senate hearings should spend less time on trying to divine ideological views—and nominees are quite right to decline to answer such queries—and more time investigating the commitment of nominees to the legacy of the Court.

1.1. Defining Judicial Review

The power of the judiciary is hard to limit explicitly because it is hard to define precisely. But it is possible to offer some qualitative observations about the nature of judicial power. Consider the types of actions themselves:

- Courts can enjoin, either by prohibiting future or declaring void existing, acts of the legislature or actions of the executive.
- Courts can command, either (in effect) writing legislation through their decisions or by forcing states or officers of the executive branch to take specific actions.Second, there are the motivations of a court in contemplating these actions:
- The legislature, or executive, has acted in a way that violates the Constitution or the body of existing precedent interpreting that Constitution.[1]
- The legislature, or executive, has acted in a way that violates the political preferences and beliefs of a majority of the justices that constitute the "court."

This suggests a simple categorization of actions—and inaction—by the Court, as depicted in table 1. The two most interesting cells in table 1 are the northeast and southwest. If a judge thinks that a law or action is constitutional but violates a personal preference, the judge

[1] In either case, it would be necessary that the action, or inaction, has evoked a legally sufficient protest from a petitioner with legal standing.

Table 1. Judge's Personal Preferences versus Constitutional Consistency

Is the Action or Inaction of the Political Branch Consonant with Dictates of the Constitution?	Personal Preferences of Judge on Court Regarding Policy Enacted by Political Branch	
	Likes Policy	Dislikes Policy
Consonant	Court never takes action	Classical judicial review: judges must frustrate own preferences and accept law
Dissonant/violation	Classical judicial review: judges must strike down law, even though judge likes law	Court always strikes down law

"should" take no action, according to the classical view of judicial review. But why would the judge forbear, just because he or she should?

Likewise, if a law or action violates the Constitution (and accumulated precedent interpreting that Constitution) but is consistent with the judge's own political view of the good, that judge "should" nullify the law. But why not refuse to act, as that is the judge's own preference?[2]

According to the classical account of judicial review, judges act, or forbear, because they serve the public interest. If courts did routinely pursue "review" that exceeded the hortatory mandates of consistency and constitutionality, then "the stream rises above its source." But in no other arena of government do we rely primarily on personal forbearance as the mechanism for controlling self-interest. In the "public choice" approach, in particular, we normally start with the assumption of narrow, self-interested policy actions if those are feasible. Can these views be reconciled? Why doesn't the stream flood its banks?

1.2. Public Choice, Public Interest, and Judicial Review

The sine qua non of the public choice approach is the confrontation of self-interested action, subject to formal and informal constraints, with the (possibly unanticipated) aggregate consequences of those actions filtered through political and economic institutions. More simply, the starting point is the assumption that individuals act to further

[2] A much more comprehensive analysis of this notion of review, with comparative examples, can be found in Vanberg (2009). And the procedural issues are expanded in Vanberg (2011). Some counterarguments for evaluating the legitimacy of judicial review are discussed in detail in Doherty and Pevnik (2013).

what they perceive as their own self-interest, even if collective benefits are left on the table. As Tullock (1984) put it, "From the earliest work in Public Choice, scholars have tended to assume that the public interest is not a major theme in the operation of government, certainly in democratic government" (89).[3]

Consequently, human beings (be they consumers, workers, bureaucrats, elected officials, or judges) cooperate in producing public goods only when they perceive it as advancing their private interest. Forbearance, or a self-imposed willingness to sacrifice one's own interest for the public good, is not a useful starting point for theorizing about government for public choice theorists.

This view did not originate with public choice, of course. As Madison and Hamilton famously observed in Federalist no. 51, "men are not angels," and good institutional design should take full advantage of the self-interest of those in government, rather than relying on their goodwill or forbearance. Hamilton noted the power of an "absolute negative" on legislation could not be entrusted to the executive:

> The provision for defense must in this, as in all other cases, be made commensurate to the danger of attack. Ambition must be made to counteract ambition. The interest of the man must be connected with the constitutional rights of the place. It may be a reflection on human nature, that such devices should be necessary to control the abuses of government. But what is government itself, but the greatest of all reflections on human nature? If men were angels, no government would be necessary. If angels were to govern men, neither external nor internal controls on government would be necessary. In framing a government which is to be administered by men over men, the great difficulty lies in this: you must first enable the government to control the governed; and in the next place oblige it to control itself. . . .
>
> An absolute negative on the legislature appears, at first view, to be the natural defense with which the executive magistrate should be armed. But perhaps it would be neither altogether safe nor alone sufficient. On ordinary occasions it might not be exerted with the requisite firmness, and on extraordinary occasions it might be perfidiously abused. May not this defect of an absolute negative be supplied by some qualified connection between this weaker department and the weaker branch of the stronger department, by which the latter may be led to support the

[3] As Epstein and Knight (2017) rightly note, often the assumption of "rationality" is nonparametric, more of an organizing principle. I am using a parameterized approach with all the false specificity and limitations entailed by such an approach.

> constitutional rights of the former, without being too much detached from the rights of its own department? (U.S. Congress n.d.)

The solution Hamilton focuses on is, as is well known, "ambition," or what modern social scientists call self-interest. Nonetheless, contrary to the characterizations of the public choice approach in the literature (e.g., Farber and Frickey 1991, 11–37), one need not presume egoistic self-interest. "Rational" preferences imply nothing more than that weak orderings over alternatives are complete and transitive. But this means that groups of individuals, particularly in "communities," might value some collective goal yet be fully consistent with rationality.

Taylor (1976, 1982) analyzed the problem of community in a way that is very useful for present purposes. He argued that the notion of "community" is a name for a complex equilibrium of a long-term game we really don't understand. His claim is that the sufficient conditions for "community" are characterized by features that include (*a*) shared norms and beliefs, (*b*) reciprocal obligations, and (*c*) direct, complex, and long-term relations among members. It is not difficult to imagine that equilibrium behavior within a community of this type is the same as that implied by an iterated, institution-free prisoner's dilemma. But how exactly might the difference be explored? And can we think of the court system, in which judicial review is embedded, as having the properties of one of Taylor's "communities"?

At a conceptual level, the answer is yes. Reciprocal obligations and direct, complex, long-term relations among judges on a court, particularly on the US Supreme Court, are clearly present. But these conditions are features of the interaction on the court itself. Where might the attitudes and preferences that satisfy the first condition, shared norms and beliefs, come from? It is possible that these shared norms might be inculcated on the bench, but it seems more likely that we look for these features in advance. More simply, then, how can we tell good judges from bad ones and then pick the good ones?

1.3. Cabals, Factions, and the Will of the People

Hamilton and Madison feared domination by faction, clearly invoked in Hamilton's call in Federalist no. 78 to protect the Constitution from the "cabals of a representative body." Although this view may seem ordinary to American ears, it was novel at the time of the founding and still very controversial in other nations. In the political science of other nations, the "will" of the people is straightforwardly embodied in the acts of the legislature. It makes no sense to think of judicial review as serving democracy in such a context. Instead, any potent form of judicial review of the legislature must by definition thwart the will of the people.

The American founders, of course, particularly Madison, viewed the will of the people as being embodied in the Constitution, not the emissions of the legislature. Once this perspective is understood, the place of the courts is clear: judicial review protects democracy and the will of the people, because it nullifies legislative acts that (would) violate the Constitution. We are brought back to Ely's paradox: the defense of the will of the people depends on a body that is in no way accountable to the people.

But if legislatures are really slaves to faction, should the judiciary be master? It would appear not, at least according to Hamilton, again from Federalist no. 78:

> [This does not] by any means suppose a superiority of the judicial to the legislative power. It only supposes that the power of the people is superior to both; and that where the will of the legislature, declared in its statutes, stands in opposition to that of the people, declared in the Constitution, the judges ought to be governed by the latter rather than the former. They ought to regulate their decisions by the fundamental laws, rather than by those which are not fundamental.

It has been pointed out by many observers that this passage contains a whiff of anthropomorphism or even mysticism (see, e.g., Bickel 1962, 16–17). Just what "will," and what "people," are we talking about? The people select legislators, and we must rely on the people speaking through their representatives for our laws. When the Court nullifies a law passed by the assembly, it acts explicitly against this expression of the majority will. "Democracy" may be defined as having more to do with equal protection under the laws or domain restrictions that put certain activities beyond the power of the law to regulate. But then the will of the majority may differ from what is demanded by "democratic" precedent.[4]

This all seems very difficult. We are left with a court that is only the equal of the legislature, which literally "checks" the legislature to

[4] The question of whether judicial review is inherently, accidentally, or potentially antidemocratic is complex. Ultimately, it comes down to the meaning and value of "democracy." Chemerinsky (1984) lays out the issues well: "The contention that judicial review is undemocratic is disingenuous at best. None of the critics of the Supreme Court's activism suggests that all judicial review should be eliminated. Yet, any judicial decision that overturns enacted by a popularly elected legislature is antimajoritarian; even judicial review based on the intent of the Framers is, by the critics' criteria, undemocratic. . . . The real question for debate is how much discretion the Court should have in interpreting the meaning of the Constitution. This is an inquiry that

ensure that laws are consistent with the will of the people, particularly as that will is embodied in the constitution and existing statutes. But in Federalist no. 78, Hamilton also recognizes that the judiciary is weak, as in the famous passage where he calls the courts the least dangerous branch:

> The judiciary, from the nature of its functions, will always be the least dangerous to the political rights of the Constitution; because it will be least in a capacity to annoy or injure them. The Executive not only dispenses the honors, but holds the sword of the community. The legislature not only commands the purse, but prescribes the rules by which the duties and rights of every citizen are to be regulated. The judiciary, on the contrary, has no influence over either the sword or the purse; no direction either of the strength or of the wealth of the society; and can take no active resolution whatever. It may truly be said to have neither FORCE nor WILL, but merely judgment; and must ultimately depend upon the aid of the executive arm even for the efficacy of its judgments. . . . The judiciary is beyond comparison the weakest of the three departments of power; . . . it can never attack with success either of the other two; and . . . all possible care is

can be answered and that is much different from the question of whether judicial review can be reconciled with majority rule. . . . A correct definition of American democracy must add to majority rule the protection of substantive values from tyranny from social majorities—an addition of crucial implications for the debate over the legitimacy of judicial review" (1209). This is a rather old subject for public choice theorists, particularly for James Buchanan, who has taken up the question in several writings. In his book with Roger Congleton, the following point is made: "There have been frequent charges that law has been politicized, that modern jurists have overstepped traditional boundaries. This alleged politicization of law has, however, not often involved explicit departure from the rule of law as such in furtherance of social purpose. Instead, the politicization charges are levied against jurists who extend the range for the application of law beyond politically proscribed limits. That is to say, jurists are accused of usurping the role of political decision makers by making changes in law rather than enforcing law that exists while remaining within the constraints imposed by generality norms. This judicial overreaching may, of course be motivated by social purposes. But jurists seemed to have remained reluctant to allow social purpose to subvert the constraints of generality directly, at least rhetorically. In civil rights cases, courts have often been willing to extend norms for equal treatment to interaction settings that have not, hitherto, been brought within previous interpretations of politically enacted statutes. Courts have, however, only rarely been willing to use overriding social purpose as an argument for providing support for unequal legal treatment" (Buchanan and Congleton 1998, 10). Other scholars have added public choice style approaches to interpretation, including Ferejohn and Weingast (1992) and Epstein and Knight (1997). Kieweit and McCubbins (1991) note that judicial review is a kind of delegation, though it is (nearly) irrevocable, save through replacement through the politics of the appointment process.

requisite to enable it to defend itself against their attacks. (U.S. Congress n.d.)

The last phrase in the quote suggests a way to escape the contradictions in the account (court is superior, court is equal, court is inferior). If the Court routinely uses its power to nullify legislation or enjoin action, when the reasons it gives for doing so have more to do with ideological preference than with constitutional nonconformity, then the Court forfeits its power. Importantly, the Court would lose its power not only to legislate or command illegitimately, but it would also lose the power to carry out its core function, the "checking" of the legislature when laws really do contravene the Constitution.[5] This problem might be exacerbated precisely if the power becomes fully institutionalized. The reason is that legislators, and perhaps even the president, might try to "have it both ways," passing laws that are politically popular under the assumption that the court will bail them out. Then, when the law is declared (rightly) unconstitutional, elected officials can simply blame the Court. Fox and Stephenson (2011) call this "political posturing," and there is some evidence (Amar and Amar 2002) of exactly this problem.[6]

1.4. Public Interest

Given that it may be costly, both in terms of their political power and in terms of satisfaction of their own ideological preferences, why would judges act in the "public interest" rather than their ideological self-interest, which they could disguise? Gordon Tullock (1984)

[5] There are not many historical examples of the US Supreme Court being ignored or rejected if it chooses to act. But one would expect, in equilibrium, for this to be true, as the Court would not. Further, the kind of example represented by President Jackson's rejection of the Court's decision in *Worcester v. Georgia* (1832, regarding Cherokee relocation) does show that the Court's power is contingent on political circumstance. I thank Dhammika Dharmapala for reminding me of this case and its importance for my argument.

[6] As Amar and Amar (2002) note, it appears that George W. Bush expected to be bailed out on the Bipartisan Campaign Reform Act, or McCain-Feingold, in 2001. As Amar and Amar put it, "During the 2000 campaign, pundit George Will explicitly asked Bush whether he thought 'a President has a duty to make an independent judgment of what is and is not constitutional, and veto bills that, in his judgment he thinks are unconstitutional.' Bush's reply was an emphatic 'I do.' When asked if he would therefore veto the version of McCain-Feingold then on the table, Bush did not equivocate: 'Yes, I would. . . . I think it does restrict free speech for individuals.' How then, did the President justify signing a bill with such constitutional flaws? In the same way that political actors for decades have been dealing with constitutional matters—by punting to the judiciary: 'I expect that the courts will resolve the legitimate legal questions as appropriate under the law' " (4).

suggested one possibility: judges may often act in the public interest because the system ensures that they have no private interest: "We make every effort to see to it that judges and juries have no material interest in the matters they try. The idea is that they should be completely unbiased. Granted that they have no interest, one might inquire how they make up their mind. The answer must, of necessity, be that they do what they think is right because they have no countervailing motive" (91).

In short, judges can have no private interest in matters they try or decide. They might as well do what they think is right because they cannot derive any benefit from the choice anyway.

But this solves only the problem of material interests. What of ideological interests? Suppose a judge tries an abortion case in a state where abortion is legal, but the judge thinks that abortion is wrong and should be illegal. How could any externally imposed rule solve this problem? If the judge owned a majority interest in a private company that produced antiabortion bumper stickers or that produced equipment used in abortion procedures, then the judge would have a material interest in the outcome and might be asked to recuse himself or herself. But how can we require recusal of a judge who has an ideology-based opinion?

1.5. *Sed quis custodiet ipsos custodes?*[7]

The problem with judicial review, in terms of constitutional design, is that we want to "check" the legislature and executive, but we do not want to endow the "custodes" (guardians) themselves with legislative or executive power. In the previous section, I agreed with Tullock (and most scholars of the courts) that divestment and recusal in matters of material interest might induce judges to act in the public interest simply by a process of elimination.

But imagine: is it possible that someone so learned in the law as to be able to carry out the checking function will not also have strong preferences? That seems unlikely. And even if it were occasionally true, it is unwise to assume that it is always true.[8] Yet some means must be found to encourage the judicial magistrates to forbear and not simply enact their personal preferences into constitutional or statutory practice.

[7] "But who will guard the guardians?" (Decius Junius Juvenal's *Satires*, 2008, VI, 38).

[8] This is argued in Madison's Federalist no. 10: "It is in vain to say that enlightened statesmen will be able to adjust these clashing interests, and render them all subservient to the public good. Enlightened statesmen will not always be at the helm. Nor, in many cases, can such an adjustment be made at all without taking into view indirect

A mythology has grown up around judicial review: any judge will respect the necessity of necessity as a trigger for review. That is, power should (can) only be exercised to avoid a greater harm or when the laws of the legislature or the actions of the executive threaten such harm. Because power can be used only in the face of such threat and only to the extent that harm is to be avoided, the stream of judicial review can never rise above the harmful source that engenders its exercise. This mythology undergirds a considerable body of legerdemain, for example:

> From the authority to ascertain and determine the law in a given case, there necessarily results, in case of conflict, the duty to declare and enforce the supreme law and reject that of an inferior act of legislation which, transcending the Constitution, is of no effect and binding upon no one. This is not the exercise of a substantive power to review and nullify acts of Congress, for no such substantive power exists. It is simply the necessary concomitant to the power to hear and dispose of a case or controversy properly before the court, to the determination of which must be brought the test and the measure of law. (*Adkins v. Children's Hospital,* 261 U.S. 525, 544 [1923], quoted in Harris 1976, 174).

It may be perfectly true that this charge of checking the excesses (and correcting the mistakes) of the legislature is the charge given to the court system. Justice Owen Roberts is succinct: if (and this is an important "if") someone formally challenges an act of Congress or the executive as being unconstitutional, then "the judicial branch of the government has only one duty—to lay the article of the Constitution which is invoked beside [the statute, rule, or action] which is challenged, and to decide whether the latter squares with the former" (*United States v. Butler,* 297 U.S. 1, (1936), quoted in Harris 1976, 174–175).

Here, then, we come to the key point. The reason that judges and legal theorists must defend the proposition that there is no formal "substantive power to review and nullify acts of Congress" is this: if such a judicial power did exist, it could not be checked. So long as the power exists only provisionally and contingently, then similarly informal checks may be enough to "guard the guardians." Obviously,

---

and remote considerations, which will rarely prevail over the immediate interest which one party may find in disregarding the rights of another or the good of the whole." (U.S. Congress n.d.)

what is required is that the guardians guard themselves. How? Why would they do that?

1.6. "A" Law versus "the" Law

Judges may care about "a" law and believe that there are better, and worse, versions for ideological reasons. Judges may also care about "the" law. Either by natural predilection or by a process of socialization (young people serve an apprenticeship as a clerk, then a lawyer, perhaps later a judge), a sense of reverence for the law is inculcated. One might be skeptical that such self-imposed constraint, bringing with it a deference toward other branches and reluctance to abuse review, will really solve the problem. Still, it is clear that members of the bar have this quality to greater and lesser extents and that one might consider this quality in deciding fitness to serve on the bench.[9]

In terms of the discussion so far, this means that at least some judges might be expected to perceive a conflict or trade-off between their professional obligations and their own ideological preferences. In pointing out the potential for such conflict, Bickel (1962) was very explicit:

> Many actions of government have *two aspects*: their immediate, necessarily intended practical effects, and their perhaps unintended or unappreciated bearing on values we hold to have more general and permanent interest. . . . But such values do not present themselves ready-made. They have a past always, to be sure, but they must be continually derived, enumerated, and seen in relevant application. . . . Courts have certain capacities for dealing with matters of principle that legislatures and executives do not possess. *Judges have, or should have, the leisure, the training, and the insulation to follow the ways of the scholar in pursuing the ends of government.* This is crucial in sorting out the enduring values of a society, and *it is not something that institutions can do well occasionally, while operating for the most part with a different set of gears.* It calls for a habit of mind, and for *undeviating institutional customs.* (16–17; emphasis added)

[9] There has been some significant but inconclusive work on the effects of "attitudes" of judges on their behavior, particularly regarding the norm of stare decisis. See, e.g., Spaeth (1995), Segal and Spaeth (1996), and Knight and Epstein (1996).

The point is that judicial review allows judges to bring to bear preferences and beliefs on the prospect of nullifying legislation or enjoining actions. There is, in fact, no way that an external constraint could prevent this; the limits must be "self-enforcing" (Weingast 1997). Furthermore, financial disclosure, divestiture, or recusal can be of no consequence because one cannot divest beliefs.

This means that judges will use preferences in deciding cases. But the nature of these preferences and beliefs is always (at least) two-dimensional, divided between a concern for the matter at hand and a larger concern for the effectiveness and legitimacy of the process. The weights attached to these two "goods" will vary, perhaps significantly, across prospective judges.

But that isn't a problem: in the US federal system, we do not choose judges by lot, and we do not elect them. Instead, the president appoints federal judges. Further, the Senate is very specifically empowered to advise and consent in the appointment of judges to the federal bench generally and most particularly to the Supreme Court.[10] Because federal judges serve "during good behavior" (Art. III, sec. 1), the process of selection is the key.

This raises a puzzle, one that is often discussed in the judicial politics literature—that is, given the amount of information (in the form of public statements, commentaries, and written opinions) that is publicly available about a candidate for the higher judicial positions such as circuit courts or the Supreme Court, why is that presidents so often appear to regret their choices? Are judges so changeable and inscrutable that their decisions should be modeled as having a random component? After all, President Eisenhower, who famously had the opportunity to make five appointments to the Supreme Court, should have been able to mold the Court to his will. Regardless of other considerations, after all, Eisenhower was able by himself to appoint a majority of the sitting justices.

But the results were unexpected. During his administration (1953–61), Eisenhower appointed five justices: Earl Warren (chief justice), John Marshall Harlan, William Brennan, Charles Evans Whittaker, and Potter Stewart. When asked after he left office about his greatest mistakes, Eisenhower said (only partly joking) that "two of them are sitting on the Supreme Court." Eisenhower was referring to Warren and Brennan, justices who had seemed conservative in their ideological views but who, once on the bench, turned out drive substantial change on several dimensions, including civil rights.

[10] US Constitution, Art. II, sec. 2, cl. 2.

What is needed is a model of judicial preferences, representing the trade-offs inherent in rendering decisions that have the force of precedent. In the following section, I investigate the implications of a model that accounts for the two-dimensional nature of the choice problem judges face in judicial review.

2. SPATIAL MODEL OF JUDICIAL REVIEW WITH PREFERENCES OVER POLICY AND EFFICACY

Quite a large number of political scientists have used spatial models to understand the Court and to represent judicial review.[11] It is tempting to imagine that the "median voter theorem" rules, for example, on the nine-member US Supreme Court, so that the preferences of the fifth justice, ranked from most to least disposed toward a position, commands the most powerful position.[12]

But, as I hope to show in the following pages, the median voter result, so useful in the application of "political" preferences, is misleading in considering the actions of judges, if only sincere preferences on policy are considered. In fact, the median voter result appears to have misled public officials, and its logic (if not its specific application) has distorted the confirmation process in Senate hearings. I will show that it is not ideological extremism, per se, that creates a problem for judicial review. In fact, it is far better to have an extremist who cares deeply about the Court's power than a moderate who is interested in policy.

It is important to insert one further comment before I present the model. The results presented in this article and, for that matter, many portions of the model itself are remarkably similar to Dharmapala and Schwartz's (2000) article. Several of their results, including their proposition 1, proposition 3, and proposition 5, are quite close to the results presented here. It is some testament to the power and consistency of the spatial modeling approach that such results can be derived entirely independently.[13]

[11] Some recent examples include Rogers (1999, 2001) and Moraski and Shipan (1999). A useful review of the spatial and other literature addressing the judiciary can be found in Shipan (1997).

[12] For background on the median voter theorem, see Hinich and Munger (1997, 21–37). One possibility, reviewed in Munger and Schaller (1997), is that voting expresses an intrinsic preference on the vote itself, as an act, rather than on an outcome. In the case of courts, it can be a problem if it is known that a large majority of other justices are already committed to vote for or, for that matter, against. But the possibility will be ignored here.

[13] Dharmapala and Schwartz completed a draft of their paper in September 2000 and presented it at the Public Choice meetings in 2001. At the time of this writing, it is still unpublished.

Let us imagine that each justice has a spatial utility function of the following form:

$$U = f(D, L). \tag{1}$$

For simplicity, let the two arguments, policy distance (D) and loss (L) of court legitimacy, be defined as separable components of a loss function. That is, D grows larger as the decision the Court publishes (x) deviates from the justices' most preferred policy (x^*). And L grows larger as x deviates from the established precedent on that policy (x_p). (Let us assume, as a matter of definition, that x, x^*, and x_p are all strictly nonnegative and continuous. In other words, the feasible policy choices are either positive or zero). Using quadratics as examples, the two arguments of the utility function might look like this:

$$D = (x^* - x)^2, \tag{2}$$

$$L = (x_p - x)^2. \tag{3}$$

The functional form specified in (1) is fairly general, as the only restriction placed on the partial derivatives is strict negativity ($f_D < 0$ and $f_L < 0$).[14] For ease of exposition, I assume further that $f_{LD} = 0$, meaning that the two effects on utility are separable.

It is worth noting, as an aside, that this assumption is too strong; I hope that relaxing it will be the subject of future work, as I discuss further in the conclusion. There are two problems with the model as it stands. First, the claim that the cross-partial is nonzero actually has an important substantive meaning, one that can be described as "legacy." In particular, the chances of an opinion being overturned figure into both the satisfaction of ideological preferences (i.e., judges may care about actual outcomes rather than what they write in an opinion that does not survive appeal or future litigation) and satisfaction of precedent (i.e., the legacy of the judge is tied to the precedents that are set and not overturned). The reason I have chosen the simpler but less realistic assumption of zero interaction is that allowing an interaction makes my ultimate claim even stronger because it is another mechanism by which the desire to satisfy purely ideological goals in opinion writing might be tempered.

Second, there is another possibility for dynamics in the model that the current static approach simply cannot handle. There is a sense in which a judge, or a group of judges, might be concerned with their legacy in the future. The 1954 case *Brown v. Board of Education of Topeka, Kansas* was sharply different from precedent and yet ensured the legacy

[14] Using the convention that $\partial f / \partial D \equiv f_D$.

of Earl Warren. Overturning a precedent in a way that becomes the new precedent could well cement the legacy of the judge(s). The point is that this article equates conformity with precedent and legacy, but almost all the truly important opinions would, by definition, belong in a third category where legacy requires breaking precedent.[15]

If we do accept the restrictive assumption of separability, we can take the total derivative of (1):

$$dU = f_D D_x dx + f_L L_x dx. \tag{4}$$

If we actually take the derivatives, using the definitions in (2) and (3), we get

$$\frac{dU}{dx} = -2[f_D(x^* - x) + f_L(x_p - x)]. \tag{5}$$

We are now in a position to state two minor results, which follow directly from (5).

Result 1. Each justice's utility-maximizing policy choice is a weighted average of the (possibly nonlinear) marginal utilities of policy distance and judicial legitimacy of that choice.

Proof. Setting the first-order condition (5) equal to zero and rearranging, we find the unconstrained ideal point of the justice:

$$x_{max} = \frac{f_D x^* + f_L x_p}{f_D + f_L} = \frac{f_D x^*}{f_D + f_L} + \frac{f_L x_p}{f_D + f_L}. \tag{6}$$

Because by assumption $f_D < 0$ and $f_L < 0$, this ratio is always nonnegative.

What this means is that the justice trades off the disutility of policy distance against the disutility of loss of the Court's legitimacy.

Result 2. Three related results on parameters also follow from (6): (*a*) If a judge has policy preferences that exactly coincide with precedent, there is no "weighted average." Instead, he or she follows precedent exactly because any marginal utility weights

[15] I thank an anonymous reviewer and my Duke colleague Georg Vanberg for independently noting this problem and for suggesting the solution to the first problem, which is noting that the current assumption understates the force of the results. The second problem awaits future research.

cancel out. (*b*) If a judge has no policy preferences, he or she follows precedent exactly. (*c*) If a judge does not care about legitimacy, he or she implements his or her own policy ideal.

Proof. (*a*) Let $x^* = x_p$, and substitute into (6):

$$x_{\max} = \frac{f_D x^* + f_L x^*}{f_D + f_L} = \frac{(f_D + f_L)}{f_D + f_L} x^* = x^* = x_p. \quad (7)$$

(*b*) Let $f_D \equiv 0$, and again substitute into (6):

$$x_{\max} = \frac{f_L}{f_L} x_p = x_p. \quad (8)$$

(*c*) Let $f_L \equiv 0$, and again substitute into (6):

$$x_{\max} = \frac{f_D}{f_D} x^* = x^*. \quad (9)$$

2.1. Capturing Political Technology: Policy Choice Maps into Legitimacy

In the previous section, for the sake of exposition, quadratic loss functions were assumed to make up the arguments of the judge's utility function. Given that the utility function itself might be some complex mapping of the values of these loss functions into utility, this is a fairly general first step. But something important is missing: the mapping from policy choices into Court legitimacy.

For deviations of policy choice from the judge's ideal point, it is sensible to use a variant of the standard quadratic, as these preferences are primitive. But the judge's preferences over policy as it affects legitimacy are derived or induced. More simply, if the judge cares about legitimacy but can only choose the policy outlined in an opinion, the judge needs an expectation about how opinions and changes in precedent will be viewed by the public.

For the sake of graphical exposition, it is useful to break out the "political technology" portion of the reaction to opinions because it allows us to portray judges' decision making as a constrained optimization problem: choose policy x to maximize utility, given the location of precedent, and the technology that maps changes in that precedent into political legitimacy of the Court.

It will prove convenient to represent the space for choice as having two dimensions. The vertical dimension is defined as deviations from the status quo policy or that policy consistent with existing precedent. This means that the origin or zero point is transformed to occur at the current policy. The horizontal dimension is legitimacy, ranging from 0 (Court slapped down, or ignored, for certain) to a maximum value of 1 if the position of the Court is completely secure.

The legitimacy of the Court is defined with reference to the status quo or policy consistent with precedent. It is perfectly possible that the Court might over time increase its legitimacy by always appearing fair and judicious, but for present purposes a more static conception of legitimacy is all that is intended. The mapping g from policy choices embodied in opinions into legitimacy is defined this way:

$$g : x \rightarrow L, \qquad L = g(x) = g(x|x_p, r, s). \tag{10}$$

As before, x is the policy choice of the Court in its opinions, and x_p is the policy associated with adherence to precedent. The other two parameters of g are worth discussing, however. The reputation of the Court, r, is the accumulated experience of the political actors in the society with the Court. The salience parameter, s, is the political importance of the particular policy being considered.

One example of a functional form that would have these properties is a generalized quadratic.

$$L = r - s(x - x_p)^2. \tag{11}$$

On the dimensions I have described earlier, with x on the vertical axis and L on the horizontal, the political legitimacy constraint defined in (11) is a left-opening parabola with a maximum of r at the point where $x = x_p$. The rate at which legitimacy declines as the Court chooses a policy different from that implied by precedent depends on the salience of the issue. As is obvious from (11), if $x = x_p$, then legitimacy is maximized at r.

The political technology constraint is depicted in figure 1. It is a kind of "feasibility set" for the judges. Any policy/legitimacy combination outside (above, below, or to the right) of the area within the parabola is feasible.[16] The more nearly vertical the technology curve, the

[16] It is important to point out that I am drawing a curve, but that curve represents a boundary on what could be a large area. The reason is any particular decision, with its compromises in wording and possible turns in the path of argument, is a blunt instrument. It is difficult to know in advance what phrases or lines of reasoning future judges, or political actors, will seize on in making decisions. Consequently, what I want to depict

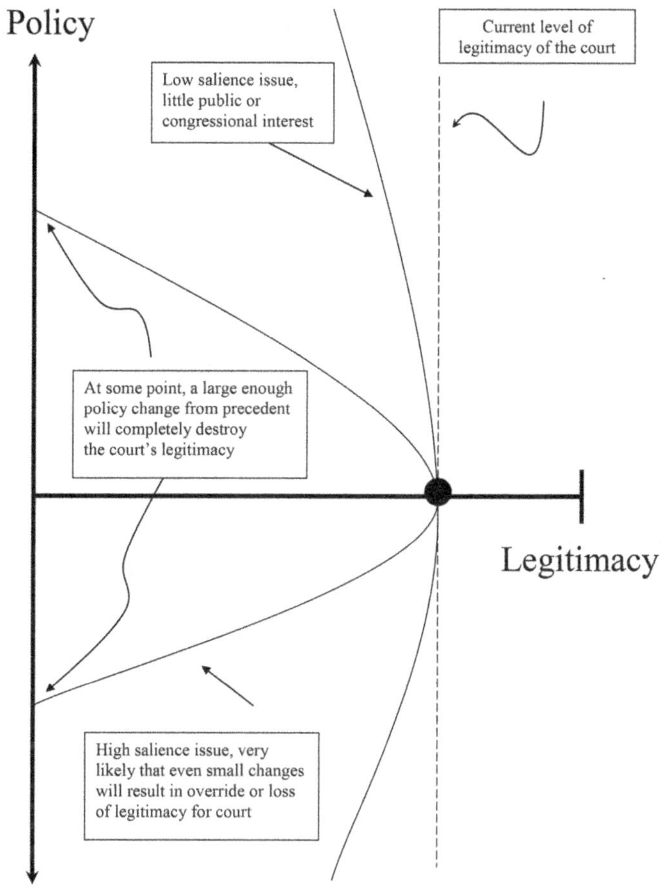

Figure 1. "Technology" of judicial review.

greater the freedom the judges have to change policy with impunity. The more concave the technology curve, the more responsive and hostile the public or the legislature is expected to be. Different issues or policy problems are likely to have dramatically different associated political sensitivities. Assuming judges value legitimacy at all, the constraint should always be binding, and we expect the actual policy choice by judges to be located somewhere on the political legitimacy frontier.

---

is the very best that the group of judges could possibly achieve in terms of effecting a policy change of a certain magnitude and minimizing the political backlash. They might very well do worse, in any given instance, landing not on the boundary of the best decision it is technically feasible to write but rather ending up inside (in fig. 1, to the left of) the boundary by an appreciable amount.

Having isolated the exogenous technological constraint that maps policy choices into legitimacy for the Court, we can now depict preferences graphically in the same policy/legitimacy space as the constraint in figure 1. Because the judge is assumed to value both legitimacy and policy proximity, the horizontal line at the policy ideal point is the inflection point in the indifference curves. To maintain the same level of utility (the definition of "indifference"), the judge will only accept deviations from his or her policy ideal if such deviations are compensated by gains in the Court's legitimacy. Consequently, the indifference curves are concave from the right (assuming diminishing marginal utility of legitimacy). To put it more simply, the slope of the indifference curves captures the trade-off between policy proximity and legitimacy in the judge's utility function.

In the example in figure 2, the judge is presented with a current precedent x_p that differs from his or her policy ideal point x^*. The solid indifference curve passing through the status quo in policy/legitimacy space describes the locus of points that the judge likes just as well as the status quo. The judge prefers any point to the right of this indifference curve and would suffer a utility loss if forced to accept any point to the

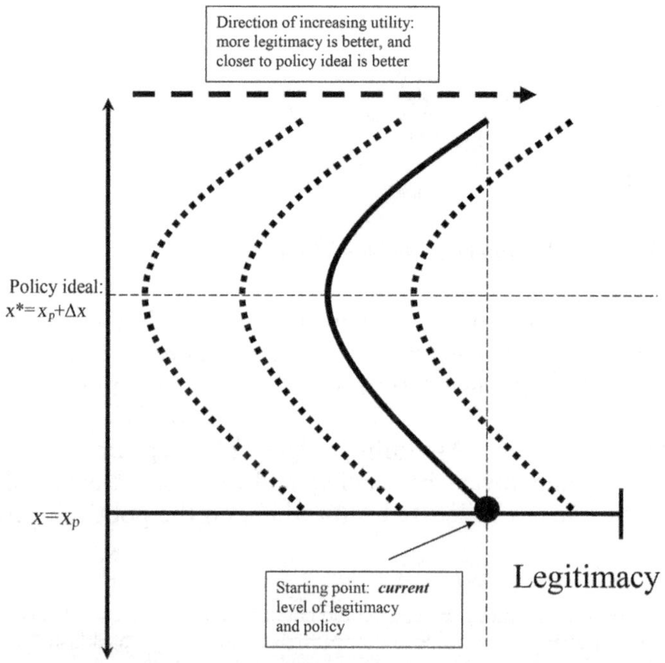

Figure 2. Representation of preferences—a representative "family" of indifference curves.

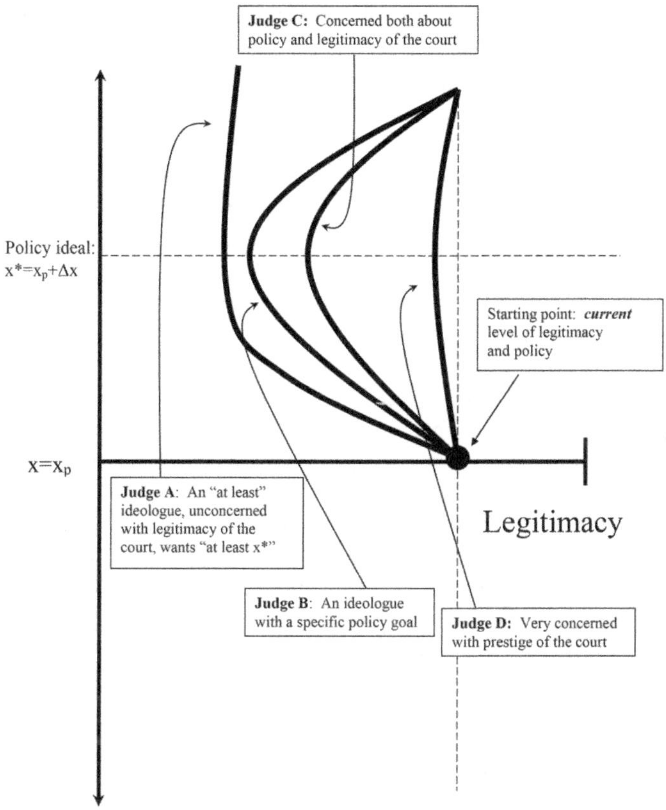

Figure 3. Representation of preferences—different judges. These indifference curves are different judges, with the same policy ideal and different marginal utility of legitimacy, not a family of indifference curves for one judge.

left, above, or below this indifference curve. The dotted indifference curves depict one possible "family" of utility function level curves with the direction of increased utility being toward the right.

We are now in a position to address the problem of choosing among judges. Which judge is best? As an illustration, I present four very different judges in figure 3. Notice that each of the four judges has the same policy ideal point x^*. They differ only in their commitment to adherence to precedent and the legitimacy of the Court. The "flatter" the indifference curve (i.e., the closer to vertical), the more the judge values the Court's legitimacy, even if it means giving up policy proximity. By contrast, the more concave the curve, the more the justice is willing to accept large decrements to the efficacy of the Court over the long run in exchange for an immediate policy gratification.

Judge A is included as an example of the representational function of the indifference curves. There is no reason to expect symmetry in preferences as a general matter. Judge A is an extreme ideologue with little concern about the Court's legitimacy. Consequently, judge A is willing to accept large losses in legitimacy for gains (from his or her perspective) in policy, as is clear from the steepness of the indifference curve through the status quo point. Furthermore, judge A does not care much about "overshooting": policies even more extreme than judge A's ideal point are not so bad and do not require large compensating increases in legitimacy to preserve indifference. Having raised the possibility of preference asymmetry, however, I ignore it for the rest of the article.

Judge B is highly ideological, though less so than judge A. Judge B's indifference curve through the status quo is highly concave to the right, reflecting a concern for policy that outweighs concern for the Court's viability as a political institution. Judge C is more moderate but still is willing to trade off the constitutional effectiveness of the Court to achieve short-term policy goals. Judge D, drawn here with a nearly vertical indifference curve, will tolerate only very small losses in legitimacy to achieve even large gains in policy proximity.

The key point is that these four judges would be literally indistinguishable if they answered a survey on policy preferences or if one accurately inferred their policy views from previous writings. All four have a policy ideal located at x^*, after all. This is a larger question than the usual complaint about judges, when they refuse to answer policy questions at all.[17] So, even if judges answered policy questions honestly and completely, these four very different judges would be indistinguishable.

Yet, as can easily be shown, the difference matters. To see why, we need to combine the preference representation of the Court with the constraint imposed by political technology. For each judge, we are looking for some intersection between the set of outcomes preferred to the status quo and the set of feasible decisions. We then aggregate up to a decision by the entire Court by asking whether there exists such an intersection, or overlapping basis for an opinion, for a majority of the Court's members. Figure 4 presents a simple example of judicial review decision making with three judges.

The example in figure 4 illustrates the main result of this article: preferences toward legitimacy of the Court are far more important

[17] For example, in her confirmation hearings before the Senate Judiciary Committee, on her way to the Supreme Court, Ruth Bader Ginsberg answered a query this way: "It would be wrong for me to say or preview in this legislative chamber how I would cast my vote on questions the Supreme Court may be called upon to decide." (Judiciary Committee 1993).

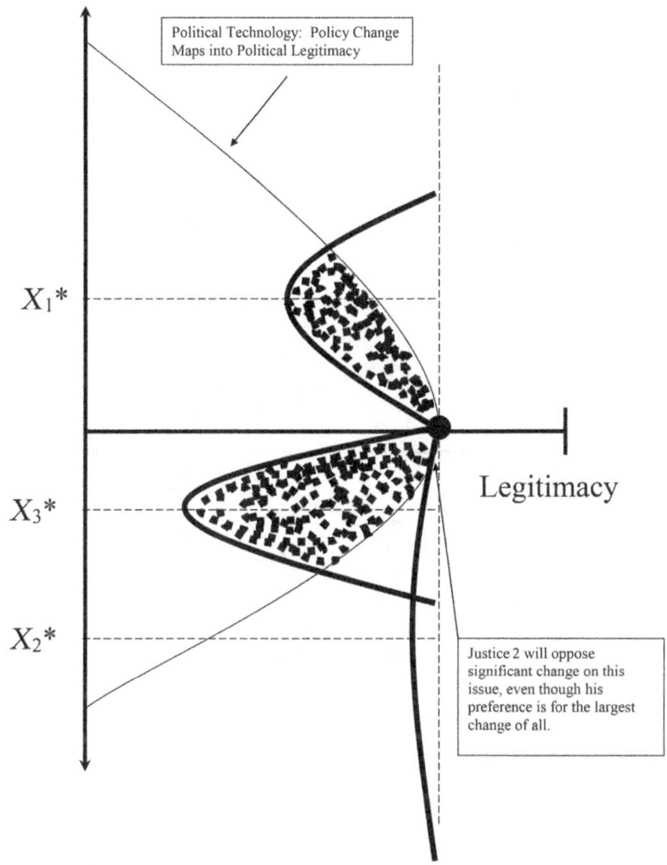

Figure 4. Feasible and preferred changes for a three-judge court: preference for policy change is nearly irrelevant.

than preferences toward policy. Notice that justice 2 is a (relative) extremist in terms of policy, because his or her ideal policy point (X_2*) is far below the status quo implied by precedent. Thus, if justice 2 were a member of Congress, we might expect an extreme voting record. But justice 2 also has very strong preferences for preserving the Court's legitimacy. Consequently, it is justice 2 who acts as the brake on large-scale judicial nullification of existing statutes. The crosshatched areas (indicating a politically feasible willingness to nullify precedent or write new policy) for justices 1 and 3 are quite large. But there is very little desire for change from justice 2, whose vote is required for a majority. On this three-judge court, either no nullification of law would take place at all, or there might some very small adjustments at the margins, with opinions written carefully and narrowly. And the judge

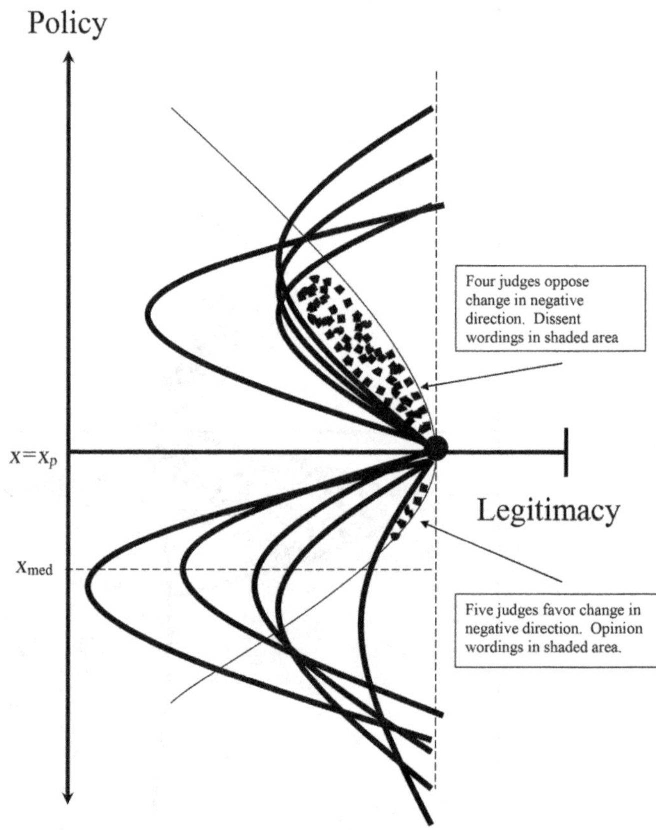

Figure 5. Feasible and preferred changes for nine justices: this is not a median voter result. Any outcome in the shaded area is possible.

preventing the overruling of precedent is the most ideologically extreme judge on the whole Court!

What about a nine-judge panel? Figure 5 is one possible configuration of preferences and technology. Five judges prefer a change in the negative direction, and four judges would prefer the status quo to such a decision. They would still more prefer a decision that would increase the policy beyond the status quo, of course. But only the majority gets to write a decision, so the four judges write a dissent. Given the preferences of the five, the decision will be narrow and circumscribed with little language that could be construed as making new law. But the dissenters will write an opinion that invokes larger principles because they are willing (according to their preferences in this particular example) to accept more of a chance of political backlash.

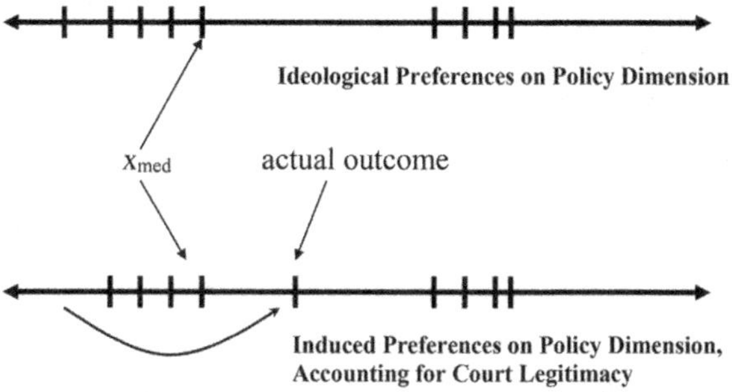

Figure 6. Median result and actual result—ideological extremists can be moderates, and moderates can be extremists.

The key thing to notice about figure 5 is that the decision bears no resemblance to the median voter model of policy (ideological) preferences sometimes used in the courts literature in political science. The median ideological preference is not the center of gravity for actual decisions by the Court. Instead, the induced preferences that account for effects on legitimacy and preferences toward legitimacy are what matter. This is illustrated in figure 6, which is adapted from figure 5. Figure 6 shows only the policy dimension of choice. The top part of the figure illustrates the naïve median voter approach, assuming that judges have accurately and honestly revealed their policy preferences either in a survey or through past writings. The bottom part of the figure shows the "true" (though possibly empirically unobservable) nature of decision making with induced rather than naïve preferences on the policy choices implied by written decisions.

The intuition presented in figure 6 leads me to the final, and main, result of the article.[18]

> **Result 3.** There is no necessary relation between the median pure policy preference and decision making by the Court, unless judges care only about policy.

> ***Proof.*** By result 1, the induced (i.e., true) policy ideal of any judge is a weighted average of policy and legitimacy considerations. Depending on the weights (a function of the marginal utilities) on policy proximity and legitimacy, the induced policy preference is always no farther away from existing precedent than the naïve policy preference. If the utility weight on legitimacy

[18] This point is one of the main claims of and is based on a very similar model as that used by Dharmapala and Schwartz (2000).

is large, extreme ideologues in policy terms may be committed centrists on the Court. Only if judges do not care about legitimacy at all (as shown in result 2*c*) does the induced ideal coincide with the naïve policy ideal.

2.2. Empirical Evidence: Do Judges Think and Act This Way?

Importantly, there is a considerable body of empirical literature that focuses on a question close to the matter that has occupied me in this section. This literature investigates the use of precedent and the "norm" of stare decisis in understanding the decisions rendered by judges. Knight and Epstein (1996) review this literature at some length, but it is worth summarizing the main conclusions here.

There are two very different ways of incorporating the idea of precedent into judicial decision making, as Knight and Epstein (1996) point out. The first is that judges rather mechanically internalize precedent, importing the set of precedents on a question into their preferences to such an extent that the two are indistinguishable. In this case, it makes no sense to distinguish between preferences and constraint imposed by preferences, because what the judge wants is what precedent dictates. The second approach, as Knight and Epstein put it, goes like this: "Precedent does not actually determine justices' preferences, but it overrides such preferences when the two diverge. That is, if justices' preferences dictate that they vote one way, but precedent dictates that they vote the other way, justices who believe in the importance of precedent should follow the precedent and not their preference" (1020).

This claim goes too far; there is a third possibility. Even if judges do not simply and entirely internalize precedent as their own preferences and do not exhibit preferences that are lexicographic in adherence to precedent, precedent and stare decisis might well still matter. That is what I have illustrated in this section: judges may perceive there to be a trade-off between their own preferences and adherence to precedent.

This distinction is not important for the empirical approach taken by Knight and Epstein (1996), however, as they focus on the explicit use of precedent by judges in making arguments and rendering decisions. Although they freely admit that this evidence is only indirect, the case they make is compelling and comprehensive. Elaborating and extending work by Segal and Spaeth (1996), as well as Segal, Cameron, and Cover (1992), Knight and Epstein note that there are three quite different stages in the process of "deciding" a case. The first is the initial hearing, where attorneys file briefs and make arguments to induce the Court to decide to hear the case in the first place. As Knight and

Epstein show, by far the most frequently used rhetorical tool in these hearings and conferences among judges is the appeal to precedent. Such invocations of precedent are far more numerous, in most cases, than use of scholarly authority or empirical evidence.

The second stage is the conference discussion, where justices meet privately to discuss the cases. Again, for the sample of cases that Knight and Epstein (1996) analyze, justices spend considerable time invoking and discussing the nature of the relevant precedents and their implications for the facts under consideration. The final stage is the circulation of drafts of the opinion and the publication of the final decision. Perhaps not surprisingly, the very highest proportion of the use of precedent as a rhetorical and persuasive tool occurs at this level.

It is perfectly possible, as Knight and Epstein (1996) point out, that the use of precedent is nothing more than a fig leaf used to disguise a naked power struggle over whose preferences will prevail. But they conclude that this is unlikely. For one thing, both justices and petitioners spend lots of time and resources investigating preferences. Second, they show that existing precedents are only rarely overturned. This is true across presidential administrations and regimes of party control of Congress, showing that precedent often binds justices, restraining the application of ideological preferences.

3. CONCLUSION: PUBLIC CHOICE AND JUDICIAL REVIEW

What is the public choice view of judicial review? The hallmark of public choice is the examination of the preferences, incentives, and constraints facing actors and consideration of the aggregate consequences of individual actions. The characterization of public choice in the legal literature has focused on the interest group model of public policy making. This is perfectly legitimate because public choice theorists have been extremely skeptical of the capacity of legislatures to resist the blandishments of interest groups. If interest groups dominate the policy process, then the substantive review of the courts might be required to balance the irresistible power of groups (Elhauge 1991; Silver 1993).

But there is nothing inherently unconstitutional about pork barrel politics, clientelism, or service to interest groups. To violate the Constitution, either some procedural rule must be violated or the law passed by Congress must infringe some fundamental right. If anything, the courts (civil and administrative) may well serve as the means by which corrupt bargains among powerful groups may be enforced, securing the new status quo against majority rule cycles or new attacks by interest groups (Crain and Tollison 1979; Zeppos 1993; McNollGast

1995; Shughart and Tollison 1998). But in order for courts to serve the function that this "interest group degeneracy" view has in mind, any notion of deference on substance and politics would have to be abandoned or be rendered so elastic that abandonment is indistinguishable. Several legal scholars have argued that the usual standard of "deference" survives the attack of the public choice monsters quite well (Easterbrook 1993; Eskridge 1993).

It is silly to compare purity of "public choicer than thou" arguments, but I have argued that the real public choice argument about judicial review is the one made in the previous pages. The real object of public choice is to explore the aggregate consequences of individually self-interested action, given the strategic context of incentives and constraints. What I have shown is that, if judges are assumed to be self-interested, certain consequences follow. A brief list of my claims follows:

- Ideologues are of two types: those with extreme policy preferences and those would serve their policy preferences, whatever they are, even at the expense of the efficacy of the judicial system. Of these, only the latter are dangerous.
- The power to "advise and consent" embedded in the US Senate is the single key provision in the judicial review process. But the Senate's only proper concern is for a genuine preference by the judge-candidate to stare decisis and the survival of the Court.
- The Court may stand long against political majorities on questions that are core constitutional principles. The reason is that many citizens, like justices, have two-dimensional preferences, valuing both policy outcomes and judicial branch efficacy.[19]
- Decision making on the Court is *not* an exercise in "median voter theorem" choice. The set of possible outcomes and the nature of wording of decisions are indeterminate with respect to a simple voting model. The existence of a nonempty bargaining

[19] Stephenson (2003) has made an interesting conjecture that might explain why citizens might value deference to courts and the power of judicial review. The argument goes like this: if there are at least two (or more) factions that alternate in power, and these changes are repeated indefinitely, then an institution of judicial review may be a "folk theorem"–like equilibrium outcome of the iterated game. This result is only suggestive, but it is potentially important, because it explains why citizens might accept and even support judicial review, even if specific outcomes of the judicial review process violate the citizens' own preferences. More simply, Stephenson gives a reason why citizen preferences might be two-dimensional also, though for different reasons. A larger version of this argument, more abstractly arguing that institutions are means of solving commitment problems, is North and Weingast (1989). My thanks to Dhammika Dharmapala for calling my attention to this point.

space, or "win set" of a status quo policy, cannot be taken for granted, even if there is a clear majority favoring policy change per se.

Ultimately, what I have tried to do is place the judicial review problem within the broader context of the public choice approach. Preferences, incentives, and constraints combine to guide choices and behavior. In writing down a model that I think captures those features better than the median voter approaches of judicial review in political science, and the various approaches taken by legal theorists, I have tried both to narrow and broaden the debate.

It is useful to consider whether the issues I have raised ever come up explicitly in legal discussions. The answer is clearly yes. At the time of this writing, the US Senate has just completed the extremely contentious confirmation process for (now) Justice Brett Kavanaugh. Separate from the concerns about youthful sexual misconduct, the American Bar Association (ABA) reconsidered its previous endorsement of Kavanaugh's qualifications in terms of judicial temperament. In particular, Kavanaugh had shown open disrespect for several of the senators who were questioning him, raising questions for some observers whether Kavanaugh appreciated the force of the "separation of powers" obligations of the Senate. The letter from the ABA (Moxley 2018) said:

> Dear Chairman Grassley and Ranking Member Feinstein:
>
> New information of a material nature regarding temperament during the September 27th hearing before the Senate Judiciary Committee has prompted a reopening of the Standing Committee's evaluation. The Committee does not expect to complete a process and re-vote prior to the scheduled Senate vote.
>
> Our original report must be read in conjunction with the foregoing. Our original rating stands.
>
> Sincerely,
>
> Paul T. Moxley (Chair of ABA Standing Committee on Federal Judiciary)

More historically, consider this striking passage in the majority opinion written in *Dickerson v. US*, 529 US 1052 (2000), a case on "Miranda warnings." Chief Justice William Rehnquist wrote the majority opinion:

> Whether or not we would agree with *Miranda*'s reasoning and its resulting rule, were we addressing the issue in the first instance, the principles of *stare decisis* weigh heavily against overruling it now. See, e.g., *Rhode Island v. Innis*, 446 U.S. 291, 304, 100

> S.Ct. 1682, 64 L.Ed.2d 297 (1980) (Burger, C. J., concurring in judgment) ("The meaning of *Miranda* has become reasonably clear and law enforcement practices have adjusted to its strictures; I would neither overrule *Miranda*, disparage it, nor extend it at this late date"). While "'*stare decisis* is not an inexorable command,'" particularly when we are interpreting the Constitution, "even in constitutional cases, the doctrine carries such persuasive force that we have always required a departure from precedent to be supported by some 'special justification.'" . . .
>
> We do not think there is such justification for overruling *Miranda*. *Miranda* has become embedded in routine police practice to the point where the warnings have become part of our national culture. See *Mitchell v. United States*, 526 U.S. 314, 331–332, 119 S.Ct. 1307, 143 L.Ed.2d 424 (1999) (Scalia, J., dissenting) (stating that the fact that a rule has found "'wide acceptance in the legal culture'" is adequate reason not to overrule" it). While we have overruled our precedents when subsequent cases have undermined their doctrinal underpinnings . . . we do not believe that this has happened to the *Miranda* decision. If anything, our subsequent cases have reduced the impact of the *Miranda* rule on legitimate law enforcement while reaffirming the decision's core ruling that unwarned statements may not be used as evidence in the prosecution's case in chief.

My real conclusion can be summarized simply: the authority that resides in the US Supreme Court, and on which the efficacy of judicial review depends, is one of many possible equilibria in a game we do not understand very well. But we recognize the Court's authority, and we have recognized it for a long time. I will close with a description of this equilibrium, from Bickel's (1962) famous account of the aftermath of the civil rights and segregation decisions of the 1950s:

> The Supreme Court's law, the southern leaders realized, could not in our system prevail—not merely in the very long run, but within the decade—if it ran counter to deeply felt popular needs or convictions, or even if it was opposed by a determined and substantial minority and received with indifference by the rest of the country. This, in the end, is how and why judicial review is consistent with the theory and practice of political democracy. This is why the Supreme Court is a court of last resort presumptively only. No doubt, in the vast majority of instances the Court prevails—not just as a result of any sort of tacit referendum; rather it just prevails, its authority accepted more or less automatically, and no matter if grudgingly. (258)

The Supreme Court has the authority to review legislation and executive actions because we all want it to have this power, even if we sometimes disagree with the specific exercise of the power as regarding some law we care about. It is therefore of the highest importance that we select justices who care about preserving this power. No other characteristic matters more.

My conclusion, then, is a reconceptualization of the theoretical dimensions and empirical measures used to evaluate the fitness and performance of justices is required. I have tried to be honest about the limitations of the approach outlined in this article, which essentially conflates attention to precedent, institutional legitimacy, and setting the legacy of the Court. These considerations should be disentangled, using more complex measures than I have suggested. After all, the logic of the approach I suggest explains the actions of Warren and Brennan, whose concern for the legacy of the Court drove them to choose a radical course, overturning the existing precedent on civil rights and public accommodation that enabled the Jim Crow system. But the particular model I advance would not allow for such an explanation because the concern for legacy aligns with concern for precedent. My defense is simply that my approach already adds an important element to previous studies that have ordered justices along an ideological dimension by treating judges' voting behavior as being honestly revelatory of primitive preferences. An even more realistic and useful model, one that differentiates precedent and legacy, awaits future work.

In addition to measuring the separate dimensions more accurately, it is important to recognize that the preferences expressed in votes are strategically contingent. The same judge who generally serves concerns for legacy by attending to precedent on some issues might, with perfect rationality, serve concerns for legacy by overturning precedents that have been superseded by political evolution or social change.

Clearly, this call for future research to address the manifest shortcomings in my own work is arrogant. But my defense is that I have tried to direct attention away from ideology as a primitive and as the sole consideration of judicial fitness. I have tried to bring judicial temperament, an old and hard-to-measure concept, "back in" by suggesting a model in which its role is clear.

REFERENCES

Amar, Akhil Reed, and Vikram David Amar. 2002. "Breaking Constitutional Faith: President Bush and Campaign Finance Reform."

FindLaw, April 5. https://supreme.findlaw.com/legal-commentary/breaking-constitutional-faith.html.

Bickel, Alexander M. 1962. *The Least Dangerous Branch: The Supreme Court at the Bar of Politics*. Indianapolis: Bobbs-Merrill.

Boudin, Louis. 1932. *Government by Judiciary*. New York: Godwin.

Buchanan, James, and Roger Congleton. 1998. *Politics by Principle, Not Interest: Towards Nondiscriminatory Democracy*. New York: Cambridge University Press.

Chemerinsky, Erwin. 1984. "The Price of Asking the Wrong Question: An Essay on Constitutional Scholarship and Judicial Review." *Texas Law Review* 62:1207–61.

Crain, W. Mark, and Robert D. Tollison. 1979. "Constitutional Change in an Interest-Group Perspective." *Journal of Legal Studies* 8:160–89.

Dharmapala, Dhammika, and Edward P. Schwartz. 2000. "A General Model of Judicial Decision-Making: Ideology, Information, and Judicial Consistency." Working paper, University of Connecticut, Department of Economics.

Doherty, Kathleen, and Ryan Pevnick. 2013. "Are There Good Procedural Objections to Judicial Review?" *Journal of Politics* 76 (1): 86–97.

Easterbrook, Frank. 1993. "The Demand for Judicial Review." *Northwestern University Law Review* 88:372–81.

Elhauge, Einer. 1991. "Does Interest Group Theory Justify More Intrusive Review?" *Yale Law Journal* 101:31–64.

Epstein, Lee, and Jack Knight. 1997. *The Choices Justices Make*. Washington, DC: CQ Press.

———. 2017. "The Economic Analysis of Judicial Behavior." In *The Oxford Handbook of US Judicial Behavior*, edited by Lee Epstein and Stefanie A. Lindquist. New York: Oxford University Press.

Eskridge, William, Jr. 1993. "The Judicial Review Game." *Northwestern University Law Review* 88:382–95.

Farber, D. A., and P. P. Frickey. 1991. *Law and Public Choice: A Critical Introduction*. Chicago: University of Chicago Press.

Ferejohn, John, and Barry Weingast. 1992. "A Positive Theory of Statutory Interpretation." *International Review of Law and Economics* 12 (2): 263–79.

Fox, Justin, and Matthew C. Stephenson. 2011. "Judicial Review as a Response to Political Posturing." *American Political Science Review* 105 (2): 397–414.

Harris, Robert. 1976. "Judicial Review: Vagaries and Varieties," *Journal of Politics* 38:173–208.

Hinich, Melvin, and Michael Munger. 1997. *Analytical Politics*. New York: Cambridge University Press.

Judiciary Committee, U.S. Senate. 1993. "Hearings Before the Committee on the Judiciary, US Senate, 103rd Congress, First Session on Nomination of Ruth Bader Ginsburg, to be Associate Justice of the Supreme Court." July 20, 21, 22, and 23, 1993. Serial No. J-103-21. https://www.congress.gov/supreme-court/GPO-CHRG-GINSBURG.pdf.

Juvenal. 2008. *The Satires*. Translated by Niall Rudd. New York: Oxford World Classics.

Kiewiet, D. Roderick, and Mathew McCubbins. 1991. *The Logic of Delegation: Congressional Parties and the Appropriations Process*. Chicago: University of Chicago Press.

Knight, Jack, and Lee Epstein. 1996. "The Norm of Stare Decisis." *American Journal of Political Science* 40:1018–35.

McNollGast (Mathew McCubbins, Roger Noll, and Barry Weingast). 1995. "Politics and the Courts: A Positive Theory of Judicial Doctrine and the Rule of Law." *Southern California Law Review* 68: 1631–83.

Moraski, Bryon J., and Charles R. Shipan. 1999. "The Politics of Supreme Court Nominations: A Theory of Institutional Constraints and Choices." *American Journal of Political Science* 43:1069–95.

Moxley, Paul T. 2018. "Letter to Senators Grassley and Feinstein, Re: Nomination of Brett M. Kavanaugh to Be Associate Justice of the Supreme Court of the United States." American Bar Association, Standing Committee on the Federal Judiciary, October 5. https://www.americanbar.org/content/dam/aba/uncategorized/GAO/2018-10-05ChairtoGrassleyFeinstein-reEvaluationofBrettKavanaugh.authcheckdam.pdf.

Munger, Michael C., and Thomas Schaller. 1997. "The Prohibition Amendments: A Natural Experiment in Interest Group Influence." *Public Choice* 90:139–63.

North, Douglass C., and Barry R. Weingast. 1989. "Constitutions and Commitment: The Evolution of Institutions Governing Public Choice in Seventeenth-Century England." *Journal of Economic History* 49:803–32.

Ramseyer, J. Mark. 1994. "The Puzzling (In)dependence of Courts: A Comparative Approach." *Journal of Legal Studies* 23:721–47.

Riker, William, and Barry Weingast. 1988. "Constitutional Regulation of Legislative Choice: The Political Consequences of Judicial Deference to Legislatures." *Virginia Law Review* 74:373–94.

Rogers, James R. 1999. "Legislative Incentives and Two-Tiered Judicial Review: A Game Theoretic Reading of Carolene Products Footnote Four." *American Journal of Political Science* 43:1096–121.

———. 2001. "Information and Judicial Review: A Signaling Game of Legislative-Judicial Interaction." *American Journal of Political Science* 45:84–99.

Segal, Jeffrey, Charles Cameron, and Albert Cover. 1992. "A Spatial Model of Roll Call Voting: Senators, Constituents, Presidents, and Interest Groups in Supreme Court Confirmations." *American Journal of Political Science* 36 (1): 96–121.

Segal, Jeffrey, and Harold J. Spaeth. 1996. "The Influence of Stare Decisis on the Votes of United State Supreme Court Justices." *American Journal of Political Science* 40:971–1003.

Shipan, Charles. 1997. *Designing Judicial Review: Interest Groups, Congress, and Communications Policy*. New York: Cambridge University Press.

Shughart, William, and Robert Tollison. 1998. "Interest Groups and the Courts." *George Mason Law Review* 6:953–69.

Silver, Charles. 1993. "Public Choice and Judicial Review." *Law and Social Inquiry* 18:165–93.

Spaeth, Harold. 1995. "The Attitudinal Model." In *Contemplating Courts*, edited by Lee Epstein. Washington, DC: CQ Press.

Stephenson, Matthew. 2003. "'When the Devil Turns . . .': The Political Foundations of Independent Judicial Review." *Journal of Legal Studies* 32:59–90.

Tanenhaus, Joseph. 1968. "Judicial Review." In *International Encyclopedia of the Social Sciences*, vol. 8, edited by David L. Sills. New York: Crowell, Collier, & Macmillan.

Taylor, Michael. 1976. *Anarchy and Cooperation*. London: Wiley.

———. 1982. *Community, Anarchy, and Liberty*. New York: Cambridge University Press.

Tullock, Gordon. 1984. "A (Partial) Rehabilitation of the Public Interest Theory." *Public Choice* 42:89–99.

U.S. Congress. n.d. "Legislative Process: Resources." Federalist Papers. https://www.congress.gov/resources/display/content/The+Federalist+Papers.

Vanberg, Georg. 2009. *The Politics of Constitutional Review in Germany*. New York: Cambridge University Press.

———. 2011. "Substance vs. Procedure: Constitutional Enforcement and Constitutional Choice." *Journal of Economic Behavior and Organization* 80:309–18.

Weingast, Barry R. 1997. "The Political Foundations of Democracy and the Rule of Law." *American Political Science Review* 91 (2): 245–63.

Worcester v. Georgia. 1832. "31 U.S. 6 Pet. 515 515. U.S. Supreme Court. Certiorari to the Superior Court for the County of Gwinett in the State of Georgia." https://www.oyez.org/cases/1789-1850/31us515.

Zeppos, Nicholas. 1993. "Deference to Political Decisionmakers and the Preferred Scope of Judicial Review." *Northwestern University Law Review* 88:296–371.

Comment on "A Stream That Rises above Its Source: Judicial Review from a Public Choice Perspective"

*Jonathan R. Macey**

1. INTRODUCTION

The scintillating question posed by Michael Munger in this article is, What do (noncorrupt) judges who are not on the take maximize when they are making judicial decisions?[1] This article is essentially about the internal trade-offs that human beings (in this case, judges) face when making decisions. Specifically, an important and enduring insight of the article is that it *costs* something for judges to decide cases simply based on their own ideological interests.

I think that Munger is right in pointing out that judges who decide cases face a trade-off in the form of a two-dimensional choice. This is a profound and important contribution.

But I think that he is mostly wrong about the nature of the trade-off. For Munger, the trade-off is between the judges' personal preferences about the outcome in a particular case and "a larger concern for the effectiveness and legitimacy of the process." In Munger's view, "justices are motivated by two considerations: their own political views and a desire to preserve the power and prestige of the Court."

For Munger, the key is that these considerations often, and perhaps inevitably, tug the judges in opposite directions and that judges'

* Yale University.

[1] The article limits its analysis to *judicial review*, which is the term used to describe the review of statutes and regulations for this purpose. However, there is nothing that prevents the analysis in the article and in this comment from applying to other forms of judicial decision-making such as statutory interpretation, common law reasoning, or the imposition of equitable remedies.

Electronically published: December 4, 2019

decision in a particular case will depend on whether their desire to give expression to personal political views is outweighed by a desire to preserve the power and prestige of the Court. I agree with Munger that there is an internal counterweight to judges' proclivity simply to give expression to their own ideological preferences when deciding opinions. But this counterweight is not a generalized desire to preserve the power and prestige of the Court. Rather, the counterweight stems from a self-interested desire on the part of judges to further their own positions and prestige within their chosen guild, which is the legal profession. Any time judges seek to benefit personally by reaching a decision that gives expression to their own ideological interests, they face a significant prospective cost in the form of a diminution in their own professional status and reputation within the legal order.

Thus, in my view, even if Munger were wrong and judges were completely indifferent to the power and prestige of the legal profession as a whole, Munger would be right in the more important general sense that they would still face a two-dimensional choice problem of precisely the sort that Munger models. However, the choice would be between the utility derived from expressing one's own political views in a judicial opinion and the decline in personal reputation within the legal profession and academy that inevitably would follow for judges who developed a reputation for following their own political views rather than the law.

2. IS IT PUBLIC CHOICE?

The article purports to be written from a public choice perspective, but it actually is written from a public interest perspective. I say this with some trepidation, of course, because Michael Munger is a towering giant in the field of public choice. I am an avid consumer of his pioneering scholarship. However, as Munger trenchantly observes:

> The sine qua non of the public choice approach is the confrontation of self-interested action, subject to formal and informal constraints, with the (possibly unanticipated) aggregate consequences of those actions filtered through political and economic institutions. The starting point is the assumption that individuals act to further what they perceive as their own self-interest, even if collective benefits are left on the table. As Tullock (1984) put it, 'From the earliest work in Public Choice, scholars have tended to assume that the public interest is not a major theme in the operation of government, certainly in democratic government' (89)."

Thus, for Munger's analysis to qualify as a public choice analysis, under the standard that he has articulated, such analysis must reflect the assumption that the judges in his analysis are acting to further their own self-interest rather than the interests of the nation or society as a whole, or some other collective. And, of course, following Gordon Tullock, such analysis must assume that judges are acting to further their own self-interest rather than the "public interest."

But Munger's model is in fact inconsistent with the public choice framework he so deftly describes. It is based on the notion that judges are motivated— and often primarily motivated—by a desire to serve a particular version of the public interest. In Munger's account the public interest being pursued by judges is the "the power and prestige of the Court." Munger uses a bit of alchemy to transform a public interest goal into self-interest by positing that judges have a preference or "desire" to serve as faithful guardians of the standing of the Court. But this alchemy denudes the public choice model of any distinctiveness or analytical power because the distinction between public choice and public interest dissolves completely if we can simply build models that assume that it is in the private interest of an economic actor such as a judge to act in the public interest. And this is what Munger does in this article.

3. THE ROLE OF PRECEDENT

My criticism that Munger's analysis is not faithful to the public choice paradigm that he purports to employ is not merely an aesthetic complaint. The fact that his analysis and model are in fact an application of public interest theory and not public choice theory makes the analysis less plausible as an account of human action. In particular, in a public choice world, in my view, due to a panoply of collective action problems, it simply is not realistic to assume, as Munger does, that a preference or desire to safeguard the power and prestige of the Court is a significant motivating factor for judges.

There is a significant free-rider problem facing any judges who would, as Munger asserts, sacrifice their own self-interest for a particular ideological outcome to enhance the power and prestige of the Court. After all, the effect of any single judicial decision on the power and prestige of the Court is likely to be so negligible as to be immeasurable. Moreover, to the extent that a decision does impact the power and prestige of the Court, the benefits of any marginal enhancement in power and prestige are necessarily shared with all judges, present and future. Any benefits from enhancing the power and prestige of the bench generally to the particular judge deciding a case as distinct from the entire population of judges are, of course, ephemeral.

Moreover, Munger's analysis suffers from the perennial analytical problem with public interest analysis in that it cannot explain why there are any problems in the world that political theory needs to address. For example, if we can assume, as Munger does, that judges want to maximize the power and prestige of the judiciary, then logic demands that we also should be able to assume that congressmen and senators have a personal preference for maximizing the power and prestige of Congress. A fortiori, presidents will prefer to maximize the power and prestige of the presidency rather than their own private agendas. And if we can write down a model in which judges want to further the power and prestige of the Court, then we can just as easily write down a model in which lobbyists act in the public interest out of a desire to further the power and prestige of their profession, such that lobbyists will be viewed as "educators" of public servants rather than as the influence peddlers that they are.

A related problem with Munger's analysis is that it is exceedingly tricky to specify precisely how a judge who wants to maximize the power and prestige of the judiciary would go about doing so. Munger asserts that the way to do this is to slavishly follow precedent. In Munger's view, although some judges will write opinions to achieve narrow, personal "ideological victories," others will write opinions "favoring preservation of tradition and precedent." But Munger himself recognizes that this is often incorrect. Munger notes that the landmark 1954 case *Brown v. Board of Education of Topeka, Kansas* broke sharply with the prevailing pro-segregationist precedent, and yet few opinions have done more to enhance the power and prestige of the Supreme Court. Munger is undoubtedly correct when he observes that his theory "equates conformity with precedent and legacy, but almost all the truly important opinions would, by definition, belong in a third category where legacy requires breaking precedent."

The point here is that, even if judges wanted to subordinate their own personal ideological preferences to enhance the power and prestige of the Court, simply following precedent would not be the right strategy. As such, Munger's assumptions about judicial preferences do not provide a useful guide to predicting what judges are doing when deciding cases.

4. LESSONS FOR THE APPOINTMENTS PROCESS

Another way in which the public interest theory creeps into Munger's analysis is in his advice to presidents and senators about how to make judicial appointments.

Munger notes that the process of selecting judges is key, and his model provides a methodology that he believes is superior to the tried and not-so-true method of selecting judges on the basis of ideological commitment. In a nutshell, his approach implies that we should favor judicial appointments for those who place the highest premium on following precedent, preserving the "legacy" of the Court and exhibiting "the judicial temperament." For Munger, "the policy implication is clear: Senate hearings should spend less time on trying to divine ideological views—and nominees are quite right to decline to answer such queries—and more time investigating the commitment of nominees to the legacy of the Court." Normatively, for Munger, "the Senate's only proper concern is for a genuine preference by the judge-candidate to stare decisis and the survival of the Court."

There is nothing wrong with this analysis in theory, but it is inconsistent with the public choice model. Of course, we would like elected officials to pick the best judges. But why should they? If the best strategy for political survival in a Darwinian electoral environment is to pick ideological judges, then that is what politicians must and will do. Munger's advice about picking judges who are devoted to precedent is tantamount to a policy prescription that counsels politicians to pick judges who care about the law rather than ideological hacks. Picking hacks allows presidents and senators to solidify their base of supporters and to win reelection.

5. THE REAL TRADE-OFF

Munger's model has a lot to say for it. As Richard Posner (1993) observed in these pages a quarter of a century ago, a successful account of judges' behavior must reflect the view that judges are "ordinary people responding rationally to ordinary incentives" who are, in a word, "rational" (1). Munger embraces this approach, in principal anyway. Following Cooter (1983), Posner notes that judges are normal humans. They care about such things as popularity, prestige, avoiding reversal, and reputation, but furthering the public interest enters into their calculus indirectly.[2]

Thus, it seems, rather than unrealistically postulate a trade-off between advancing one's ideological interests and a generalized preference for preserving "tradition and precedent" or the "prestige" and

[2] As Posner (1993) recognizes, although judges care about these things, the concept of judges acting in the "public interest" is excluded from the analysis because its inclusion would be "inconsistent" with an approach that treats judges as "ordinary" beings and follow the public interest only to the extent that doing so is consistent with enhancing their own utility. *Id.* at 13–15.

"legacy" of the Court, as Munger supposes, a more realistic model would posit a trade-off between giving vent to one's ideological preferences and specific judicial preference to further one's own prestige and reputation, particularly within the confines of judges' chosen social and professional milieu, the legal guild.

One advantage over the revision to Munger's model that I advocate here is that it can explain why judges write dissents. On one hand, the practice of writing dissents is inconsistent with Munger's model of judges because writing dissents neither furthers judges' ideological interests nor serves to strengthen the role of precedent. On the other hand, the ubiquitous practice of writing dissents clearly serves to further the prestige of the judges writing such dissents because it allows judges to avoid the reputational consequences of joining a majority opinion that they view as substandard, second-rate, anti-intellectual, or "results-oriented."

6. CONCLUSION

Judges want to be cited. They want the judicial opinions that they have authored to be featured prominently in the casebooks and legal treatises read by lawyers, law students, and law professors. They want to be invited to speak at prestigious universities here and abroad. They want honorary degrees. When judges blindly follow their own ideological preferences in rendering decisions, they risk being relegated to the ranks of "results-oriented" judges whose views are neither followed nor respected. This is the real trade-off that judges face when tempted to give free reign to their personal ideologies when rendering decisions.

REFERENCES

Cooter, Robert D. 1983. "The Objectives of Private and Public Judges." *Public Choice* 41 (1): 107–32.

Posner, Richard A. 1993. "What Do Judges and Justices Maximize? (The Same Thing Everybody Else Does)." *Supreme Court Economic Review* 3 (1): 1–41.

Is Campaign Spending a Cause or an Effect? Reexamining the Empirical Foundations of *Buckley v. Valeo* (1976)

*Anna Harvey**

The Supreme Court's campaign finance jurisprudence rests on a distinction between spending restrictions (generally struck) and contribution restrictions (often upheld). In Buckley v. Valeo *(1976), the case originating this distinction, the majority rejected an "anti-distortion" rationale for spending restrictions, claiming that campaign spending is merely an effect of candidate support, not a cause of candidate support. If this claim is true, then removing restrictions on campaign spending should have no discernible causal impacts. This article tests the* Buckley *majority's empirical claim using its own ruling, which struck limits on campaign spending in state elections in 26 states. Estimates consistently suggest that the* Buckley*-induced removal of state limits on campaign spending led to increased Republican vote shares, increased Republican candidate entry, and decreased Democratic candidate entry in state legislative and gubernatorial elections in states affected by the ruling, as well as increased Republican House vote shares and the election of more conservative House incumbents in states both affected by the ruling and holding concurrent federal and state elections. These findings suggest that the rationale for the core distinction in the Supreme Court's campaign finance jurisprudence has little empirical foundation.*

* Professor of Politics; Director, Public Safety Lab; New York University; email: anna.harvey@nyu.edu.

Electronically published: October 11, 2019
 978-0-226-64653-4/2019/0027-0005$10.00

1. INTRODUCTION

The Supreme Court's campaign finance jurisprudence rests on a doctrinal distinction between contribution and spending limits. According to this distinction, contribution limits can sufficiently serve the government's interest in preventing corruption so as to offset their potential negative impacts on speech rights. Spending limits, by contrast, do not serve the government's interest in preventing corruption. Moreover, the Court's majorities have failed to find any other governmental interest sufficiently served by spending limits so as to justify their potential negative impacts on speech rights (Alschuler et al. 2018). In practice, although contribution limits are often upheld, every spending limit that has come before the Court has been struck.[1]

In *Buckley v. Valeo*, 424 U.S. 1 (1976), the case originating this distinction, the majority considered and rejected an "anti-distortion" governmental interest in restricting spending in elections, claiming that campaign spending is unlikely to distort electoral outcomes because it is an effect of candidate support, not a cause of candidate support. According to the *Buckley* majority, "The financial resources available to a candidate's campaign, like the number of volunteers recruited, will normally vary with the size and intensity of the candidate's support. There is nothing invidious, improper, or unhealthy in permitting such funds to be spent to carry the candidate's message to the electorate" (424 U.S., at 56). In a footnote, the *Buckley* majority cited with approval an opinion dissenting in part from the appellate court's ruling in the case, stating that "if a senatorial candidate can raise $1 from each voter, what evil is exacerbated by allowing that candidate to use all that money for political communication? I know of none" (424 U.S., at 56, quoting 171 U.S. App. D.C., at 268, 519 F.2d, at 917 [Tamm, J.]). Ten years later, the Court repeated its empirical claim in *Federal Election Commission v. Massachusetts Citizens for Life*, 479 U.S. 238 (1986) (*MCFL*), striking restrictions on independent spending as applied to an antiabortion organization and declaring, "Political 'free trade' does not necessarily require that all who participate in the political marketplace do so with exactly equal resources. See *NCPAC*, supra (invalidating limits on independent spending by political committees), *Buckley*, 424 U.S., at 39–51 (striking

[1] The Court struck down spending limits in *Buckley v. Valeo*, 424 U.S. 1 (1976); *First National Bank of Boston v. Bellotti*, 435 U.S. 765 (1978); *FEC v. National Conservative Political Action Committee*, 470 U.S. 480 (1985); *Federal Election Commission v. Massachusetts Citizens for Life*, 479 U.S. 238 (1986); *Colorado Republican Federal Campaign Committee v. FEC (Colorado 1)*, 518 U.S. 604 (1996); and *Citizens United v. Federal Election Commission*, 558 U.S. 310 (2010).

down expenditure limits in 1971 Campaign Act). *Relative availability of funds is after all a rough barometer of public support"* (479 U.S., at 258, emphasis added).

If, in fact, the "relative availability of funds" to a campaign is "a rough barometer of public support," as declared by the *MCFL* majority, then spending on behalf of a candidate, whether by the candidate's own campaign or by independent organizations, is an effect of support for that candidate. It does not cause support for the candidate. If this claim is true, then removing spending restrictions in elections should have no causal impacts.

Recent studies, however, have identified substantial causal impacts from the Court's ruling in *Citizens United v. Federal Election Commission*, 558 U.S. 310 (2010), striking restrictions on independent spending by corporations and unions in 23 states. Klumpp, Mialon, and Williams (2016), for example, found that the ruling increased the probability that Republican state legislative incumbents ran for reelection, decreased the probability that Democratic state legislative candidates contested races, and increased the probability that Republican state legislative candidates won election. Harvey and Mattia (forthcoming) further found that the ruling led to the election of more conservative Republican state legislators in states affected by the ruling relative to states unaffected by the ruling. These findings indicate that the removal of restrictions on independent spending by corporations and unions in the wake of *Citizens United* in fact had significant causal impacts. At least in this context, spending is not merely an effect of preexisting candidate support but rather causes increased candidate support.

To date, however, no study has examined the Court's empirical claim in the context of the removal of campaign spending restrictions (as opposed to independent spending restrictions). This article uses the *Buckley* ruling itself to test its majority's assertion that the removal of restrictions on campaign expenditures will not impact electoral outcomes. In *Buckley*, the Court struck the limits on campaign spending in federal elections that had been enacted in the Federal Election Campaign Act (FECA) amendments of 1974. Because the 1974 amendments were challenged immediately after they became effective in January 1975, and because the Court's ruling in *Buckley* was issued in January 1976, the campaign spending limits never took effect for federal elections. Yet because the ruling in *Buckley* was based on a sweeping First Amendment argument, the ruling also struck statutes in 26 states limiting campaign spending in state legislative and gubernatorial races. As of the 1976 state legislative and gubernatorial elections, these spending caps were no longer in effect.

The effects of *Buckley*'s ruling are estimated using both conventional difference in differences (DD) designs and coarsened exact matching (CEM) on pretreatment levels of and trends in Republican electoral success and Republican extremism. The results suggest that the *Buckley*-induced removal of state limits on campaign spending led to increased Republican vote shares in state legislative and gubernatorial elections and to increased Republican candidate entry and decreased Democratic candidate entry in state legislative elections. *Buckley*'s effects on candidate entry were of the largest magnitude in districts won by the opposing party in the previous election, a finding consistent with the greater insulation of incumbents from the effects of changes in campaign spending restrictions. Results are generally robust to the exclusion of southern states, to the restriction of the sample to only those states whose laws regulating campaign spending restrictions remained unchanged between 1950 and 1976, to the inclusion of indicators for the pretreatment presence of other state-level campaign finance statutes, and to the use of 1978 rather than 1976 as the first postruling election.

Further, *Buckley* had no effect on Republican vote shares in House elections held in states with no concurrent state elections but had effects of comparable magnitude to those observed for state elections in House elections held concurrently with state elections. DD and CEM analyses of House Dynamic Weighted Nominal Three-Step Estimation (DW-NOMINATE) scores indicate that *Buckley*'s ruling also appears to have led to the election of relatively more conservative House incumbents in the states both affected by the ruling and holding concurrent federal and state elections. These findings are robust to the exclusion of southern states and to preruling placebo tests. Overall, the findings suggest that the rationale for the core distinction in the Supreme Court's campaign finance jurisprudence subjecting spending restrictions to greater scrutiny than contribution restrictions has little empirical foundation.

2. *BUCKLEY V. VALEO* (1976)

FECA, as amended in 1974, inter alia limited general and primary campaign expenditures by candidates for federal office to various specified amounts, depending on the office sought. In *Buckley v. Valeo*, 424 U.S. 1, decided on January 30, 1976, the Supreme Court ruled that "the First Amendment requires the invalidation of the Act's . . . ceilings on over-all campaign expenditures, since those provisions place substantial and direct restrictions on the ability of candidates, citizens, and associations to engage in protected political expression, restrictions that the First Amendment cannot tolerate" (424 U.S. 3). Because the

1974 FECA amendments did not become effective until January 1975, the campaign spending limits never took effect for federal elections.

But the sweeping First Amendment ruling in *Buckley* did impact the campaign spending ceilings for state legislative and gubernatorial races on the books in 26 states in 1976, rendering these ceilings invalid for the 1976 state election cycle. Table 1 reports the states that had mandatory expenditure limits in 1976 and the date of the first

Table 1. States with Mandatory Expenditure Limits in 1976

State	Date Statute(s) Enacted
Alabama	1950
Florida	1972
Indiana	1950
Iowa	1950
Kansas	1950
Maine	1972
Maryland	1950
Massachusetts	1950
Michigan	1950
Minnesota	1950
Mississippi	1970
Missouri	1950
Montana	1950
New Hampshire	1950
New Jersey	1950
New York	1950
North Dakota	1950
Ohio	1950
Oregon	1950
South Dakota	1950
Utah	1974
Vermont	1970
Wisconsin	1950
Wyoming	1950

Source: Primo and Milyo (2006).

election in which each statute took effect (with 1950 being the first year for which data are available). Figure A1 maps a reduced form of the pattern of enactment and repeal of campaign spending limits.

According to the *Buckley* majority, its ruling striking these state-level spending restrictions should have had little impact. There is, however, substantial circumstantial evidence suggesting that the majority may have been wrong. In the first congressional election held after the ruling, the conservatism of congressional Republicans began what would become a steady and steep increase, an increase largely caused by an influx of increasingly conservative Republican freshmen. Congressional Democrats have moved only gradually to the left over the same period (see figs. 1 and 2). These phenomena have been widely noted yet remain largely unexplained (Barber and McCarty 2015).

Despite relatively strong theory predicting electoral returns to moderation (Downs 1957), Republican House candidates began to attract more electoral support as they became more conservative in the mid-1970s. As the proportion of moderate House Republicans began a sustained decline with the cohort elected in the 1976 elections, the Republican share of the national House popular vote began a period of relatively sustained growth, reaching a 64-year high in 2010. We do not observe the same negative correlation between

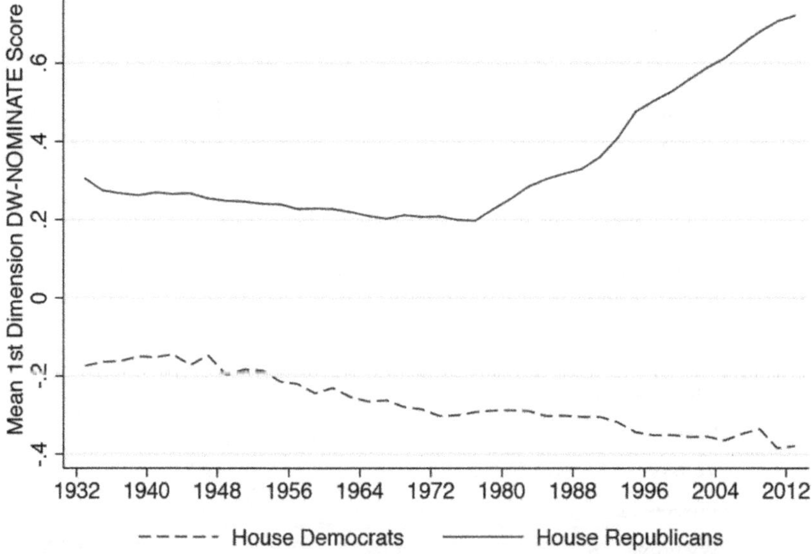

Figure 1. DW-NOMINATE party means (McCarty, Poole, and Rosenthal 1997). Color version available as an online enhancement.

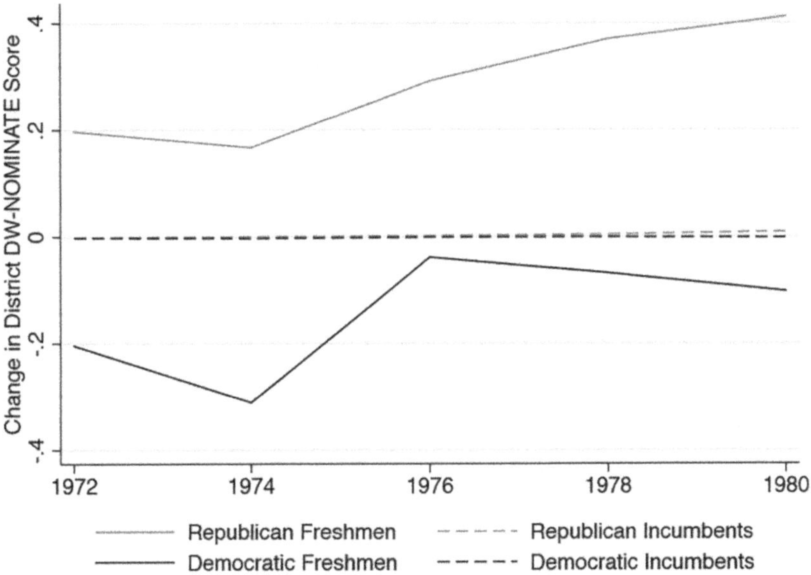

Figure 2. Interelection change in district-level House DW-NOMINATE scores. Color version available as an online enhancement.

the proportion of moderate House Democrats and the Democratic share of the House popular vote (see figs. 3 and 4). The apparent correlation in the aggregate between increasing Republican extremism and increasing Republican electoral success and the absence of this correlation for Democrats also remain unexplained.

A prominent anecdotal explanation for these trends is that, in approximately the mid-1970s, increasingly wealthy donors began to more aggressively promote the election of increasingly conservative Republican representatives, largely to protect donor wealth (Mayer 2016). It is true that the flow of money into federal campaigns has increased dramatically since the mid-1970s (see fig. A2). Given the nature of the findings about the impact of *Citizens United* and given the timing of the Court's ruling in *Buckley*, it is perhaps not implausible that the latter ruling may have contributed causally to these trends. Yet to date there is no evidence of the *Buckley* ruling's causal impacts.

3. IDENTIFYING THE CAUSAL IMPACT OF CAMPAIGN SPENDING

Numerous empirical studies have sought to estimate the impacts of campaign spending on outcomes (for reviews of this literature, see

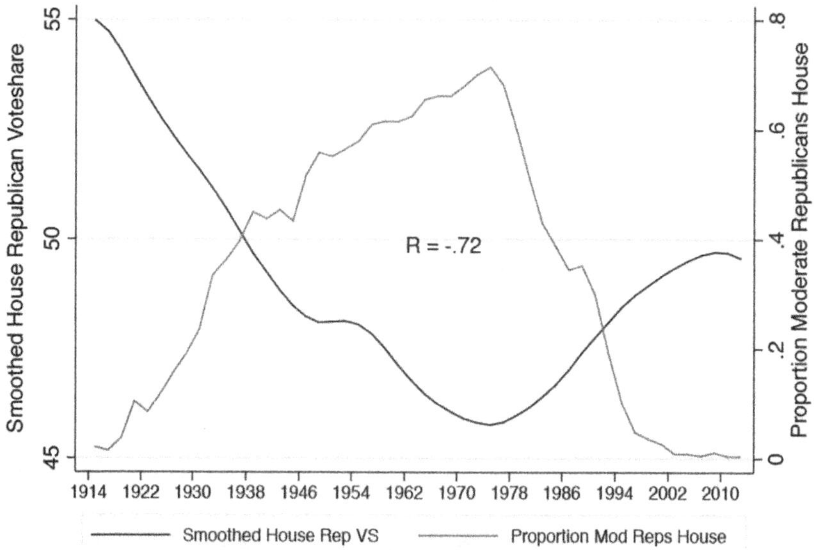

Figure 3. Republican (R) House vote shares (VS) and moderate (mod) Republicans (ICPSR 2013; McCarty, Poole, and Rosenthal 1997). Color version available as an online enhancement.

Ansolabehere, de Figueiredo, and Snyder 2003; Stratmann 2005, 2018). However, these studies have struggled with questions of causal identification (Stratmann 2018). Amassed campaign contributions can affect outcomes from the sidelines without ever being spent; the mere knowledge that a candidate has money to spend may affect an opposing candidate's entry and spending choices, confounding estimates of spending on outcomes (Fox and Rothenberg 2011). Conversely, candidates may be more likely to spend when they are falling behind in voter support, again confounding estimates of the possibly positive impacts of spending on vote shares (Stratmann 2018).

Some studies have used changes in state-level campaign finance statutes to identify effects of contributions and spending on outcomes. These studies have generally found that statutory limits on campaign finance tend to benefit Democratic candidates. Besley and Case (2003) found, for example, that state statutes restricting corporate campaign contributions were positively associated with the Democratic seat share in both chambers of state legislatures between 1950 and 2000. Hall (2016) found that state statutes prohibiting corporate contributions between 1990 and 2012 were associated with higher Democratic seat shares in state legislatures. As already noted, Klumpp et al. (2016) found that *Citizens United* (2010), striking bans on corporate and union independent expenditures, was associated

Figure 4. Democratic (D) House vote shares (VS) and moderate (mod) Democrats (ICPSR 2013); McCarty et al. 1997). Color version available as an online enhancement.

with increases in the probabilities that Republican incumbents ran for reelection and that Republican candidates won office in state lower house legislative elections between 2000 and 2012 and with decreases in the probability that Democratic candidates contested races in state lower house legislative elections over the same period. Harvey and Mattia (forthcoming) found that *Citizens United* (2010) led to the election of more conservative Republican state legislators in states affected by the ruling relative to states not affected by the ruling.

Restrictions on money in elections might disproportionately benefit liberal candidates for two reasons. First, in a right-skewed income distribution we would expect the median donor to favor less redistribution, relative to the median voter, and therefore to disproportionately support less redistributive candidates (Feddersen and Gul 2014). Second, money spent during campaigns can affect electoral outcomes. Both experimental and quasi-experimental evidence suggests that campaigns can have significant effects on voter turnout (Enos and Fowler 2018; Green, McGrath, and Aronow 2013; Spenkuch and Toniatti 2018) and voter preferences (Gerber et al. 2011). Greater access to campaign money by more conservative candidates might then enable relatively more effective efforts to increase the turnout of more conservative voters and/or to shift the short-term preferences of voters in a more conservative direction.

We might then expect that the Court's ruling in *Buckley*, repealing inter alia 26 state statutes restricting campaign spending in state elections, would likewise have increased the probability of Republican electoral victories, Republican candidate entry, and the conservatism of Republican incumbents and have decreased the probability of Democratic electoral victories and Democratic candidate entry. The empirical focus here is on these reduced-form questions, rather than on the flow of money that presumably mediated between the restrictions' repeal and electoral outcomes, because of the difficulties inherent in identifying the causal impact of campaign money.[2] Disclosure of money in state elections is uneven, and those few states with thorough disclosure in the 1970s do not have digitized records available for this period (Spencer and Wood 2014). Perhaps more importantly, even if these records were fully available, we would still be unable to make inferences from them. As already noted, money can affect electoral outcomes from the sidelines without ever being spent; the mere knowledge that state campaigns could spend without limit after *Buckley* may have affected outcomes (Fox and Rothenberg 2011). Conversely, correlations between campaign expenditures and outcomes do not imply causal effects (Stratmann 2018).

4. STATE LEGISLATIVE AND GUBERNATORIAL ELECTIONS

Our first question of interest concerns *Buckley*'s impact on state legislative and gubernatorial elections.

4.1. Data

District-level Republican shares of the two-party vote in state legislative elections and county-level Republican shares of the two-party vote in gubernatorial elections (both scaled to lie between 0 and 1) are here used as measures of net Republican electoral success in state elections. Republican vote shares are presumably endogenous to the particular candidates contesting any given race (Hall and Snyder 2015). Yet candidate entry may itself have been endogenous to restrictions on campaign spending. If Republican candidates in state elections stood to benefit disproportionately from unrestricted campaign spending after *Buckley*, then the lifting of restrictions on such spending may have led to increased Republican and decreased Democratic candidate entry. District-level Republican and Democratic candidate

[2] For a similar approach applied to *Citizens United v. FEC* (2010), see Klumpp, Mialon, and Williams (2016) and Harvey and Mattia (forthcoming).

entries in state legislative elections, measured as dummy variables equal to 1 if there is a Republican (Democratic) candidate contesting a race, are also analyzed independently as measures of Republican electoral success.

State legislative election data are available at the district level from Klarner et al. (2013). Because of the possibility of redistricting occurring as of the 1972 election cycle, the pretreatment sample is limited to the 4-year period between 1972 and 1975, inclusive; the posttreatment sample is correspondingly limited to the 6-year period between 1976 and 1981, inclusive. Nebraska is dropped because of its nonpartisan unicameralism. Races not held in single member districts are also dropped.[3] Gubernatorial election data are available from ICPSR Study 3371.[4]

Figures 5–8 and table A1 report averaged outcome data by year and treatment status for the 1972, 1974, and 1976 elections. On every measure, Republicans experienced gains in the 1976 state legislative and gubernatorial elections held in the treated states relative to those held in the control states. In state legislative elections, illustrated in figure 5, the average Republican vote share remained unchanged between 1974 and 1976 in the control states. But in the treated states, the average Republican vote share increased by almost 5 percentage points. In gubernatorial elections, illustrated in figure 6, the average Republican vote share also remained unchanged between 1974 and 1976 in the control states but increased by almost 4 percentage points in the treated states. Republican candidate entry in state legislative elections, illustrated in figure 7, decreased by 3 percentage

[3] In the remaining panel, all states other than Alabama, Louisiana, Maryland, and Mississippi held lower chamber elections every 2 years during the period of interest, with only Kentucky and Virginia holding their biennial elections, and Louisiana and Mississippi holding their quadrennial elections, in odd-numbered years. All states other than Alabama, Louisiana, Maryland, Mississippi, Michigan, Kansas, South Carolina, Minnesota, New Jersey, Virginia, and Hawaii also held upper chamber elections every 2 years during the period of interest, with only Kentucky holding its biennial elections, and Louisiana, Mississippi, New Jersey, and Virginia holding their quadrennial elections, in odd-numbered years.

[4] States holding gubernatorial elections every 2 years in even-numbered years during this time frame are Arkansas, Illinois, New Hampshire, Rhode Island, and Vermont. States holding gubernatorial elections every 4 years starting in 1972 are Delaware, Indiana, Missouri, North Dakota, Louisiana, North Carolina, West Virginia, Montana, Utah, and Washington; starting in 1974 are Connecticut, Maine, Massachusetts, New York, Pennsylvania, Michigan, Ohio, Wisconsin, Iowa, Kansas, Nebraska, South Dakota, Alabama, Florida, Georgia, South Carolina, Texas, Maryland, Oklahoma, Tennessee, Arizona, Colorado, Idaho, Nevada, New Mexico, Wyoming, California, Oregon, Alaska, and Hawaii; starting in 1971 are Kentucky, Louisiana, and Mississippi; and starting in 1973 are New Jersey and Virginia.

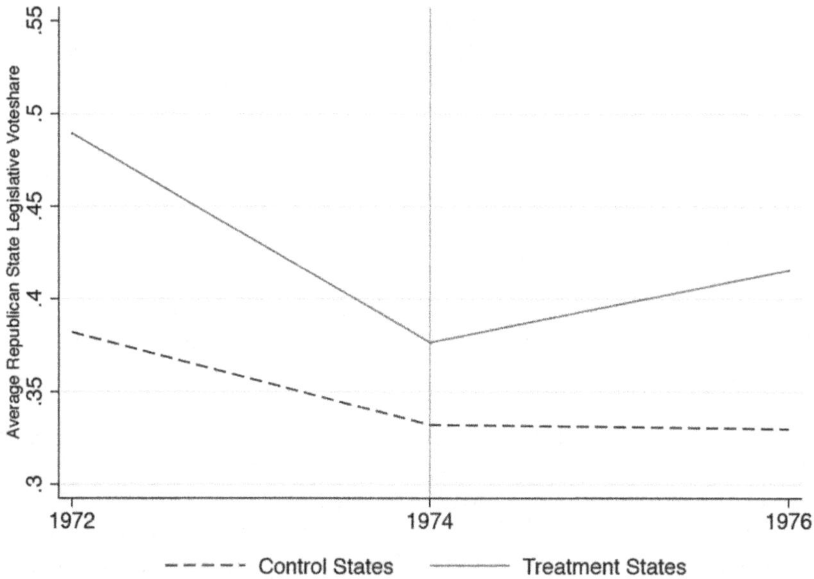

Figure 5. Average Republican state legislative vote shares. Color version available as an online enhancement.

points between 1974 and 1976 in the control states but increased by 5 percentage points in the treated states. Democratic candidate entry in state legislative elections, illustrated in figure 8, remained unchanged between 1974 and 1976 in the control states but decreased by 3 percentage points in the treated states.

Figures 5–8 also suggest that states that had enacted campaign spending limits were not trending in a more pro-Republican direction prior to *Buckley* relative to states that had not enacted spending limits. In fact, in the state elections held just prior to *Buckley*, Republicans appear either to have been losing electoral support faster in the treated states relative to the control states (Republican legislative vote shares and Democratic legislative candidate entry) or to have been losing electoral support at the same rate in the treated states as in the control states (Republican gubernatorial vote shares and Republican legislative candidate entry).[5]

[5] Independently of these trends, Republicans experienced higher average levels of pretreatment electoral success in states that had enacted campaign spending limits relative to states that had not. This may be because most of the state campaign spending limits in force in the treated states prior to the ruling in *Buckley* were enacted prior to the 1950s, during a period in which the racial/regional dimension of conflict in American politics was both important and on which the Republican Party was located to the left of the Democratic Party (McCarty, Poole, and Rosenthal 2006). States

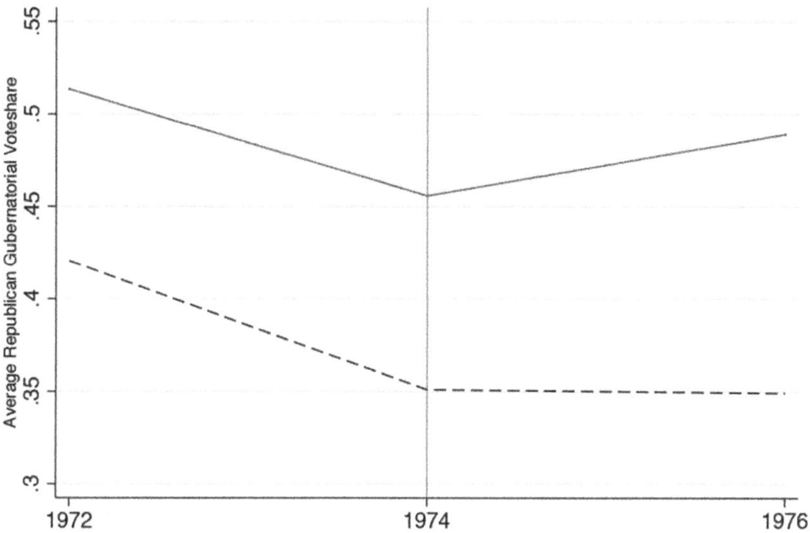

Figure 6. Average Republican gubernatorial vote shares. Color version available as an online enhancement.

The raw data, however, do not control for unit-specific variation in levels of or trends in pretreatment Republican electoral strength. The analyses in the next section attempt to address these issues.

4.2. Difference in Differences Analysis

The DD design, which uses the full span of years from 1972 to 1981, addresses the issue of national-level trends that might have affected Republican electoral success in state legislative and gubernatorial races in the 1970s.

The outcomes of interest are district-level Republican vote shares in state legislative elections, county-level vote shares in gubernatorial elections, Republican candidate entry (0/1) in state legislative elections, and Democratic candidate entry (0/1) in state legislative elections. These outcomes are defined by district i in state s during year t and are assumed to be generated by the following equation:

$$\text{Vote share/Entry}_{ist} = \beta[\text{Spending Limit}_s \times \text{Post-}\mathit{Buckley}_t] + \alpha_{is} + \mu_t + \varphi_s t + \varepsilon_{ist} \quad (1)$$

enacting campaign spending limits during this period may have been those with greater support for the Republican Party's more liberal position on this dimension.

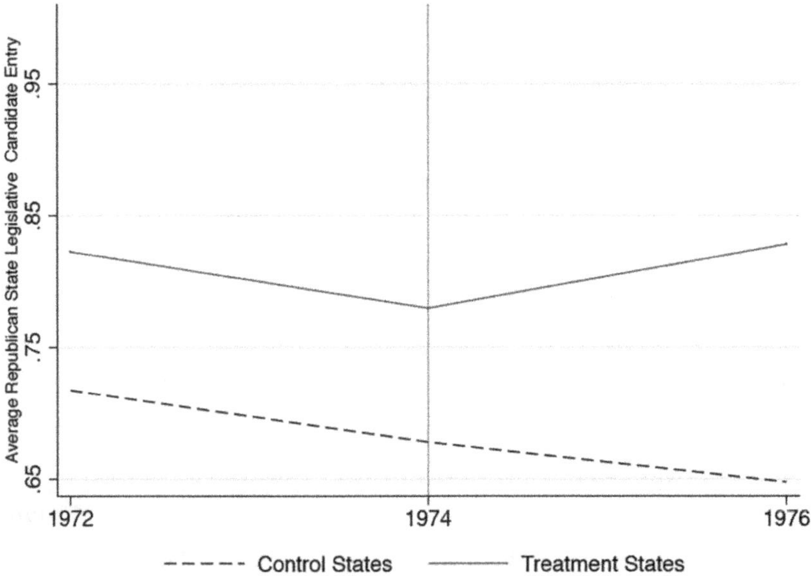

Figure 7. Average Republican state legislative candidate entry. Color version available as an online enhancement.

Spending Limit_s is a dummy variable equal to 1 if state s had a spending limit in place before the Court's ruling in *Buckley*; Post-$\textit{Buckley}_t$ is a dummy variable equal to 1 if the election year is 1976 or later. District/county fixed effects α_{is} (which subsume state fixed effects) are included to address the fixed differences in levels of Republican electoral support across both states and districts/counties (as evident in figs. 5–8 and table A1). Election-year fixed effects μ_t are included to absorb partisan shocks specific to the election year unrelated to *Buckley*.

Figures 5–8 appear to suggest that, on average, the treated states were not trending in a more Republican-friendly direction prior to treatment relative to control states. However, it is also the case that control and treated states do not appear to have had parallel pretreatment trends. To address the issue of nonparallel pretreatment trends, equation (1) includes state-specific linear time trends $\varphi_s t$. The error term is ε_{ist}. All models are estimated using ordinary least squares (OLS) with robust standard errors clustered on states.

The coefficient on the interaction term [Spending Limit_s × Post-$\textit{Buckley}_t$] estimates the average within-district/county posttreatment change in Republican electoral success in treated states relative to that in control states. Figure 9 reports these coefficients for

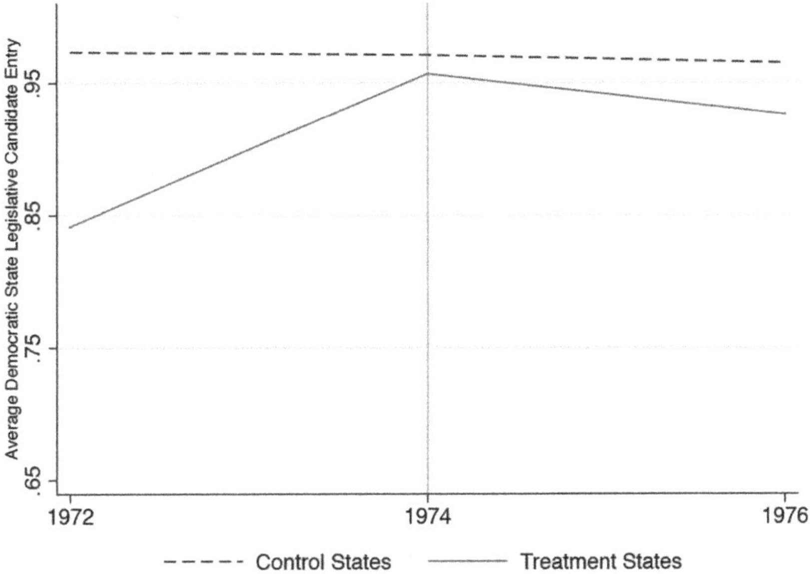

Figure 8. Average Democratic state legislative candidate entry. Color version available as an online enhancement.

the four outcomes of interest along with 95% confidence intervals. The raw differences evident in figures 5–8 largely survive the DD analysis. After including district/county and year-specific fixed effects and state-specific time trends, both Republican state legislative and Republican gubernatorial vote shares are on average 3 percentage points higher in treated states posttreatment relative to control states posttreatment. Republican state legislative candidates were on average 8 percentage points more likely to contest races in the treated states posttreatment relative to the control states post treatment. Finally, Democratic state legislative candidates were on average 1 percentage point less likely to contest races in the treated states posttreatment relative to the control states posttreatment, although this estimate is not distinguishable from 0 at conventional significance levels.

Pooling districts typically won by the Republican Party with those typically won by the Democratic Party may be obscuring effects on candidate entry. With their institutional means of promoting their candidacies, incumbents are likely to be less sensitive to changes in campaign spending regulations (Benoit and Marsh 2008). We would expect to see *Buckley*'s largest effects on candidate entry in state legislative districts typically won by the opposing party. Figure 10 subsets state legislative races by the identity of the typical winning party

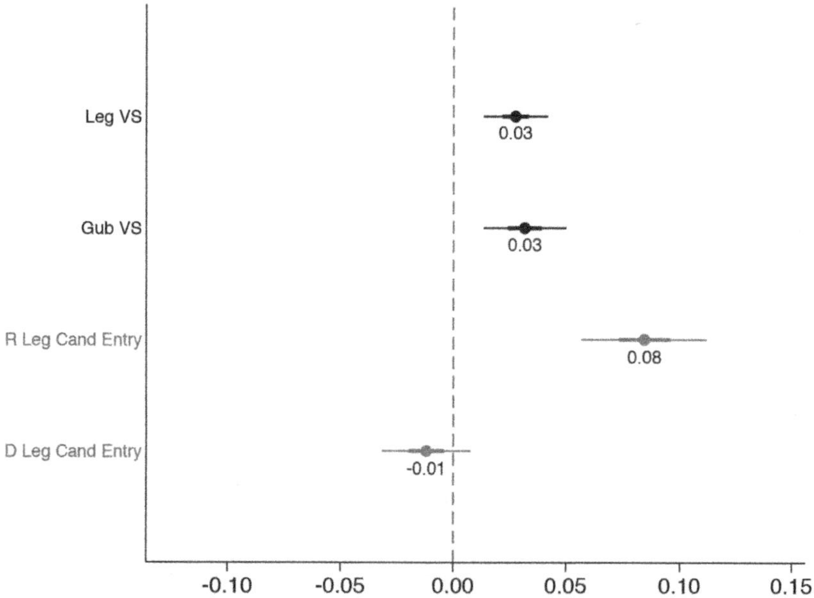

Figure 9. Republican electoral success in state elections, 1972–81. Ordinary least squares difference in differences estimates of the change in Republican electoral success in treated states posttreatment. Robust standard errors clustered on states. All models include district/county fixed effects, year fixed effects, and state-specific linear time trends. State legislative vote share, *n* = 20,488; gubernatorial vote share, *n* = 7,023; state legislative candidate entry, *n* = 21,561. Cand = candidate; D = Democratic; Gub = gubernatorial; Leg = legislative; R = Republican; VS = vote shares. Color version available as an online enhancement.

during the pretreatment period, grouping state legislative districts wherein the Democratic Party won at least one pretreatment election and districts wherein the Democratic Party won no pretreatment elections.[6] All models include district and year-specific fixed effects and state-specific time trends; coefficients on the interaction term are reported with 95% confidence intervals.

Figure 10 suggests that *Buckley*'s effect on Republican candidate entry was somewhat larger in state legislative districts won at least once by the Democratic Party during the pretreatment period, although its effect on Democratic candidate entry was clearly larger in state legislative districts always won by the Republican Party during the pretreatment period. Republican candidate entry is 9 percentage points higher in the treated states posttreatment in state legislative

[6] Other strategies for subsetting the data produce similar results.

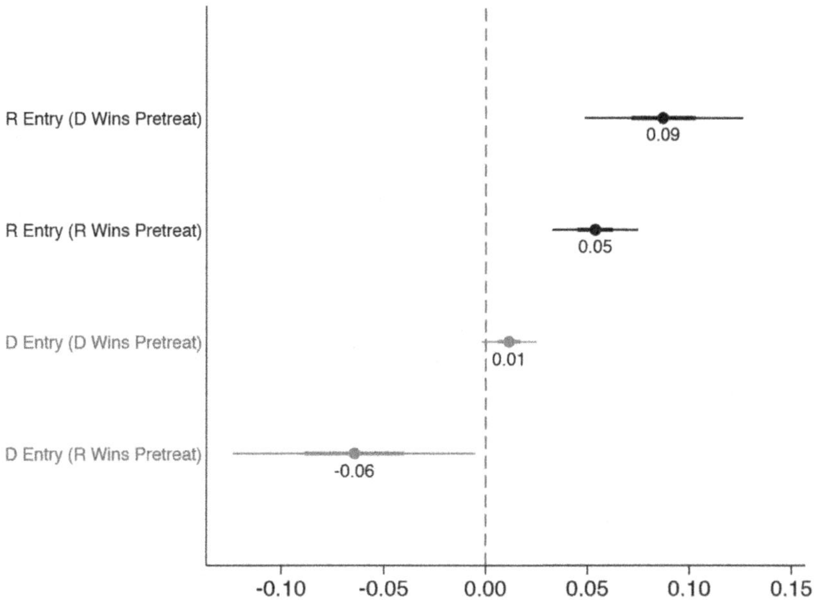

Figure 10. Candidate entry in state legislative elections (subsetted), 1972–81. Ordinary least squares difference in differences estimates of the change in state legislative candidate entry in treated states posttreatment. Robust standard errors clustered on states. All models include district fixed effects, year fixed effects, and state-specific linear time trends. "D Wins Pretreat" (n = 15,168) includes those state legislative districts wherein the Democratic Party won at least one pretreatment election; "R Wins Pretreat" (n = 6,393) includes those state legislative districts wherein the Democratic Party won no pretreatment elections. Color version available as an online enhancement.

districts won at least once by the Democratic Party during the pretreatment period and is 5 percentage points higher in the treated states posttreatment in state legislative districts always won by the Republican Party during the pretreatment period. Democratic candidate entry is 6 percentage points lower in the treated states posttreatment in state legislative districts always won by the Republican Party during the pretreatment period and is essentially unchanged in state legislative districts won at least once by the Democratic Party during the pretreatment period.

In short, the DD estimates indicate that the raw differences in vote shares across control and treatment states observed in figures 5–8 survive a more demanding econometric analysis largely intact, with the caveat that *Buckley*'s effects on Democratic candidate entry appear to be limited to districts won by the Republican Party during the preruling period.

4.3. Coarsened Exact Matching

Equation (1) includes state-specific linear time trends to address the issue of nonparallel pretreatment trends. However, this strategy allows for the inclusion of districts or counties in both the treatment and control groups that are sufficiently anomalous in their pretreatment trends as to have no clear counterparts in the corresponding group. Pruning these anomalous districts/counties from the sample can improve estimates of causal effects (Ho et al. 2007; Iacus, King, and Porro 2012).

Preprocessing is implemented on the cross-section of 2,646 state legislative districts for which we have vote share and candidate entry data for the 1972, 1974, and 1976 elections, and on the cross-section of 2,681 counties for which we have gubernatorial vote share data for the 1968, 1972, and 1976 elections or for the 1970, 1974, and 1978 elections. In the treated states are 1,360 of these 2,646 state legislative districts and 1,190 of these 2,681 counties (those with spending limits struck by *Buckley*).

Table A2 reports on the pretreatment similarities between the treated and control districts or counties in these two samples, reporting balance statistics for both the full cross-sections and the cross-sections resulting from pruning using CEM on pretreatment levels of and trends in Republican electoral success. For state legislative elections, preprocessing using CEM was performed on the following district-level variables: average Republican state legislative vote shares for 1972 and 1974, change in Republican state legislative vote shares between 1972 and 1974, average Republican state legislative candidate entry for 1972 and 1974, change in Republican state legislative candidate entry between 1972 and 1974, average Democratic state legislative candidate entry for 1972 and 1974, and change in Democratic state legislative candidate entry between 1972 and 1974. For counties, preprocessing using CEM was performed on both averages of and changes in Republican gubernatorial vote shares between 1968 and 1972 or between 1970 and 1974, depending on a state's election cycle.[7]

For the CEM analyses the dependent variables from equation (1) are transformed into first differences. For state legislative elections, the dependent variables are the district-level changes in Republican vote shares, Republican candidate entry, and Democratic entry

[7] For both cross sections, Sturge's rule was used to coarsen or bin these variables, but results are robust to other coarsening strategies, including Scott's rule, the Freedman-Diaconis rule, and Shimazaki-Shinomoto's rule. Only observations with nonmissing values for all variables were included in the CEM analyses.

between the 1974 and 1976 elections. For gubernatorial elections, the dependent variable is the county-level change in Republican vote shares between either 1976 and 1972 or 1978 and 1974. These differenced outcomes are assumed to be generated by the following equation:

$$\Delta \text{Vote share/Entry}_{is} = \beta \text{Spending Limit}_s + \gamma X_i + \varepsilon_{is} \quad (2)$$

The term γX_i represents the set (or a subset) of the district- or county-level pretreatment variables used to prune the two samples. Equation (2) is estimated using OLS with weights derived from CEM on all pretreatment variables reported in table A2.

Figures 11 and 12 report estimates of the coefficients on Spending Limit_s from equation (2), along with 95% confidence intervals, using the samples of state legislative districts and counties pruned by CEM. Estimates of *Buckley*'s effect are comparable to those reported

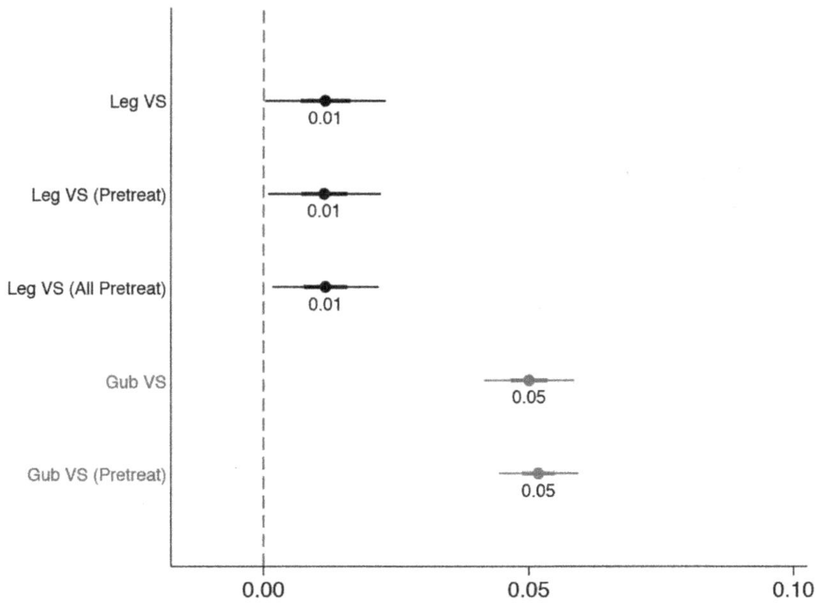

Figure 11. Change in Republican vote shares in state elections, coarsened exact matching (CEM) estimates. CEM-pruned ordinary least squares estimates of the relative change in Republican vote shares in treated states posttreatment. "Pretreat" models include levels of and trends in pretreatment vote shares; "All Pretreat" models include all pretreatment variables as controls. Legislative district, *n* = 2,613; gubernatorial county, *n* = 2,474. Gub = gubernatorial; Leg = legislative; VS = vote shares. Color version available as an online enhancement.

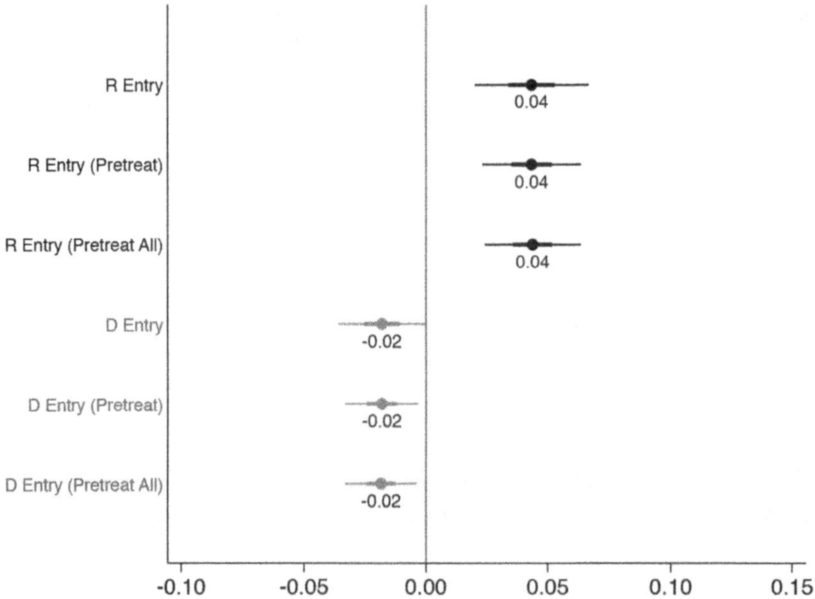

Figure 12. Change in candidate entry in state legislative elections, coarsened exact matching (CEM) estimates. CEM-pruned ordinary least squares estimates of the relative change in state legislative candidate entry in treated states posttreatment. "Pretreat" models include levels of and trends in pretreatment Republican (R)/Democratic (D) candidate entry; "Pretreat All" models include all pretreatment variables as controls. n = 2,613. Color version available as an online enhancement.

in figure 9. Republican vote shares in state legislative districts rose by approximately 1 percentage point between 1974 and 1976 in states affected by *Buckley* relative to states not affected by the ruling. County-level Republican vote shares in gubernatorial elections rose by approximately 5 percentage points between the periods of 1972–76 and 1974–78 in states affected by *Buckley* relative to states not affected by the ruling. Republican candidate entry in state legislative elections increased by approximately 4 percentage points between 1974 and 1976 in states affected by *Buckley* relative to states not affected by the ruling. Finally, Democratic candidate entry in state legislative elections decreased by 2 percentage points between 1974 and 1976 in states affected by *Buckley* relative to states not affected by the ruling.

Figure 13 reports estimates of *Buckley*'s effect on legislative candidate entry, with 95% confidence intervals, using samples subsetted by the winning party in 1974 and pruned by CEM implemented separately on each subsample, using the six pretreatment variables used to

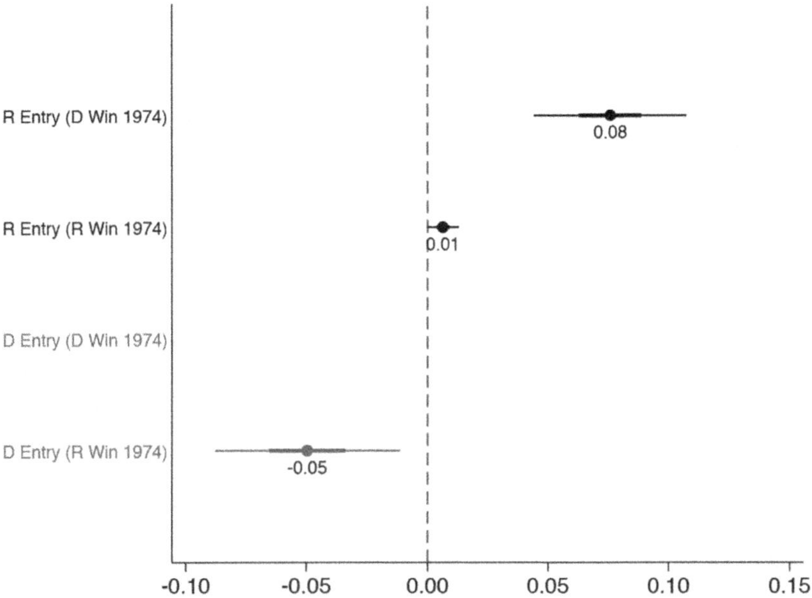

Figure 13. Change in candidate entry in state legislative elections, subsetted, coarsened exact matching (CEM) estimates. CEM-pruned estimates of the change in state legislative candidate entry in treated states posttreatment, for the subsamples of districts won in 1974 by the Democratic Party (D; *n* = 1,697) or the Republican Party (R; *n* = 920). All models include all pretreatment matching variables as controls. Color version available as an online enhancement.

prune the full sample.[8] The estimates are again qualitatively similar to those reported in figure 10. As in figure 10, we see that there is a larger effect of *Buckley* on Republican candidate entry in districts won by the Democratic Party in 1974 relative to districts won by the Republican Party; in the former districts Republican candidate entry increased by 8 percentage points in 1976 in treated districts relative to control districts; in the latter districts Republican candidate entry increased by only 1 percentage point in treated districts relative to control districts.

Also as in figure 10, there is a larger effect of *Buckley* on Democratic candidate entry in districts won by the Republican Party in

[8] In the subsample of those 941 districts won by the Republican Party in 1974, the unmatched $\mathcal{L}_1$ is 0.20; after pruning 8 control and 13 treated districts using Sturge's rule tod bin the matching variables, the $\mathcal{L}_1$ statistic is reduced to 0.12. In the subsample of those 1,722 districts won by the Democratic Party in 1974, the unmatched $\mathcal{L}_1$ is 0.29; after pruning 11 control and 14 treated districts using Sturge's rule to bin the matching variables, the $\mathcal{L}_1$ statistic is reduced to 0.17.

1974 relative to districts won by the Democratic Party; in the former districts Democratic candidate entry decreased by 5 percentage points in 1976 in treated districts relative to control districts; in the latter districts, there is insufficient variation in Democratic candidate entry to be able to estimate the model (virtually all such districts saw Democratic candidate entry in 1976).

4.4. Robustness

We can challenge these estimates in several ways. First, states that enacted campaign spending caps were more likely to be drawn from the nonsouthern states; control states were more likely to be drawn from the southern states (defining the South as the 11 former Confederate states). With Jimmy Carter on the top of the Democratic ticket in 1976, voters in southern states may have been less likely to vote Republican down the ticket; this might produce the findings reported earlier. Figure A3 replicates figure 9, excluding the 11 former Confederate states. Results are generally similar to those reported in figure 9.

Second, we can further address the possibility that 1976 was an anomalous election by using 1978 as the first postruling election. Figure A4 replicates figure 9, using the changes between the 1974 and 1978 elections as the quantities of interest. Results are again generally similar to those reported in figure 9; although *Buckley*'s estimated effects on legislative and gubernatorial vote shares are smaller than those reported in figure 9, they remain significant at conventional levels.

Third, restricting the sample to only those states whose statutes regulating campaign expenditure limits remained unchanged from the start of data availability in 1950 to the Court's ruling in *Buckley* can partially address the possibility that states may have responded to partisan electoral trends by changing their statutes.[9] Figure A5 replicates figure 9 using this reduced sample. Results remain largely unchanged.

Finally, adding indicators for the pretreatment presence of other state-level campaign finance statutes addresses one possible source of omitted variable bias. Figure A6 replicates figure 9, controlling for the presence in 1974 of state statutes mandating disclosure, restricting individual donations to candidates, and restricting corporate and union donations to candidates.[10] Again, estimates are qualitatively similar to those reported without these controls.

[9] The states included in this reduced sample are those shaded (treated) and white (control) in fig. A1.

[10] No states had public funding provisions for state elections in effect prior to 1976.

5. US HOUSE ELECTIONS

5.1. County-Level Vote shares in House Elections

Buckley's strike of state statutes restricting campaign spending had no direct effect on federal elections. But it may have had indirect spillover effects if increased spending by Republican candidates in state legislative and gubernatorial elections in the treated states increased pro-Republican turnout and/or induced pro-Republican changes in voter preferences in federal elections being held concurrently with state elections.

The possibility of spillover effects in those federal elections held concurrently with state elections offers an opportunity to further probe the possibility that the findings reported earlier were simply the result of differing trends in voter preferences, trends unrelated to the Supreme Court's ruling in *Buckley v. Valeo*. If this were the case, presumably we would see similar patterns in Republican electoral success across treated and control states even in those federal elections held in states with no concurrent state legislative or gubernatorial elections. Conversely, if the findings reported earlier were in fact the product of *Buckley*'s ruling, we would expect to see effects in federal elections similar to those observed for state elections only in those states holding concurrent state and federal elections and not in those states with no concurrent state legislative or gubernatorial elections.[11]

Figure 14 reports average county-level vote shares in House elections, using only the set of five states not holding concurrent state legislative or gubernatorial elections in 1976.[12] There is no apparent evidence of an effect of *Buckley* in these elections, analogous to that observed in state legislative and gubernatorial elections. If anything, Republican vote shares decreased more in this set of treated states after *Buckley* relative to this set of control states; the average Republican vote share increased by 12 percentage points between 1974 and 1976 in the control states but increased by only 2 percentage points in the treated states.[13]

[11] The concurrence of state electoral calendars with federal electoral calendars is almost perfectly uncorrelated with treatment status ($r = 0.01$ for concurrent federal/legislative elections and $r = 0.02$ for concurrent federal/legislative/gubernatorial elections).

[12] These states are New Jersey, Maryland, Kentucky, Virginia, and Alabama. The analogous sample for Senate elections is not reported due to small sample size.

[13] Although this difference may suggest a difference between treated and control states not due to *Buckley*, this difference disappears when we remove southern states from the sample, reported in fig. A7.

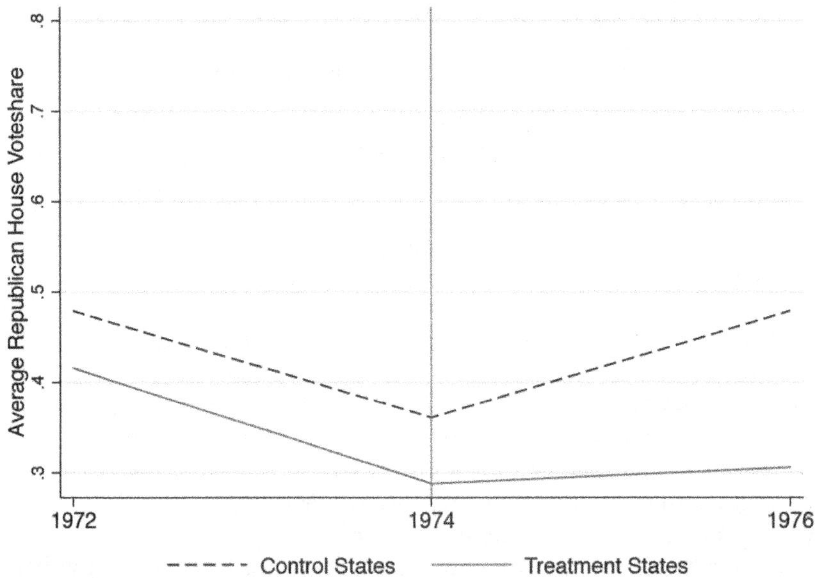

Figure 14. Average county-level Republican House vote share states with no concurrent 1976 state elections. Color version available as an online enhancement.

Figure 15 reports average county-level vote shares in House elections using only the set of 15 states holding concurrent state legislative and gubernatorial elections in 1976.[14] There is no evidence of a preruling pro-Republican trend in vote shares in the treated states relative to the control states. However, we see apparent evidence of a small effect of *Buckley* analogous to that observed in state legislative and gubernatorial elections. In the sample of states holding concurrent legislative and gubernatorial elections, the average Republican vote share increased by 4 percentage points between 1974 and 1976 in the control states but increased by 5.5 percentage points in the treated states.

Figure 16 reports OLS and CEM-pruned estimates of the coefficients on Spending Limit_s from equation (2), along with 90% confidence intervals, using the sample of counties for which we have vote share data for the 1972, 1974, and 1976 House elections. The dependent variable is the change in county-level Republican House vote shares between 1974 and 1976. The "no concurrent" coefficients are

[14] States holding state legislative and gubernatorial elections concurrently with federal elections in 1976 are New Hampshire, Rhode Island, Vermont, Delaware, Illinois, Indiana, Missouri, North Dakota, Arkansas, Louisiana, North Carolina, West Virginia, Montana, Utah, and Washington.

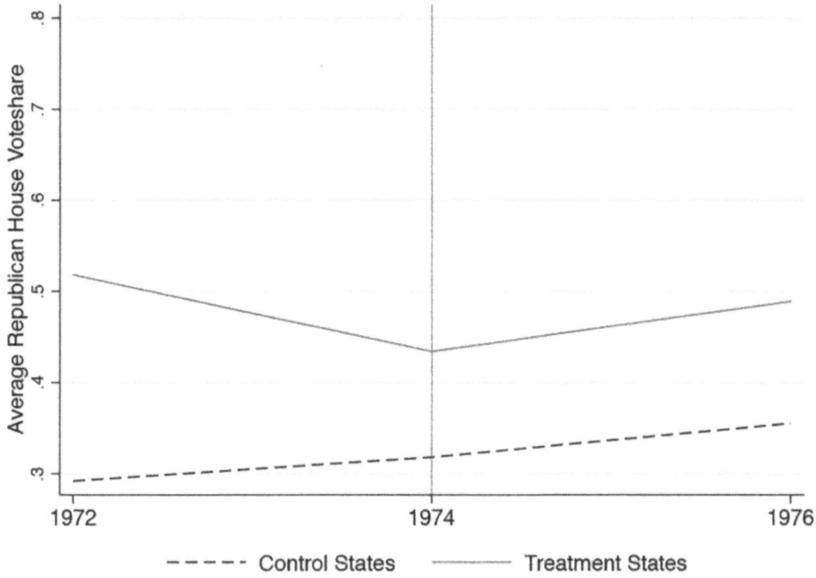

Figure 15. Average county-level Republican House vote share states with concurrent 1976 state elections. Color version available as an online enhancement.

estimated using only the sample of states not holding concurrent state legislative or gubernatorial elections in 1976. In the CEM model, this sample of 365 counties is preprocessed using CEM on the average levels of and changes in county-level Republican House vote shares in 1972 and 1974.[15] There is no evidence of increased Republican vote shares in the treated states posttreatment relative to the control states posttreatment. Instead, as was seen in figure 14, Republican vote shares actually decrease more in the treated states posttreatment relative to the control states posttreatment.

The "concurrent" coefficients are estimated using only the sample of states holding concurrent state legislative and gubernatorial elections in 1976. In the CEM model, this sample of 811 counties was also preprocessed using CEM on the average levels of and changes in county-level Republican House vote shares in 1972 and 1974.[16] Here we see increased Republican vote shares in the treated states posttreatment relative to the control states posttreatment; first differences in county-level Republican House vote shares between 1974

[15] The unmatched $\mathcal{L}_1$ is 0.42; after pruning 33 control and 9 treated counties using Sturge's rule to bin the matching variables, the $\mathcal{L}_1$ statistic is reduced to 0.24.

[16] The unmatched $\mathcal{L}_1$ is 0.51; after pruning 151 control and 11 treated counties using Sturge's rule to bin the matching variables, the $\mathcal{L}_1$ statistic is reduced to 0.28.

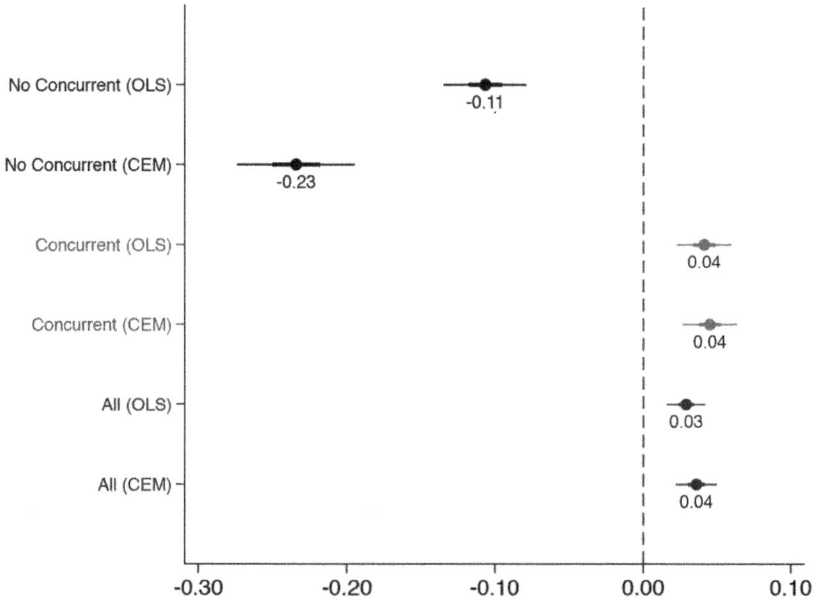

Figure 16. Change in county-level Republican House vote shares, ordinary least squares (OLS)/coarsened exact matching (CEM) estimates. OLS and CEM-pruned OLS estimates of the relative changes in county-level House Republican vote shares in treated states posttreatment. All models include all pretreatment matching variables as controls. Robust standard errors clustered on states; 90% confidence intervals. Color version available as an online enhancement.

and 1976 are 4 percentage points larger in the treated states relative to the control states.

Finally, the "all" coefficients are estimated using the full sample of counties, in which treatment is defined as a county's location in a state that had a limit on campaign spending struck by the Court's ruling in *Buckley* and that held state legislative and gubernatorial elections in 1976. This sample of 2,934 counties was again preprocessed using CEM on the average levels of and changes in county-level Republican House vote shares in 1972 and 1974.[17] Here again we see increased Republican vote shares posttreatment relative to all other states posttreatment. First differences in county-level Republican House vote shares between 1974 and 1976 are 3–4 percentage points higher in the treated states holding concurrent elections in 1976 relative to all other states. Figure A7 replicates the CEM models from

[17] The unmatched $\mathcal{L}_1$ is 0.51; after pruning 1,032 control counties using Sturge's rule to bin the matching variables, the $\mathcal{L}_1$ statistic is reduced to 0.28.

figure 16 using only the sample of nonsouthern states; results are nearly identical to those reported in figure 16.

These vote share estimates for concurrently held congressional elections are comparable in magnitude to the vote share estimates for gubernatorial elections, indicating large spillover effects of *Buckley* in concurrent congressional elections. This is consistent with greater pro-Republican campaign spending mobilizing more pro-Republican turnout in all concurrently held post-*Buckley* elections in the treated states relative to the control states (Spenkuch and Toniatti 2018) and/or inducing greater short-term increases in pro-Republican candidate preferences in the treated states relative to the control states (Gerber et al. 2011).

5.2. House DW-NOMINATE Scores

The vote share evidence is consistent with the hypothesis that *Buckley*'s repeal of state-level campaign spending limits benefitted not only Republican candidates running in state legislative and gubernatorial elections in the repeal states but also Republican candidates running in those federal elections being held concurrently with state elections in the repeal states. In the repeal states with concurrent federal elections, relative increases in Republican spending in state elections may have generated relative increases in pro-Republican turnout and/or short-term voter preferences, increases that may have benefitted all Republican candidates on the ballot in those states.

The remaining hypothesis of interest is that the increased ability to spend in the repeal states may have generated more conservative policy positions among posttreatment state candidates vying for the support of newly relevant conservative donors. We lack the estimates of state legislators' preferences for this period that would allow us to estimate *Buckley*'s effect on the same. However, given the apparent spillover effects in concurrently held federal elections, we can estimate this effect on House incumbents. If state legislative and gubernatorial candidates moved to the right in the treated states posttreatment and were using donor funds to generate voter turnout and/or short-term preferences for their more conservative candidacies, these more conservative electorates may have induced House candidates to also move to the right in those treated states with posttreatment concurrent federal elections.

Figures 17 and 18 report average House DW-NOMINATE scores across treated and control states for the sets of states not holding and holding concurrent state legislative or gubernatorial elections in 1976. As we would expect, there is no apparent evidence of an effect of *Buckley* on DW-NOMINATE scores in the states not holding

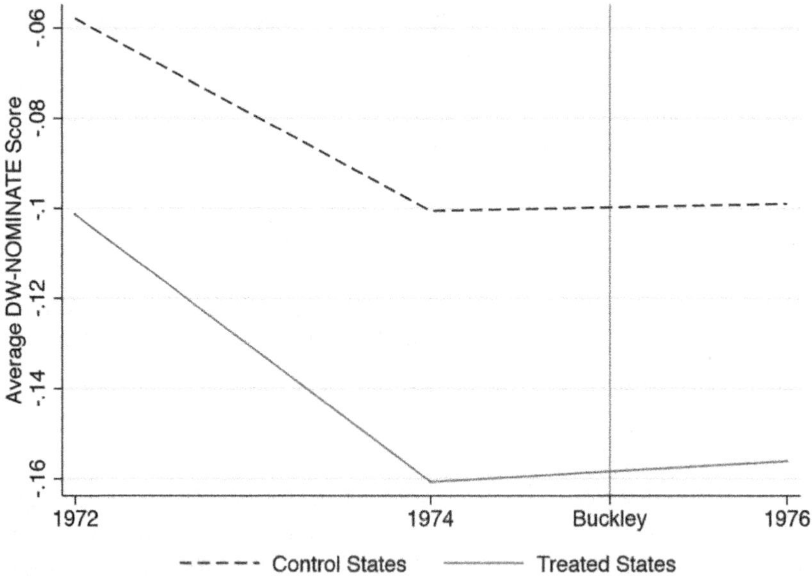

Figure 17. Average DW-NOMINATE scores in states with no concurrent 1976 state elections. Color version available as an online enhancement.

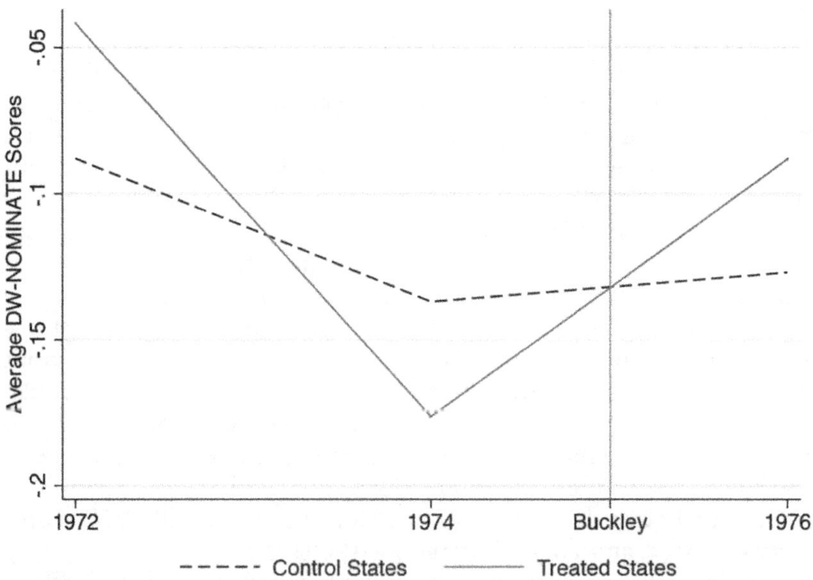

Figure 18. Average DW-NOMINATE scores in states with concurrent 1976 state elections. Color version available as an online enhancement.

concurrent elections in 1976; trends are almost precisely parallel across the two sets of states. However, there is a sharp movement rightward in DW-NOMINATE scores in the treated states postruling in states holding concurrent elections in 1976, a movement that is not mirrored in the control states.

Figure 19 reports DD estimates from equation (1) of the coefficient on Spending $\text{Limit}_s \times \text{Post-}Buckley_t$, along with 90% confidence intervals, for states not holding concurrent elections in 1976, states holding concurrent elections, and all states, in which treatment is defined as a district's location in a state that both had a limit on campaign spending struck by the Court's ruling in *Buckley* and held state legislative and gubernatorial elections in 1976. In states not holding concurrent state elections, DW-NOMINATE scores in treated states moved slightly to the left after the 1976 elections relative to scores in the control states. In states holding concurrent state elections, however, DW-NOMINATE scores moved 0.06 point to the right postruling in treated states relative to a baseline DW-NOMINATE average

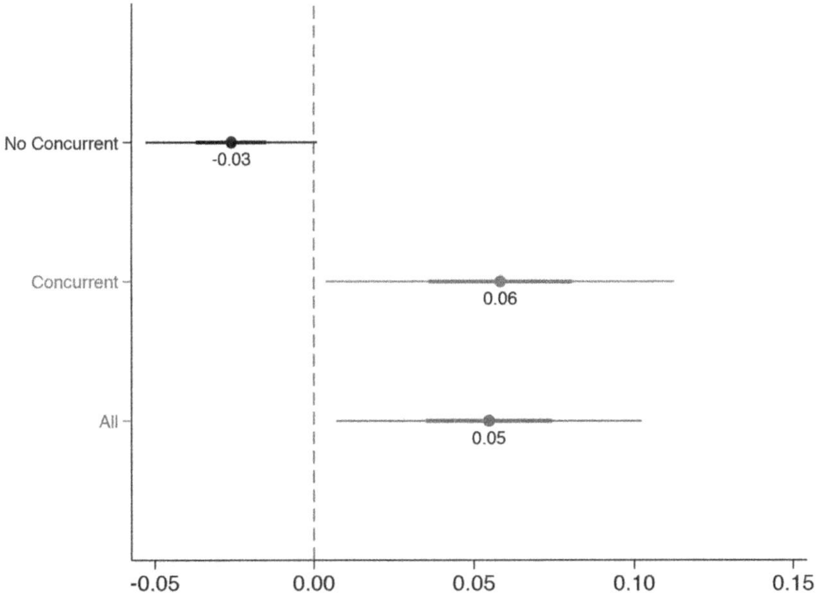

Figure 19. Difference in differences (DD) estimates; DW-NOMINATE scores 1972–80. Ordinary least squares DD estimates of the relative changes in district-level House DW-NOMINATE scores, 1972–80, for districts located in states not holding concurrent elections in 1976, districts located in states holding concurrent elections, and districts in all states, in which treatment is defined as location in a treated state holding concurrent elections in 1976. All models include district and year fixed effects; 90% confidence intervals reported. Color version available as an online enhancement.

of −0.10 point in the control states. The same pattern is seen in the estimates using all states, defining treatment as a treated state holding concurrent state elections in 1976; DW-NOMINATE scores moved 0.05 point to the right postruling in treated/concurrent states, again relative to a baseline DW-NOMINATE average of −0.10 in the control states.

Figure 20 reports OLS and CEM-pruned OLS estimates of the coefficients on spending limit$_s$ from equation (2), along with 90% confidence intervals. The dependent variable is the change in district-level DW-NOMINATE scores between 1974 and 1976. The "no concurrent" coefficients are estimated using only the sample of states not holding concurrent state legislative or gubernatorial elections in 1976; the "concurrent" coefficients are estimated using only the sample of

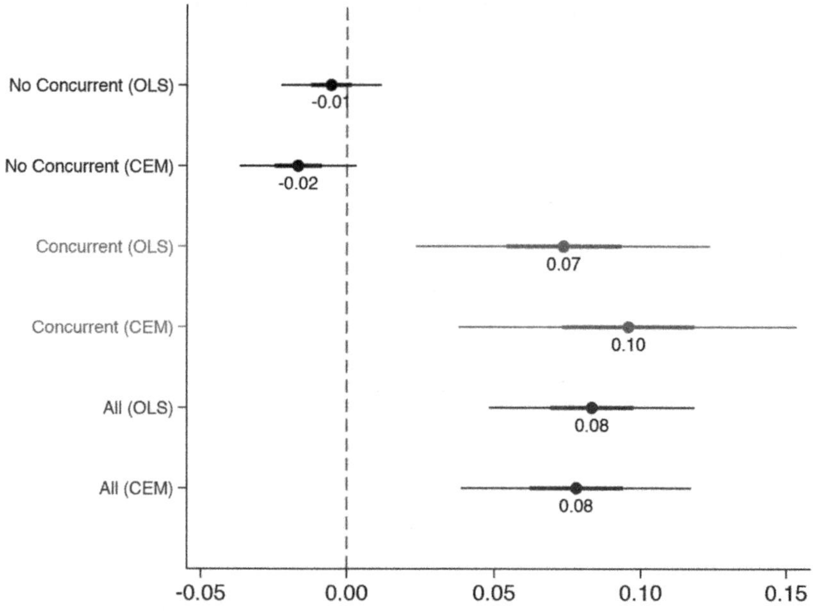

Figure 20. Ordinary least squares (OLS)/coarsened exact matching (CEM) estimates; change in DW-NOMINATE scores 1974–76. OLS and CEM-pruned OLS estimates of the relative changes in district-level House DW-NOMINATE scores between the ninety-fourth and ninety-fifth Congresses, for districts located in states not holding concurrent elections in 1976, districts located in states holding concurrent elections, and districts in all states, in which treatment is defined as location in a treated state holding concurrent elections in 1976. Districts in CEM models are matched based on average levels of and changes in DW-NOMINATE scores across the ninety-third and ninety-fourth Congresses. All models include preruling matching variables as controls; robust standard errors clustered on states; 90% confidence intervals reported. Color version available as an online enhancement.

states holding concurrent state legislative and gubernatorial elections in 1976; the "all" coefficients are estimated using the full sample of counties, in which treatment is defined as a district's location in a state that had a limit on campaign spending struck by the Court's ruling in *Buckley* and that held state legislative and gubernatorial elections in 1976. In the CEM models, samples are preprocessed using CEM on the average levels of and changes in district-level DW-NOMINATE scores in 1972 and 1974. All models include preruling matching variables as controls; robust standard errors are clustered on states.

There is no evidence of an effect of *Buckley* in the treated states posttreatment, relative to the control states posttreatment, in states not holding concurrent elections in 1976. However, in the models taking into account the concurrence of state and federal elections, DW-NOMINATE scores move 0.07–0.10 point more to the right in treated states posttreatment relative to a baseline increase in conservatism in the control states of 0.01 DW-NOMINATE point. The same pattern is seen in the estimates using all states, defining treatment as a treated state holding concurrent state elections in 1976; DW-NOMINATE scores moved 0.08 point more to the right postruling in treated/concurrent states relative to a baseline increase in conservatism in the control states of 0.01 DW-NOMINATE point.

5.3. Robustness

We can challenge the results reported in figure 20 in two ways. First, we can exclude southern states on the theory noted earlier that the presence of Jimmy Carter at the top of the ticket may be a confounder. Figure A8 replicates figure 20 after excluding the southern states; results are nearly identical to those reported for the full sample.

Second, we can conduct a preruling placebo test, assuming that a placebo *Buckley v. Valeo* ruling took place between the 1972 and 1974 congressional elections. If we see estimates similar to those reported in figure 20, we can assume that the latter estimates were not in fact the result of the Court's ruling in January 1976 but instead were simply the continuation of preruling trends. Figure A9 replicates figure 20 for the preruling period. Treated states are defined as those states with state-level campaign spending restrictions in 1974; concurrent states are defined as those states holding legislative and gubernatorial elections concurrently with federal elections in 1974. All CEM estimates were preprocessed using Sturge's rule on the average levels of and changes in districts' DW-NOMINATE scores in the ninety-second and ninety-third Congresses. There is no evidence of a preruling conservative shift in DW-NOMINATE scores in the treated states relative to the control states.

6. DISCUSSION

In the Supreme Court's campaign finance jurisprudence, contribution limits have often been held to sufficiently serve the government's interest in preventing corruption so as to warrant their potential negative impacts on speech rights. Spending limits, by contrast, have not been seen as sufficiently deterrent of corruption so as to warrant the same treatment. Moreover, the Court's majorities have failed to find any other governmental interest sufficiently served by spending limits to justify their potential negative impacts on speech rights. In *Buckley v. Valeo* (1976), the majority considered and rejected an "anti-distortion" governmental interest, claiming that campaign spending is unlikely to distort electoral outcomes because it is an effect of candidate support, not a cause. As the Court stated this empirical claim in *MCFL* (1986), the "relative availability of funds is after all a rough barometer of public support" (479 U.S., at 258).

If, in fact, the "relative availability of funds" to a campaign is "a rough barometer of public support," as declared by the *MCFL* majority, then removing spending restrictions in elections should have no causal impacts. Of specific interest here, the Supreme Court's ruling in *Buckley*, striking campaign spending restrictions in 26 states, should have had no causal impacts.

Yet the findings reported here indicate that the *Buckley* ruling in fact had significant impacts in state legislative, gubernatorial, and congressional elections. The *Buckley*-induced removal of state limits on campaign spending led to increased Republican vote shares in state legislative and gubernatorial elections, to increased Republican candidate entry and decreased Democratic candidate entry in state legislative elections, and to both increased Republican House vote shares and the election of relatively more conservative House incumbents in the states both affected by the ruling and holding concurrent federal and state elections. Overall, the findings suggest that the rationale for the core distinction in the Supreme Court's campaign finance jurisprudence, subjecting spending restrictions to greater scrutiny than contribution restrictions, has little empirical foundation.

APPENDIX

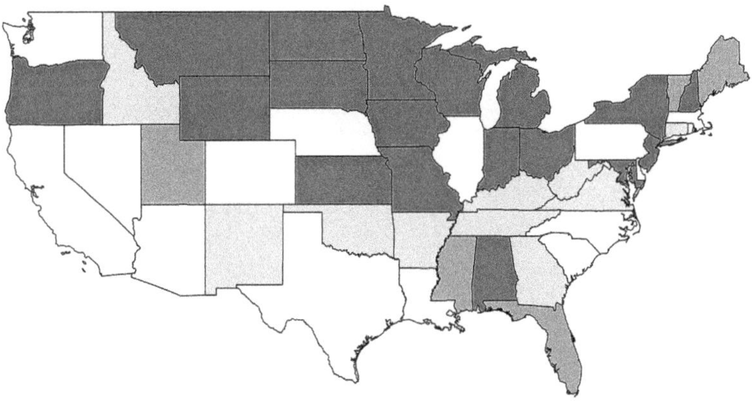

Figure A1. States enacting mandatory expenditure limits (Primo and Milyo 2006). Dark grey = states that enacted spending limits prior to 1950 and did not change them prior to 1976; medium grey = states that enacted spending limits between 1950 and 1976; light grey = states that had spending limits at some point between 1950 and 1976 but repealed them before *Buckley*; white = states that had no spending limits between 1950 and 1976. Color version available as an online enhancement.

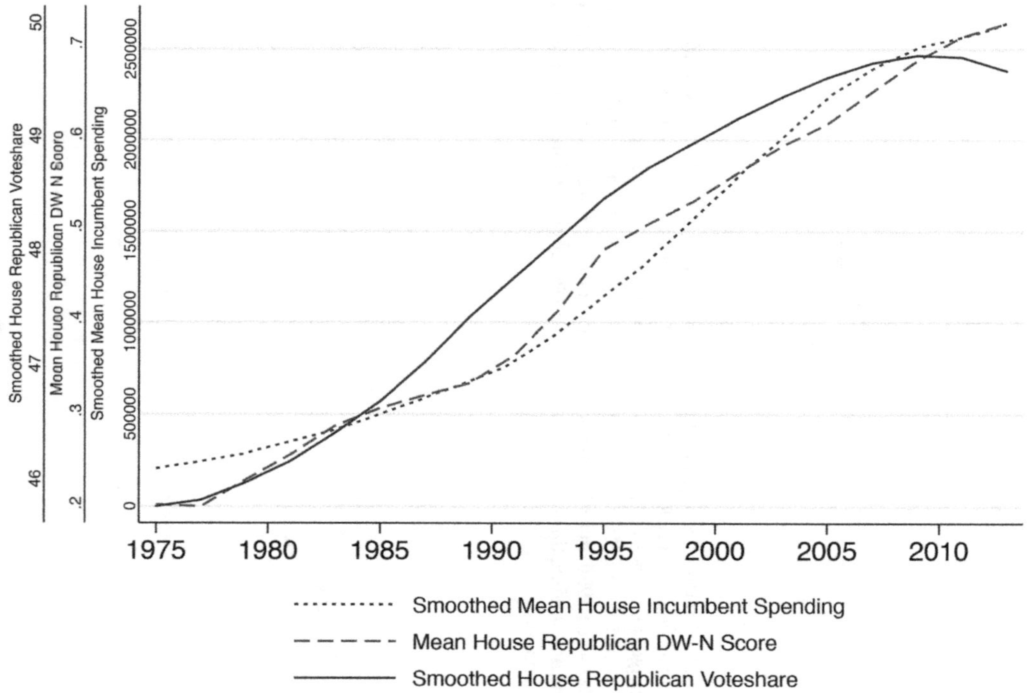

Figure A2. National Republican House vote share, mean House incumbent spending, and mean House Republican DW-NOMINATE scores (ICPSR 2013; Center for Responsive Politics 2015). Color version available as an online enhancement.

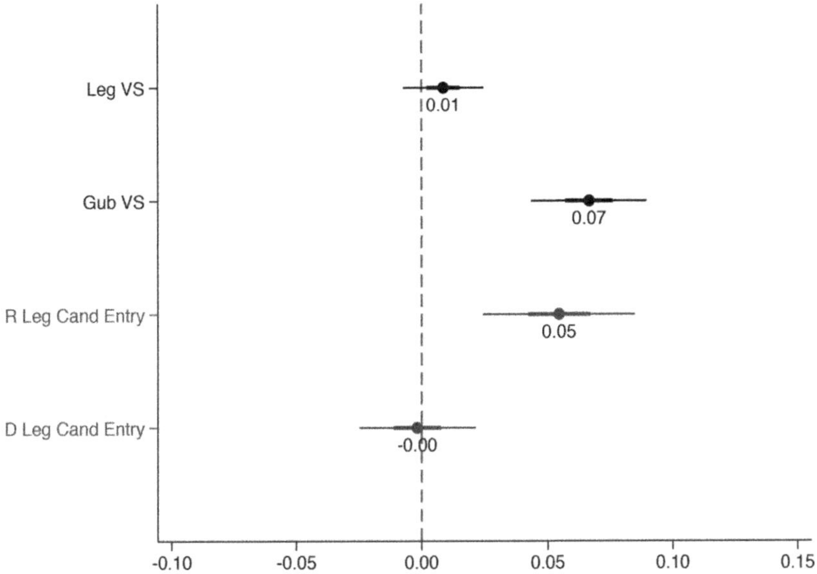

Figure A3. Republican electoral success in nonsouthern state elections, 1972–81. Ordinary least squares difference in differences estimates of the change in Republican electoral success in nonsouthern treated states posttreatment. All models include district/county fixed effects, year fixed effects, and state-specific linear time trends; 90% and 50% confidence intervals reported. Cand = candidate; D = Democratic; Gub = gubernatorial; Leg = legislative; R = Republican; VS = vote shares. Color version available as an online enhancement.

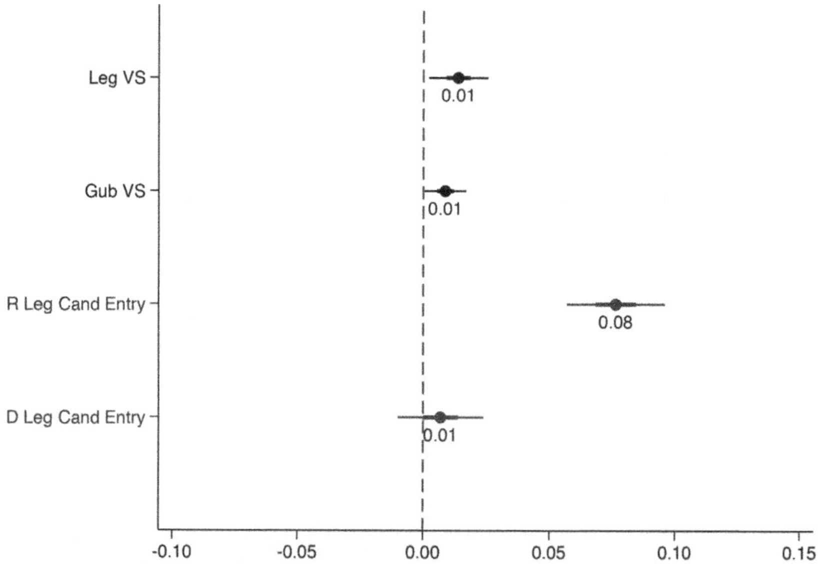

Figure A4. **Change in Republican vote shares in 1978 and 1974 state elections, coarsened exact matching (CEM) estimates. CEM-pruned ordinary least squares estimates of the relative change in Republican vote shares in treated states posttreatment, using 1978 as first posttreatment election. "Pretreat" models include levels of and trends in pretreatment vote shares. "Pretreat All" models include all pretreatment variables as controls. Cand = candidate; D = Democratic; Gub = gubernatorial; Leg = legislative; R = Republican; VS = vote shares. Color version available as an online enhancement.**

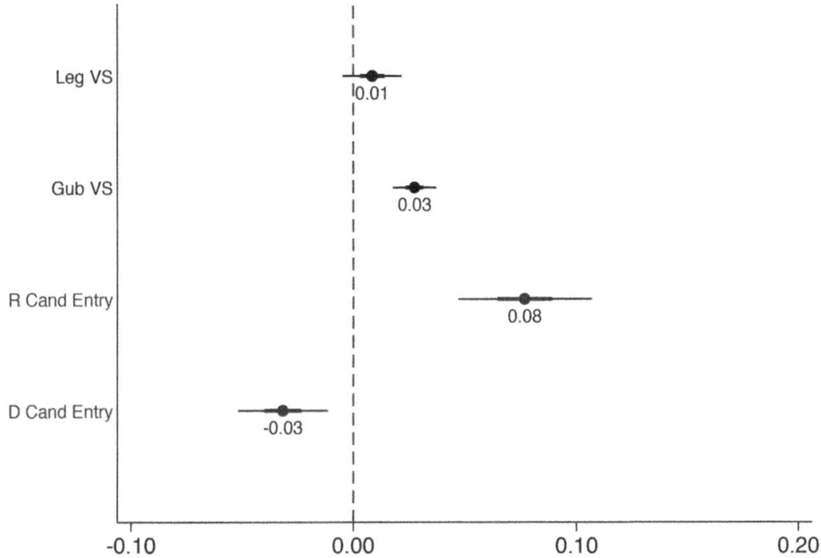

Figure A5. **Change in Republican electoral success in state elections, coarsened exact matching (CEM) estimates, states with campaign spending statutes unchanged since 1950. CEM-pruned ordinary least squares (OLS) estimates of the change in Republican electoral success in state elections in treated states posttreatment, using only those states whose laws regulating campaign expenditure limits remained unchanged between 1950 and 1976. All results are from OLS regressions using weights derived from coarsened exact matching on average Republican vote share 1972–74 and change in Republican vote share 1972–74 (state legislative vote share, *n* = 1,927); average Republican vote share 1972–74 and change in Republican vote share 1968–72 or 1970–74 (gubernatorial vote share, *n* = 1,929); average Republican/Democratic legislative candidate entry 1972–74 and change in Republican/Democratic legislative candidate entry 1972–74 (candidate entry, *n* = 2,104). Cand = candidate; D = Democratic; Gub = gubernatorial; Leg = legislative; R = Republican; VS = vote shares. Color version available as an online enhancement.**

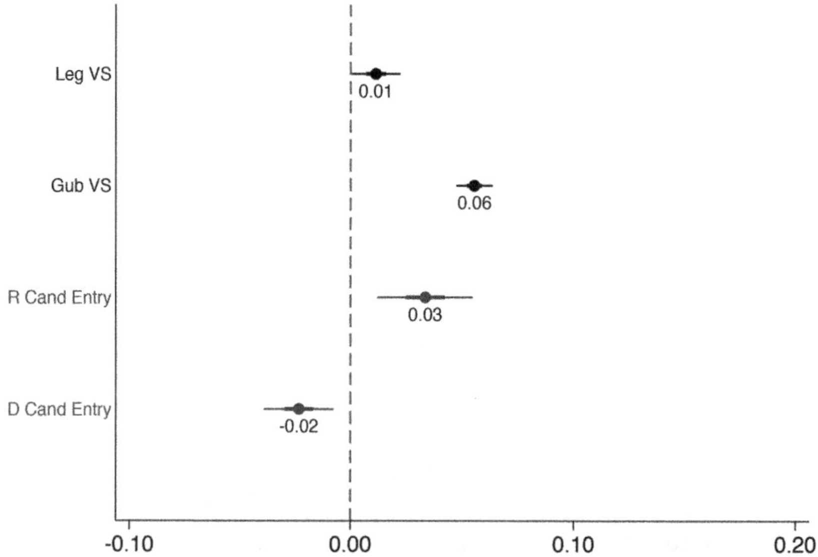

Figure A6. **Change in Republican electoral success in state elections, coarsened exact matching (CEM) estimates, controlling for pretreatment presence of other campaign finance statutes. CEM-pruned ordinary least squares (OLS) estimates of the change in Republican electoral success in state elections in treated states posttreatment controlling for the presence in 1974 of statutes requiring disclosure, restricting individual contributions to candidates, and restricting corporate and union contributions to candidates. All results are from OLS regressions using weights derived from CEM on all pretreatment variables reported in table A2. Legislative district, *n* = 2,613; gubernatorial county, *n* = 2,474. Cand = candidate; D = Democratic; Gub = gubernatorial; Leg = legislative; R = Republican; VS = vote shares. Color version available as an online enhancement.**

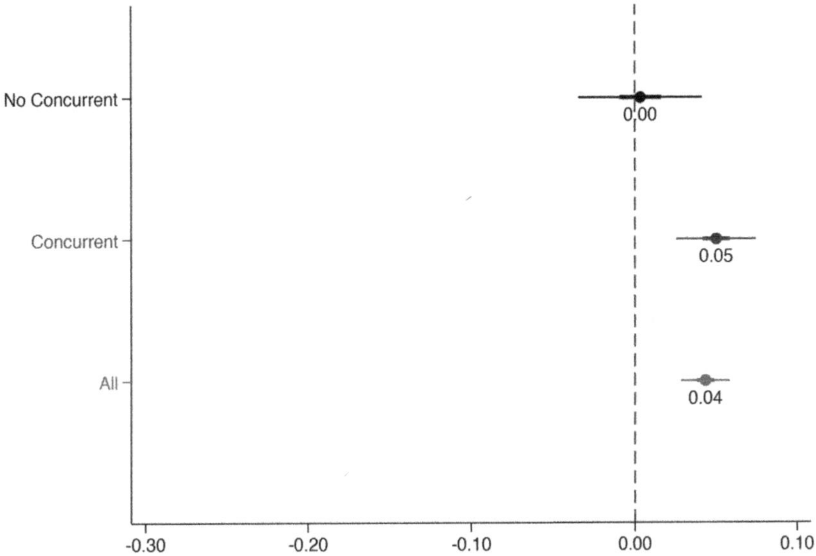

Figure A7. Change in nonsouthern county-level Republican House vote shares, coarsened exact matching (CEM) estimates. CEM-pruned ordinary least squares estimates of the relative changes in county-level House Republican vote shares in treated states posttreatment. All models include all pretreatment matching variables as controls. Southern states are excluded. Color version available as an online enhancement.

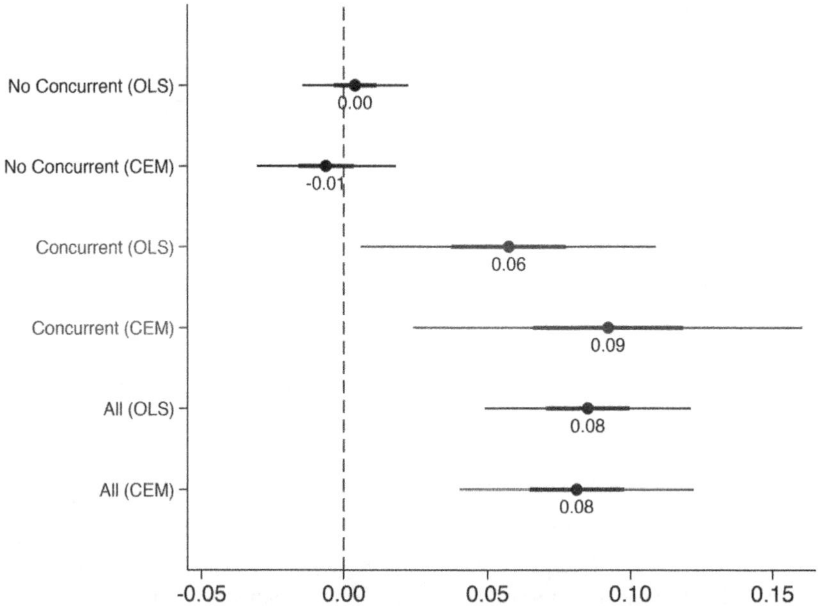

Figure A8. Ordinary least squares (OLS)/coarsened exact matching (CEM) estimates; change in DW-NOMINATE scores, 1974–1976, nonsouthern states only. OLS and CEM-pruned OLS estimates of the relative changes in district-level House DW-NOMINATE scores between the ninety-fourth and ninety-fifth Congresses, nonsouthern states only, for districts located in states not holding concurrent elections in 1976, districts located in states holding concurrent elections, and districts in all states, in which treatment is defined as location in a treated state holding concurrent elections in 1976. Districts in CEM models are matched based on average levels of and changes in DW-NOMINATE scores across the ninety-third and ninety-fourth Congresses. All models include preruling matching variables as controls; robust standard errors clustered on states; 90% confidence intervals reported. Color version available as an online enhancement.

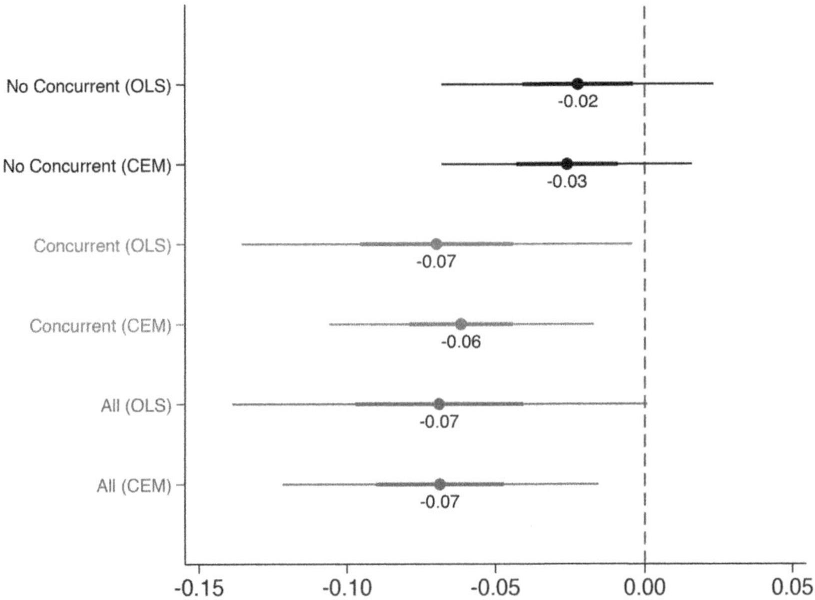

Figure A9. Ordinary least squares (OLS)/coarsened exact matching (CEM) estimates; change in DW-NOMINATE scores, 1972–1974, preruling placebo test. OLS and CEM-pruned OLS estimates of the relative changes in district-level House DW-NOMINATE scores between the ninety-third and ninety-fourth Congresses. All models include all pretreatment matching variables as controls. Robust standard errors clustered on states; 90% confidence intervals reported. Color version available as an online enhancement.

Table A1. Descriptive Statistics

	Control States	*n*	Treated States	*n*	Difference
Average Republican legislative vote share:					
1972	.38	1,834	.49	1,728	.11**
1974	.33	1,715	.38	2,290	.04**
1976	.33	1,779	.42	2,149	.09**
Average Republican gubernatorial vote share:					
1972	.42	696	.51	640	.09**
1974	.35	1,133	.46	934	.10**
1976	.35	443	.49	450	.14**

Table A1. *(continued)*

	Control States	n	Treated States	n	Difference
Average Republican legislative candidate entry:					
1972	.72	1,992	.82	1,939	.11**
1974	.68	1,869	.78	2,304	.10**
1976	.65	1,947	.83	2,166	.18**
Average Democratic legislative candidate entry:					
1972	.97	1,992	.84	1,939	.13**
1974	.97	1,869	.96	2,304	.01*
1976	.97	1,947	.93	2,166	.04**

State legislative/gubernatorial outcomes are averaged across all state legislative districts/counties reporting nonmissing data in specified years.
$^{*}p < .05$.
$^{**}p < .01$.

Table A2. CEM Balance Statistics

	Unmatched Sample	Matched Sample
State legislative elections:		
$\mathcal{L}_1$	.30	.19
Avg R VS, 1972–74 $\mathcal{L}_1$	.15	.05
Change in R VS, 1972–74 $\mathcal{L}_1$	.13	.08
Avg R cand entry, 1972–74 $\mathcal{L}_1$	.10	.00
Change in R cand entry, 1972–74 $\mathcal{L}_1$	.02	.00
Avg D cand entry, 1972–74 $\mathcal{L}_1$	.04	.00
Change in D cand entry, 1972–74 $\mathcal{L}_1$	.03	.00
Number of strata	64	48
n control	1,286	1,262
n treated	1,360	1,351
Gubernatorial elections:		
$\mathcal{L}_1$	.52	.26
Avg R VS, 1968–72 or 1970–74 $\mathcal{L}_1$	.38	.07
Change in R VS, 1968–72 or 1970–74 $\mathcal{L}_1$	.34	.09

Table A2. *(continued)*

	Unmatched Sample	Matched Sample
Number of strata	83	47
n control	1,491	1,366
n treated	1,190	1,108

CEM performed using Sturge's rule on all variables. The overall $\mathcal{L}_1$ statistics measure the distance or lack of overlap between the multidimensional distributions of these variables across the treatment and control groups, within each cross-section (Iacus et al. 2012). For example, before pruning, the overall $\mathcal{L}_1$ for the sample of state legislative districts is 0.30, indicating that only 70% of the two multidimensional distributions overlap. After pruning, the overall $\mathcal{L}_1$ is reduced to 0.19, indicating that 81% of the distributions overlap, with a loss of 9 treated and 24 control districts. Avg = average; cand = candidate; D = Democratic; R = Republican; VS = vote shares.

REFERENCES

Alschuler, Albert W., Laurence H. Tribe, Norman L. Eisen, and Richard W. Painter. 2018. "Why Limits on Contributions to Super PACs Should Survive *Citizens United*." *Fordham Law Review* 86:2299.

Ansolabehere, Stephen, John M. de Figueiredo, and James M. Snyder Jr. 2003. "Why Is There So Little Money in US Politics?" *Journal of Economic Perspectives* 17 (1): 105–30.

Barber, Michael J., and Nolan McCarty. 2015. "Causes and Consequences of Polarization." In *Solutions to Political Polarization in America*, edited by Nathaniel Persily, 15–58. New York: Cambridge University Press.

Benoit, Kenneth, and Michael Marsh. 2008. "The Campaign Value of Incumbency: A New Solution to the Puzzle of Less Effective Incumbent Spending." *American Journal of Political Science* 52 (4): 874–90.

Besley, Timothy, and Anne Case. 2003. "Political Institutions and Policy Choices: Evidence from the States." *Journal of Economic Literature* 41 (1): 7–73.

Center for Responsive Politics. 2015. OpenSecrets.org.

Downs, Anthony. 1957. *An Economic Theory of Democracy*. New York: HarperCollins.

Enos, Ryan D., and Anthony Fowler. 2018. "Aggregate Effects of Large-Scale Campaigns on Voter Turnout." *Political Science Research and Methods* 6 (4): 733–51.

Feddersen, Timothy, and Faruk Gul. 2014. "Polarization and Income Inequality: A Dynamic Model of Unequal Democracy." Working paper, Northwestern University.

Federal Election Campaign Act of 1971, 86 Stat. 3, as amended by the Federal Election Campaign Act Amendments of 1974, 88 Stat. 1263 (1974).

Fox, Justin, and Lawrence Rothenberg. 2011. "Influence without Bribes: A Noncontracting Model of Campaign Giving and Policymaking." *Political Analysis* 19 (3): 325–41.

Gerber, Alan S., James G. Gimpel, Donald P. Green, and Daron R. Shaw. 2011. "How Large and Long-lasting Are the Persuasive Effects of Televised Campaign Ads? Results from a Randomized Field Experiment." *American Political Science Review* 105 (1): 135–50.

Green, Donald P., Mary C. McGrath, and Peter M. Aronow. 2013. "Field Experiments and the Study of Voter Turnout." *Journal of Elections, Public Opinion, and Parties* 23 (1): 27–48.

Hall, Andrew B. 2016. "Systemic Effects of Campaign Spending: Evidence from Corporate Contribution Bans in US State Legislatures." *Political Science Research and Methods* 4 (2): 343–59.

Hall, Andrew B., and James M. Snyder. 2015. "How Much of the Incumbency Advantage Is Due to Scare-Off?" *Political Science Research and Methods* 3 (3): 493–514.

Harvey, Anna, and Taylor Mattia. Forthcoming. "Does Money Have a Republican Bias? Estimating the Causal Impact of *Citizens United* on State Legislative Preferences." *Public Choice.*

Ho, Daniel E., Kosuke Imai, Gary King, and Elizabeth Stuart. 2007. "Matching as Nonparametric Preprocessing for Reducing Model Dependence in Parametric Causal Inference." *Political Analysis* 15 (3): 199–236.

Iacus, Stefano M., Gary King, and Giuseppe Porro. 2012. "Causal Inference without Balance Checking: Coarsened Exact Matching." *Political Analysis* 20:1–24.

Inter-University Consortium for Political and Social Research. 2013. *General Election Data for the United States, 1950–1990.* Ann Arbor, MI: Inter-University Consortium for Political and Social Research [distributor]. https://doi.org/10.3886/ICPSR00013.v2.

Klarner, Carl, Williams Berry, Thomas Carsey, Malcolm Jewell, Richard Niemi, Lynda Powell, and James Snyder. 2013. "State Legislative Election Returns Data, 1967–2010." Harvard Dataverse, V1. http://hdl.handle.net/1902.1/20401.

Klumpp, Tilman, Hugo M. Mialon, and Michael A. Williams. 2016. "The Business of American Democracy: *Citizens United*, Independent Spending, and Elections." *Journal of Law and Economics* 59 (1): 1–43.

Mayer, Jane. 2016. *Dark Money: The Hidden History of the Billionaires behind the Rise of the Radical Right*. New York: Doubleday.

McCarty, Nolan, Keith T. Poole, and Howard Rosenthal. 1997. *Income Redistribution and the Realignment of American Politics*. Washington, DC: American Enterprise Institute.

McCarty, Nolan, Keith T. Poole, and Howard Rosenthal. 2006. *Polarized America: The Dance of Ideology and Unequal Riches*. Cambridge, MA: MIT Press.

Primo, David M., and Jeffrey Milyo. 2006. "Campaign Finance Laws and Political Efficacy: Evidence from the States." *Election Law Journal* 5 (1): 23–39.

Spencer, Douglas M., and Abby K. Wood. 2014. "*Citizens United*, States Divided: An Empirical Analysis of Independent Political Spending." *Indiana Law Journal* 89:315–72.

Spenkuch, Jorg L., and David Toniatti. 2018. "Political Advertising and Election Results." *Quarterly Journal of Economics* 133 (4): 1981–2035.

Stratmann, Thomas. 2005. "Some Talk: Money in Politics. A (Partial) Review of the Literature." *Public Choice* 124:135–56.

———. 2018. "Campaign Finance." In *Oxford Handbook of Public Choice*, edited by Roger D. Congleton, Bernard N. Grofman, and Stefan Voigt. New York: Oxford University Press.

Testing for the Effect of Campaign Expenditure Limits

Thomas Stratmann[*]

The consequences of campaign expenditure limits are an understudied area in the field of campaign finance. The article "Is Campaign Spending a Cause or an Effect? Reexamining the Empirical Foundations of *Buckley v. Valeo* (1976)" by Anna Harvey is a welcome and interesting contribution to this field of study. Harvey's article covers a lot of ground. It analyzes the effect of campaign expenditure limits on electoral outcomes for state House races, governor races, and federal races, and on US House of Representatives DW-NOMINATE scores. In this discussion of the article, I focus on the methodology employed and suggest future work that can build on the current article.

In 1976 the Supreme Court found that campaign expenditure limits in electoral races are unconstitutional. Twenty-six states had these limits prior to 1976, both for state legislative and gubernatorial elections. After 1976, these 26 states were forced to repeal their expenditure limits. Harvey exploits these repeals in her empirical analysis by studying elections in the majority of the 50 states between 1972 and 1981. A large part of the empirical analysis in this article uses state and year fixed effects to identify the effect of the 1976 Supreme Court decision and uses outcome in a state House district in a given state in a given year as the unit of observation.

The article suggests that repeal of expenditure limits for state legislative races had an effect on electoral outcomes and political competition. In particular, the results show that campaign expenditure limits hurt Republican candidates in terms of vote shares and political

* George Mason University.

Electronically published: December 4, 2019
 978-0-226-64653-4/2019/0027-0006$10.00

participation. The hypothesized mechanism is with the lifting of expenditure limits Republican candidates are able to spend larger amounts on their election campaigns, which in turn generates a larger vote share. A related idea proposed in this article is that the lifting of limits leads to entry by more Republican candidates because the lifting of limits allows them not to be subject to caps on spending. Although the regression results in the article support these hypotheses, it would be nice to have additional supporting evidence. For example, prior to 1976, were Republican candidates, as opposed to Democratic candidates, more likely to bump up against the spending limits? Another piece of supporting evidence might come from testing whether the effect found in this article was stronger in those states that had more stringent campaign expenditure limits.

If expenditure limits have a bite, that is, if limits are in effect binding, their removal may motivate potential candidates to enter a race. The belief that they are binding may also motivate potential candidates to enter the race. It would be nice to have more evidence whether, prior to *Buckley v. Valeo*, expenditure limits were binding and, if so, for what percentage of all candidates, perhaps broken down by incumbents, challengers, and candidates in open seat races. And it would be good to know something of the "conceived wisdom" at that time, perhaps from newspaper articles, to what extent expenditure limits had a bite. However, these data are difficult to come by. One way to get to the issue for whom expenditure limits were binding prior to the 1976 decision is to analyze whether the striking down of expenditure limits had an asymmetric effect for a major party candidate entry versus a minor party entry, for incumbents versus challengers, or for entry in open seat races. For example, if major party candidates face fewer constraints in raising campaign contributions relative to minor party candidates and, consequently, major party candidates spend more on their campaigns, then lifting of expenditure restrictions may increase major party candidate entry.

Hopefully, future theoretical work might provide more guidance for empirical work on campaign expenditure limits. In particular, theoretical work might suggest additional channels and mechanisms of how expenditure limits might matter for electoral outcomes and under what type of circumstances expenditure limits matter for political competition and participation. Other measures of competitiveness in addition to those in Harvey's article could be examined as well, such as incumbency reelection rates, the frequency of competitive elections, and the frequency of open seat races.

Other avenues of future research may examine whether the documented effect occurs because Republicans experienced an increase in campaign contributions, which in turn resulted in more spending. Or, assuming expenditure limits were binding, did Republican supporters contribute less to their preferred candidate prior to *Buckley* because they knew that their contributions could not be spent because of expenditure limits?

For the analysis in this article, it is of interest to unpack the coefficient of interest, that is, to show the dynamics. Given the span of the data analyzed, different coefficients can be estimated for the two elections prior to the *Buckley* decision and for the three election years after that decision. This way we can better understand whether the estimated effect is because of an immediate change after the 1976 decision as opposed to a gradual adjustment over time. Or perhaps there was a large immediate effect that was attenuated over time. The descriptive statistics suggest that there was a onetime bump in entry, right after the Supreme Court decision, and a fairly stable pattern after 1976. It would be nice to see if such a statistical analysis would be consistent with these descriptive statistics.

Given that some states have fewer than 100 House races (e.g., California) and others have more than 300 House races (e.g., New Hampshire), a regression analysis that uses a House race as a unit of observation will weigh the campaign expenditure law in states with a larger number of races more heavily. An alternative to the approach taken in the article would be to make the unit of observation a state in a given year, an approach which weights each state equally. Which approach is correct depends on the research question and hypotheses. At the same time, from a welfare perspective, districts composed of smaller populations are underweighted in a regression analysis that has a district as a unit of observation, as are low population states where the unit of observation a state. Which specification is correct will depend on the hypotheses being tested and the research question of interest.

It would be nice to learn a bit more about what other elements of state election laws were changed when states adjusted their statutes in response to *Buckley v. Valeo*. For example, did states that removed their campaign expenditure limits increase, at the same time, their contribution limits from individuals, corporations, unions, or political action committees? Did they change public funding provisions or alter other aspects of their election laws, such as candidate ballot access or signature requirements?

As in all studies that examine changes of a particular law, the concern is whether the particular introduction or removal of the law is the only thing that changed in the same legislative period, whether other laws were introduced at the same time, or whether regulatory procedures changed, which could account for some or all of the estimated effect. Harvey is clearly aware of these issues, as evidenced by offering a number of robustness tests. I would have liked to see some of the robustness tests shown as the main specification in the article rather than in an appendix.

From reading this article, it is my understanding that the Supreme Court suggested that contribution limits are justified because of corruption concerns, but that campaign expenditures as a function of campaign contributions (i.e., underlying electoral support) were ruled not to be subject to caps. Put differently, the Supreme Court reasoned that campaign spending merely reflects the underlying support of the candidate and, thus, does not merit being limited. Although I follow the Court's logic, I do not quite understand the view put forth in this article; that is, with this decision and line of reasoning, the Supreme Court implied that expenditure limits do not matter for election outcomes.

Suppose campaign contributions are an expression of preference, as suggested by the Supreme Court. The way I understand the 1976 decision is that the justices opine that expenditure limits curtail the expression of preferences. But does this opinion imply that the justices assumed that by allowing additional expressions of preferences, one would not expect that removing such limits would result in changes in electoral outcomes? However, this is a matter of interpretation of Supreme Court assumptions used when making a decision and does not take anything away from the advance in our understanding of campaign expenditure limits to which this article makes a valuable contribution.

Judicial Choice among Cases for Certiorari

*Álvaro Bustos**
Tonja Jacobi†

How does the Supreme Court choose among cases to grant cert? In a model with a strategic Supreme Court, a continuum of rule-following lower courts, a set of potential cases for revision, and a distribution of future lower court cases, we show that the Court takes the case that will most significantly shape future lower court case outcomes in the direction that the Court prefers. That is, the Court grants cert to the case with maximum salience. If the Court is rather liberal (or conservative), then the most salient case is that which moves the discretionary range of the legal standard as far left (or right) as possible. But if the Court is moderate, then the most salient case will be a function of the skewedness of the distribution of ideologies of the lower courts and the likelihood that future cases will fall within the adjusted discretionary range. The extent of the political alignment of lower courts affects not only substantive lawmaking by the Supreme Court but also the earlier decision of whether to grant a given case cert to begin with.

* Álvaro Bustos is a professor in the School of Management at Pontificia Universidad Católica de Chile.

† Tonja Jacobi is a professor of law at Northwestern University Pritzker Law School. We thank attendees for their comments at the 2019 Supreme Court Economic Review Roundtable held at George Mason University, the 2016 Political Economy of the American Judiciary Conference held at Northwestern University, and the 2016 Latin American Workshop of Law and Economics held at Universidad de Los Andes, Colombia.

Electronically published: December 9, 2019
 978-0-226-64653-4/2019/0027-0007$10.00

1. INTRODUCTION

Public choice of legal issues has long focused on questions of how the Supreme Court shapes its own agenda (e.g., Jacobi 2008; Stearns and Zywicki 2009). Since the 1970s, an extensive empirical literature on certiorari has developed, establishing that ideology significantly shapes a justice's vote on whether to take a case (e.g., Boucher and Segal 1990), as does the ideological positions of the other justices (e.g., Caldeira, Wright, and Zorn 1999). But almost all of this analysis considers the dichotomous decision of whether or not to take a case (e.g., Linzer 1979; McGuire and Caldeira 1993), rather than the public choice question of how to choose between cases that each represent an opportunity to shape doctrine in a given area as well as an opportunity cost.[1] With a limited docket, there are deep economic and legal consequences in taking any given case and not taking other cases. This article considers how the justices choose among cases for cert.

To do so, we utilize a model of doctrinal development that captures common-law decision-making as a gradually diminishing range of discretion: in a unidimensional plane, there are two extreme intervals of determined cases, which bind future decision-making, and an internal interval of remaining discretion, in which lower court judges have freedom to choose (Baker and Mezzetti 2012; Niblett 2013). Each Supreme Court determination further reduces the discretionary range in one direction or the other. This model is an ideal vehicle for analyzing choice over cert because it enables us to represent, in a very simple fashion, the factors that are central to that decision: individual judicial ideology, the overall ideological preferences of the Supreme Court, the level of alignment between the Court and the lower court judges, the range of feasible outcomes of a case, the potential doctrinal impact of a decision, and the distribution of likely future cases. We show that this last factor, although previously seldom considered, is a very important one and leads to results that are not obvious.

When the Court decides which of two cases to take, it is also deciding whether to alter the upper or the lower bound of the doctrinal range. Each option decreases the discretionary range, to a greater or lesser extent, and also shapes the nature of the remaining doctrinal range: altering the lower bar makes the remaining discretionary range more conservative, and altering the upper bar makes the remaining

[1] But see Daughety and Reinganum (2006); Cameron, Segal, and Songer (2000); and Spitzer and Talley (2000), who address the certiorari decision as a strategic game played by the Supreme Court and the lower courts (both appeal and first instance) in which information plays a central role.

discretionary range more liberal. What will ensure that the Court prefers to change the lower bar rather than the upper bar? The answer depends primarily on two factors: first, the extent to which the Court is ideologically aligned with the lower court judges, who will sincerely decide future cases within the newly decreased discretionary range set by the upper and lower bars, one of which will be altered; and, second, the distribution of future cases that the lower courts face. Together, these two factors affect the salience of the chosen case and how significant it can be in shaping future lower court case outcomes in the direction that the Court prefers.

Importantly, when the Supreme Court decides which cases it should consider, it will not always choose cases that move the case law maximally in the direction of the preferences of the current justices. Each case decided by the Court eliminates some of the discretion of lower courts, as it gradually clarifies the law. When lower courts have ideological views that are compatible with the Supreme Court, then the value to the Court of narrowing the discretionary range is mitigated. Then the Court will be better off focusing on cases in which the lower courts are more likely to diverge from the Supreme Court's preferences. Political alignment between the Supreme Court and the lower courts has been shown to affect optimal decisions relating to application of substantive doctrine, such as applying Chevron deference (Cohen and Spitzer 1994), as well as how those doctrines are optimally shaped, for instance, using rules versus standards (Jacobi and Tiller 2007); this article shows that it can also affect the earlier decision of whether to hear a given case.

In particular, we find that ideologically extreme Courts grant cert to cases that unequivocally move the opposite boundary of the discretionary range as close as possible to the ideology of the Court. In contrast, ideologically moderate Courts might decide to move either boundary of the range. The reason for this finding is extreme Courts understand that lower courts with opposing ideologies can be constrained by imposing a discretionary range that is closer to the ideology of the Court because then more cases will be decided by the lower courts in the way that the Court wants. Moderate Courts will face the danger of undesirable lower court rulings in both directions and so will instead focus on granting cert to cases that will adjust the lower court discretion in a way to maximize impact over their future decisions.

We also examine the relative influence of the distribution of expected future cases and lower court ideology. We find that for the Court to alter the lower bar, it is sufficient that all or most of the lower court judges are liberal, regardless of the distribution of the cases (as long as the leftward distribution of cases is nonzero). However, the reverse is not true: it is not sufficient that all of the cases be likely to arise at the liberal end of the distribution, regardless of the ideologies of the judges. When the distribution of the cases and the lower court judges are concentrated in opposite directions, the two factors play off against each other but the ideology of the lower courts dominates. Then the Court may want to change the lower bound, even if the impact of changing the lower bound is small (the distribution of cases tends to the right), as long as the distribution of the ideologies of the lower courts tends sufficiently leftward. Thus, overall, it is not the distribution but the salience of the cases that matters—that is, the expected effect of the new standard as a product of the number of cases.

This helps explain some seeming puzzles that we see in judicial behavior. In some areas, such as criminal procedure, the Court regularly expends resources taking numerous cases that each make tiny changes in doctrine. In contrast, for a long time, scholars commented that patent law was neglected by the Court and overdue for doctrinal adjustment. Our findings shed new light on these contrasting judicial strategies. In some areas the Court will give close attention to seemingly almost insignificant doctrinal changes, whereas in others it will seemingly neglect opportunities for large doctrinal shifts. More specifically, our baseline model can be extended to show that the opportunity cost of forsaking large changes in one area of law may be compensated by even small changes in other areas because the distribution of expected cases and lower court ideologies can be very different in the different areas of law.[2]

The rest of the article is organized as follows. Section 2 provides additional background and discusses key elements of our model. Section 3 presents the model. Section 4 solves the model and derives the main results. The model is flexible enough to support various extensions. Section 5 presents and discusses seven extensions, showing which assumptions are harmless and which vary the conditions for granting cert: strategic lower courts, cases that cross multiple legal issues, potential overlap between the upper and lower boundaries, a three-justice Court, imperfect knowledge of future lower court cases, changes in the number of petitions for review, and permitting confirmations as well as reversals. In section 6, we conclude.

2. KEY CONCEPTS AND BACKGROUND

This section describes the relevant literature, assumptions, our setup, and extensions.

[2] See sec. 5.2, where we allow the Court to choose cases that relate to different areas of law.

2.1. Model Framework and Advantages

We incorporate the choice of certiorari into a model of legal evolution developed by Baker and Mezzetti (2012) and Niblett (2013). These authors model judicial learning and doctrinal evolution where sincere judges attempt to hone in on an exogenous optimal threshold between dichotomous outcomes, such as liability and nonliability, which they can only estimate through deciding a series of cases. Prior Supreme Court doctrine establishes high and low bounds, which translate into settled rules: cases above the upper threshold or below the lower threshold will be invalid; cases within the undetermined range are decided at the discretion of the lower court judge. When a new case is decided by the Supreme Court, its ruling sets the new upper or lower bound. Baker and Mezzetti and Niblett use this framework to model doctrinal development. We use it to model choice over cases.

The model is flexible enough to capture not only the standard liberal-conservative division but also variants on the left-right divide, such as individual rights versus state power division, considered here, or a proregulation versus libertarian division, considered later in this article. Consider, for example, Fourth Amendment doctrine concerning when a search warrant is required. A decision that a warrant is presumptively required before police can enter a home initially sets the upper boundary, elucidating a constitutional liberty; a decision that a warrant exemption exists for a public emergency sets the lower boundary, permitting greater state action. A subsequent decision that bringing a drug-sniffing dog onto the curtilage of the home requires a warrant moves the upper bar to the left, moving the remaining discretionary zone leftward, expanding constitutional rights. A decision that a caravan fits within the car exception, and thus does not get the presumption of the home protection, moves the lower bar to the right, expanding state regulatory power. Gradually, the discretionary range decreases. All else being equal, then, a conservative or statist (liberal or libertarian) justice deciding between two cases will want to take the case that will allow the Court to move the lower (upper) boundary farther to the right (left). But we show there is greater complexity to these strategies when the median justice is moderate.

Niblett (2013, 304) argues that this essential framework captures the law and economics view of the common law as a decentralized, sequential evolutionary process of incremental information acquisition, which eventually converges on a legal rule. Expanding Baker and Mezzetti's (2012) and Niblett's model to consider interaction of case types and court ideologies not only further develops that model, but it also contributes more broadly to the certiorari literature in three ways.

First, it allows us to consider the reality of judicial choice between cases. Previously, scholars have examined the factors that go into the up or down vote on a given petition; however, this ignores the trade-offs involved in choosing any given case instead of other alternatives.[3] The Supreme Court receives 7,000 to 8,000 petitions for review each year but chooses approximately 1% for full review. Scholars often disregard unpaid petitions, which traditionally made up half of the Court's cert pool and more recently constitutes three quarters of petitions as frivolous, although this characterization is disputed (Watson 2006). Even ignoring unpaid petitions still leaves approximately 2,000 petitions for the Court to cull down to approximately 80 cases. Even though the size of the Supreme Court's docket has been dropping in recent decades and is predicted to likely remain low (Owens and Simon 2012), the justices report searching for ways to deny each petition, because of the "small amount of available argument time in the face of so many petitions" (Perry 1991, 218–19). This suggests there is still a trade-off between cases, and so in assessing the "certworthiness" of any one petition, the Court must also consider the relative merits and opportunity costs of its other options.[4]

Second, the framework by Baker and Mezzetti (2012) and Niblett (2013) allows us to put the choice over cases and the outcomes that will flow from taking any given case within the existing and ever-changing doctrinal space of which those outcomes will become part. The model maps the doctrinal space as ever decreasing, as more issues are determined over time and to the extent stare decisis is respected (see sec. 2.2). This constitutes a fundamental constraint on the impact of any given decision and thus is a major factor over whether any chosen case will have doctrinal significance, yet it is not included in the standard model of cert, in which each case is treated as if decided discretely. The doctrinal landscape defines the potential of, and the limitations for, every case and thus is an important consideration.

Third, utilizing Baker and Mezzetti's (2012) and Niblett's (2013) model allows us to capture other factors within a very simple framework that have been previously shown to affect the choice over cert. This includes both the legal side of the equation with existing doctrinal contours and potential doctrinal impact, as well as the policy

[3] Daughety and Reinganum (2006) and Cameron, Segal, and Songer (2000) consider that there exists an opportunity cost every time the Court chooses any given case but that cost is a constant not related to central issues such as the evolution of the legal doctrine, the decision of the courts, and ultimately the selection among cases.

[4] Perhaps a trade-off always exists simply because different factors affect the opportunity cost of each case, such as work minimization (Posner 1993).

side with the justices' own ideological preferences and the relative ideological positions of the lower court judges. We vary the model by having strategic rather than sincere Supreme Court judges who follow their policy preferences rather than seeking some exogenously defined ideal threshold. We consider the effect of strategic lower court judges as an extension. In addition, we show that the expected distribution of future cases will also have an important effect, a factor that has received far less consideration previously.

In addition to contributing to the cert literature, the results of this model might be of value to the legislative and executive branches in the nomination and confirmation process. The model uncovers nontrivial ways in which the political agents can shape the evolution of Supreme Court doctrine indirectly by influencing the ideological composition of lower courts (see also McNollgast 1995).

2.2. Assumptions

The model involves three core assumptions, which we briefly explore here in turn: that the Court will face two sets of cases; that deciding either case will shape the doctrinal discretionary range, which gradually reduces; and that only cases in the discretionary range will be appealed to the Supreme Court.

We characterize each case as the a priori probability that a court with a random, uniformly distributed ideology will decide that case with a liberal decision.[5] Numerous models exist for how courts translate status quos (usually lower court decisions) into majority opinion outcomes (see Jacobi 2009), and we do not replicate that here. For simplicity, we restrict our analysis to the choice between two sets of cases. In one-dimensional preference space, one case on any topic will dominate each set; thus, we treat the choice as between two cases, one at each doctrinal boundary. This is, of course, a simplifying assumption, because minor factual differences between cases could make one case more attractive to a given justice even if it presents a weaker opportunity to shift doctrine in the direction that a justice most prefers. However, the evidence of the Court delaying to address certain cases through its various avoidance doctrines and the justices' own admission of delaying while searching for appropriate vehicles (see Perry

[5] Ultimately the case type relates to its facts. For example, if the question is whether certain evidence should be excluded, the a priori probability that evidence seized in a case where the police had a warrant and clear probable cause will be deemed admissible is much higher than the a priori probability of admissibility where the same evidence was seized without a warrant or clear probable cause.

1991) both support the idea that the justices will seek the one case that offers the best opportunity to address a given issue.[6]

This implies that the revision of a given case can change the discretionary range in only one direction. This is a strong assumption but there are at least three reasons to take this approach. First, allowing for a case revision to modify either end of the discretionary range would permit one of the modifications to introduce a onetime drastic change in the discretionary range. Given the judicial norms of incrementalism, minimalism, percolation, and avoidance, an assumption that favors smaller rather than larger changes is appropriate.[7] Second, by working with these two tethered sets of cases, we are able to capture the Court's choice between whether to alter the upper bar or the lower bar, and so are able to derive interesting and sensitive predictions of how the Court decides between two contending cases for cert. Third, modeling the Court as able to alter either bar is a very complex inquiry, which we have addressed in a stand-alone working paper (Bustos and Jacobi 2019). For now, in section 5.7 we discuss a generalization of our model and show that without this assumption, many of our results hold; some others are particular cases of a more general formulation.

Initially we model the two cases as from one given area of law, but later we consider choice between cases in different areas (see sec. 5.2). Thus we assume that justices do not have complete flexibility in choosing between every possible case outcome on the ideological continuum. This makes sense both because case outcomes need to reflect the position of the majority coalition and also because judges are often restrained in their choice over outcome by the facts of the case, by the procedure of the case particularly whether a particular position has been argued below (Epstein, Segal, and Johnson 1996), as well as by legitimacy constraints; for instance, a justice cannot choose to rule "yes if the party is white, no if the party is black" (Jacobi and Tiller 2007).

In addition, we assume that both lower court judges and the Supreme Court justices are bound by rules of stare decisis; that is, the undecided region can only be contracted with each subsequent case and not expanded. Although this constraint is somewhat artificial, it is mostly an accurate description: the justices rejecting their own

[6] To the extent that the cases are not fungible in this way, raising slightly different legal issues because of the differences in the facts, it makes sense to think of those issues as subtopics; then the Court could be choosing to modify the same ideological range more than once, in which case the model applies iteratively to the smaller subset of cases.

[7] This does not mean that large changes in the discretionary range cannot take place within our model, but without the assumption that a case can change only one end, those changes could be very dramatic. For more detail, see sec. 2.3 and n. 9.

reasoning is unusual and costly, and they have established high standards for doing so, including that there has been such significant factual change as to render the fundamental reasoning of the initial rule "intolerable" or "no more than a remnant of abandoned doctrine" (*Planned Parenthood v. Casey*, 505 U.S. 833 [1992]). Baker and Mezzetti (2012) show that reliance on precedent actually arises endogenously, so that judges can conserve resources (528), and that even allowing for revision (i.e., disobedience) of precedent, ordinarily there will be stabilization of precedent anyway (533).[8] Consequently, only cases within the discretionary range are appealed to the higher Court.

Putting these elements together, we treat the Court as choosing between two cases that will change the doctrinal boundaries in different ways. The new boundary will in turn determine the range available to the lower courts in future cases and, thus, the distribution of future Supreme Court options. All other major assumptions are relaxed in section 5.

2.3. Setup—Illustration

To illustrate how our model operates, suppose for simplicity that the doctrinal question is what speed constitutes unsafe driving.

As shown in figure 1, the existing discretionary range is 20–80: speeds below 20 miles per hour (mph) are clearly lawful, whereas speeds above 80 mph are unlawful. Our model assumes that the Court will only face petitions with speeds occurring between 20 and 80. The Court faces a set of cases, where the minimum is being tested—we call this set $\underline{\Theta}$—and a set of cases where the maximum is being tested—we call this $\overline{\Theta}$. Suppose $\underline{\Theta}$ includes cases with speeds 21, 22, and 28 with $\theta_B = 28$, and $\overline{\Theta}$ includes speeds 75, 76, and 78, with $\theta_{B+1} = 75$.[9] We will use the subindex B, which stands for border case, to denote the case facts that are the most extreme within $\underline{\Theta}$ that can change the lower boundary of the discretionary range; analogously, $B + 1$ denotes the case facts that are the most extreme within $\overline{\Theta}$ that can change the upper boundary of the discretionary range.

[8] They model judges as optimizing between error and decision costs and theorize that errors in precedent may arise if judges do not look closely enough at cases, so as to avoid decision costs (Baker and Mezzetti 2012, 532). They show that as long as decision costs are at least half of error costs, precedent will nonetheless stabilize (Baker and Mezzetti 2012, 533).

[9] Note that if we allowed for any of the points in $\underline{\Theta}$, say, 22, to also be part of $\overline{\Theta}$, then through a Court decision, the upper boundary of the discretionary range could be shifted from 80 to 22 with one decision. We believe these rather dramatic changes are contrary to judicial norms, as discussed, and rule them out up front. That said, in sec. 5.7 we study the implications of relaxing that assumption.

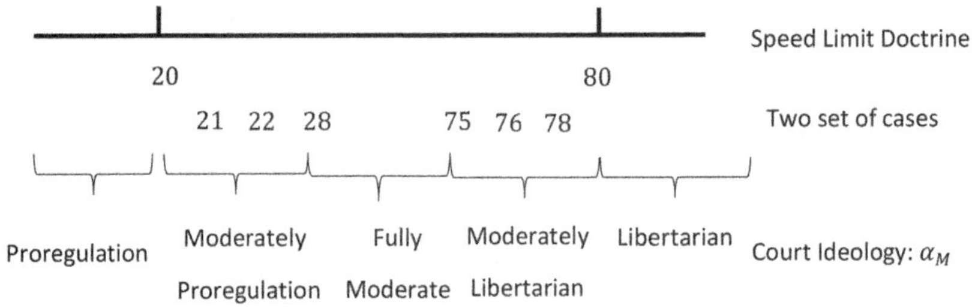

Figure 1. Illustration of the model

The Court has an optimal speed of *M*, in which *M* stands for the median's ideal. As discussed, the model does not simply need to apply to a liberal-conservative continuum: here, we model a regulatory-libertarian continuum, where libertarians (arguably a branch of conservatives) oppose government restrictions on driving speeds, and proregulators (many liberals) favor government intervention for safety purposes. We call preferences that are lower than 20 or higher than 80 "extreme." *M* is "fully moderate" when it is between 28 and 75—between the two closest of the cases in each set. A "moderately proregulation" (or moderately liberal) *M* is more than 20 but less than 28. Similarly, *M* is "moderately libertarian" (or moderately conservative) when it is under 80 but over 75 (it is under 28 but over 20).

Intuition suggests that the median justice of the Court, weighing two potential cases for cert, would prefer the case that eliminates the maximum extent of the discretionary range that is far from his or her ideological preference, thus binding future lower court judges most stringently to the justice's preferences. We show that this is the optimal decision when the Court is extreme, relative to prior doctrinal determinations. However, we show that when the Court is moderate, then the choice between cases will depend on both the expected heterogeneity of future cases and the position of the Court's ideology relative to the distribution of lower court judges' ideologies. When *M* is moderately libertarian/conservative, the Court will want to move the lower threshold to the right as long as the distribution of the ideologies of the lower courts is sufficiently clustered to the left or when the probability of future cases occurring to the left is high. The reverse applies to moderately proregulation/liberal courts.

Our model predicts that, from most likely to least likely, the likelihood of changing the lower bound conditional on the ideology of the Supreme Court is (1) moderately conservative Court, (2) fully moderate Court, and (3) moderately liberal Court.

3. THE MODEL

3.1. Players and Legal Standard

The Supreme Court has ideology represented by its median $\alpha_M \in [0,1]$ in which 0 means most liberal and 1 means most conservative.[10] In addition, there exists a continuum of lower courts with ideologies $\alpha_L \in [0,1]$ distributed according to density $F(\alpha_L) = R^+$, $F(\alpha_L) = \int_0^{\alpha_L} f(x)dx$ and $F(1) = 1$, $F(0) = 0$. Ideologies are common knowledge.[11]

Initially, the legal standard is defined by parameters $\{\underline{\theta}, \overline{\theta}\}$ with $0 \leq \underline{\theta} \leq \overline{\theta} \leq 1$ such that all cases $\theta \in [0,1]$ in which $\theta < \underline{\theta}$ must be decided by the lower courts with a conservative decision, and all cases in which $\theta > \overline{\theta}$ must be decided by the lower courts with a liberal decision; the lower courts have freedom to decide the case with a liberal or conservative decision in all the cases in which $\theta \in [\underline{\theta}, \overline{\theta}]$. We call $[\underline{\theta}, \overline{\theta}]$ the discretion interval (see Bustos and Jacobi 2015).[12]

3.2. Cases and Decisions

In the first period, the Supreme Court faces a set of potential cases $\Theta = \{\theta_1, \dots, \theta_N\}$ such that $\theta_i > \theta_j$ if $i > j$ and $\theta_i, \theta_j \in [\underline{\theta}, \overline{\theta}]$ for all i, j. From this set of cases the Court chooses one that we call θ^*, to which it grants cert. Because at this point we consider that all the cases relate to the same legal issue/topic, they all share the same legal standard $\{\underline{\theta}, \overline{\theta}\}$. We relax this in the extensions in section 5.2. The decision of the Court modifies the standard in the following way: if $\theta^* \leq \theta_B$, then $\underline{\theta} = \theta^*$ and if $\theta^* > \theta_B$, then $\overline{\theta} = \theta^*$ in which $\theta_B \in \Theta$. The intuition behind this adjustment of the standard is simple. The subset of cases $\underline{\Theta} = \{\theta_1, \dots, \theta_B\}$ includes cases that give the Court the opportunity to revise the lower bound of the legal standard (cases that have been decided conservative by lower courts) whereas the subset of cases $\overline{\Theta} = \{\theta_{B+1}, \dots, \theta_N\}$ includes cases that give the Court the opportunity to revise the upper bound of the legal standard (cases that have been decided liberal by lower courts). Evidently, $\underline{\Theta} \cup \overline{\Theta} = \Theta$ and $\underline{\Theta} \cap \overline{\Theta} = \varnothing$. Later we relax this last assumption in section 5.3.

In the second period, each lower court faces a case $\mu \in [0,1]$ that is distributed according to density $g(\mu) \in R^+$, $G(\mu) = \int_0^{\mu} g(x)dx$ and $G(1) = 1$,

[10] Because our model is symmetric, we can exchange the meaning of the notation to 0 as most conservative and 1 to most liberal.

[11] This is not a universal assumption in the literature. For example, Carrubba and Clark (2012) and McNollgast (1995) assume that the lower courts' preferences are not known.

[12] We are ruling out the possibility that the decisions of lower courts will directly shape the discretion interval (be a source of legal rules).

$G(0) = 0$. We assume that the lower courts are obedient and follow the legal standard. That is, if $\mu < \underline{\theta}$, the lower court votes conservative regardless of its own ideological preferences. If $> \overline{\theta}$, the lower court votes liberal regardless of its own ideological preferences. But if $\mu \in [\underline{\theta}, \overline{\theta}]$, the court votes according to its preferences. That is, if $\alpha_L < \mu$, it makes a liberal decision, but it makes a conservative decision if $\alpha_L > \mu$. Notice that the probability that the lower court type α_L votes conservative is $G(\underline{\theta})$ if $\alpha_L < \underline{\theta}$, it is $G(\alpha_L)$ if $\alpha_L \in [\underline{\theta}, \overline{\theta}]$, and it is $G(\overline{\theta})$ if $\alpha_L > \overline{\theta}$.

3.3. Payoffs

The Supreme Court gets payoff 1 when a lower court decides a case in the way in which it would like and 0 otherwise. The Court would like a case to be decided liberal when $\alpha_M < \mu$ and conservative when $\mu < \alpha_M$. Table 1 summarizes the expected utility of the Court, which we denote $U(\alpha_m)$, before it makes any adjustment to the standard.

We only explain the calculation when $\alpha_M < \underline{\theta}$. The details for the other cases can be found in the appendix. When $\alpha_M < \underline{\theta}$, the Court expects to get utility

$$\int_0^{\alpha_M} 1 \cdot g(\mu)d\mu + \int_{\alpha_M}^{\underline{\theta}} 0 \cdot g(\mu)d\mu + \int_{\underline{\theta}}^{\overline{\theta}} \left(\int_0^{\mu} 1 \cdot f(x)dx + \int_{\mu}^{1} 0 \cdot f(x)dx \right) g(\mu)d\mu$$
$$+ \int_{\overline{\theta}}^{1} 1 \cdot g(\mu)d\mu,$$

which is

$$G(\alpha_M) + 1 - G(\overline{\theta}) + \int_{\underline{\theta}}^{\overline{\theta}} F(\mu)g(\mu)d\mu.$$

The first expression $G(\alpha_M)$ refers to the cases $(\mu < \underline{\theta})$ that, as the Supreme Court wants, will be decided conservative by the lower courts; the second expression $1 - G(\overline{\theta})$ refers to the cases $(\mu > \overline{\theta})$ that, as the Supreme Court wants, will be decided liberal by the lower courts. The

Table 1. Supreme Court Expected Payoff $U(\alpha_M)$

When	Then
$\alpha_M < \underline{\theta}$	$G(\alpha_M) + 1 - G(\overline{\theta}) + \int_{\underline{\theta}}^{\overline{\theta}} F(\mu)g(\mu)d\mu$
$\alpha_M \in [\underline{\theta}, \overline{\theta}]$	$G(\underline{\theta}) + 1 - G(\overline{\theta}) + \int_{\underline{\theta}}^{\alpha_M} (1 - F(\mu))g(\mu)d\mu + \int_{\alpha_M}^{\overline{\theta}} F(\mu)g(\mu)d\mu$
$\alpha_M > \overline{\theta}$	$G(\underline{\theta}) + 1 - G(\alpha_M) + \int_{\underline{\theta}}^{\overline{\theta}} (1 - F(\mu))g(\mu)d\mu$

third expression, $\int_{\underline{\theta}}^{\overline{\theta}} F(\mu)g(\mu)d\mu$, refers to the cases that within the discretion interval will be decided by the lower courts as the Court wants, that is, those where the lower courts' ideologies are to the left of the case. Mathematically, the expression is the expected cumulative distribution of the judges' ideology when cases belong to the interval $[\underline{\theta}, \overline{\theta}]$.[13]

4. SOLUTION OF THE MODEL

4.1. Main Results

We need to characterize different scenarios for the ideology of the Supreme Court. We consider the situation in which the Court is liberal: $\alpha_M < \underline{\theta}$; that is, the preference of the median of the Court is to the left of the lower doctrinal bound. In that scenario it is easy to show that the case the Court chooses for cert is $\theta^* = \theta_{B+1}$. To see this, notice that it is in the best interest of the Court to move the discretion interval as far left as possible. The reason is that the lower court gets 0 for all the cases in the interval $[\alpha_M, \underline{\theta}]$ because all those cases are decided by the lower courts with a conservative decision, but the Court would like a liberal decision. In the interval $[\overline{\theta}, 1]$ all the lower courts always decide cases as the Court would like, whereas in the interval $[\underline{\theta}, \overline{\theta}]$ only some of the lower courts (the most liberal) will decide the cases as the Court wants. The best outcome for the Court is to move both the lower and the upper bounds of the discretion interval as far left as possible. That said, the Court cannot move the lower bound farther left because $\theta_1 > \underline{\theta}$. Hence, the best the Court can do regarding the lower bound is to leave it as it is. But the Court can move the upper bound to the left, and the maximum effect takes place when $\overline{\theta} = \theta_{B+1}$.

Using analogous logic, if the Court is conservative $\alpha_M > \overline{\theta}$, then it prefers to move the lower bound as far right as possible, which is equivalent to $\underline{\theta} = \theta_B$. Notice that this result for a Court of either extreme ideology (liberal or conservative) does not depend on the distribution of future cases *or* the distribution of lower courts' ideologies.

Now we discuss the more interesting scenario when the ideology of the Court falls within the discretion interval. We consider three scenarios where $\alpha_M \in [\underline{\theta}, \overline{\theta}]$: the Court is moderately liberal, fully moderate, or moderately conservative, within the discretion interval, in contrast to the extreme variants described earlier. In the first scenario, the ideology of the Court is moderately left $(\underline{\theta} \leq \theta_i < \alpha_M < \theta_{i+1} \leq \ldots$

[13] More accurately, it is $(G(\overline{\theta}) - G(\underline{\theta}))E(F(\mu)|\mu \in [\underline{\theta}, \overline{\theta}])$. Notice that table 1 tells us that the utility of Court -α_M increases the closer $\{\underline{\theta}, \overline{\theta}\}$ is to α_M. For example, when $\alpha_M \in [\underline{\theta}, \overline{\theta}]$, then $\{\partial U(\alpha_M)/\partial\underline{\theta}\} = F(\underline{\theta})g(\underline{\theta}) > 0$ and $\{\partial U(\alpha_M)/\partial\overline{\theta}\} = -(1 - F(\overline{\theta}))g(\overline{\theta}) < 0$.

$\leq \theta_B \leq \theta_{B+1})$, which means that the Court is more liberal than the most extreme (farther right) case within $\underline{\Theta}$. In the second scenario, which mirrors the first, the ideology of the Court is moderately right $\theta_B \leq \theta_{B+1} \leq \ldots \leq \theta_j < \alpha_M < \theta_{j+1} \leq \overline{\theta}$, which means that the ideology of the Court is more conservative than the most extreme (farther left) case within $\overline{\Theta}$.[14] The third scenario is that the Court is ideologically fully moderate (i.e., moderate within the range of possibilities where the Court's ideology lies in the discretion interval) with its ideology located between the two sets of cases such that $\theta_B \leq \alpha_M \leq \theta_{B+1}$. We show that in all of these scenarios, the selection of the case that the Court wants to review centrally depends on both the heterogeneity of case types and the heterogeneity of lower court judges' ideologies. Contrary to intuition, it is neither the ideological proximity between the Court and the optimal case (see corollary 1) nor the desire to reduce the size of the discretion interval (see corollary 2) that drives the Court's decision.

As the logic behind the results is very similar in all three scenarios, here we explain the intuition when the ideology of the Court is fully moderate $(\theta_B \leq \alpha_M \leq \theta_{B+1})$. Proposition 1 formally characterizes the cases chosen by the Court in all scenarios.

Using the logic of the cases already explained in which $\alpha_M \leq \underline{\theta}$ and $\overline{\theta} \leq \alpha_M$, it is easy to understand that a fully moderate Court chooses between cases θ_B and θ_{B+1} because all cases in $\underline{\Theta}$ and to the left of θ_B are dominated by θ_B and all the cases in $\overline{\Theta}$ and to the right of θ_{B+1} are dominated by θ_{B+1}. Table 2 presents a detailed comparison of the expected utility that the Supreme Court obtains if it chooses θ_B or θ_{B+1}. In the comparison of utilities, we need to distinguish cases that fall within four intervals of the set $[\underline{\theta}, \overline{\theta}]$.

Looking first only at the interval $[\underline{\theta}, \theta_B]$, the Court prefers to review θ_B instead of θ_{B+1} because in the first alternative the discretion interval becomes $[\theta_B, \overline{\theta}]$ rather than $[\underline{\theta}, \theta_{B+1}]$. In the first alternative, lower courts decide all the cases within $[\underline{\theta}, \theta_B]$ as the Court would like with a conservative decision. Instead, in the second alternative (if θ_{B+1} is reviewed) the lower courts decide the cases in $[\underline{\theta}, \theta_B]$ according to their own preferences; that is, only the courts with ideologies $\alpha_L \geq \theta$ decide as the Supreme Court would like. Following the same logic but because the incentives are reversed, now looking at the interval $[\theta_{B+1}, \overline{\theta}]$ the Court prefers to review θ_{B+1} instead of θ_B. That is because by choosing θ_{B+1} the Court has certainty that the lower courts will decide as it wants, with a liberal decision, whereas by choosing θ_B, the lower courts will decide as the Court would want only with a certain probability. In the other two regions ($[\theta_B, \alpha_M]$ and $[\alpha_M, \theta_{B+1}]$), the Court is

[14] Note that the cases in which $\underline{\theta} < \alpha_M < \theta_1 \leq \ldots \leq \theta_B \leq \theta_{B+1}$ and $\theta_B \leq \theta_{B+1} \leq \ldots \leq \theta_j < \alpha_M < \overline{\theta}$ are also included here.

Table 2. Supreme Court Expected Payoffs

Case Interval	Expected Utility (θ_B)	Expected Utility (θ_{B+1})
$[\underline{\theta}, \theta_B]$	$G(\theta_B) - G(\underline{\theta})$	$\int_{\underline{\theta}}^{\theta_B}(\int_{\mu}^{1} f(x)dx)g(\mu)d\mu$
$[\theta_B, \alpha_M]$	$\int_{\theta_B}^{\alpha_M}(\int_{\mu}^{1} f(x)dx)g(\mu)d\mu$	$\int_{\theta_B}^{\alpha_M}(\int_{\mu}^{1} f(x)dx)g(\mu)d\mu$
$[\alpha_M, \theta_{B+1}]$	$\int_{\alpha_M}^{\theta_{B+1}}(\int_{0}^{\mu} f(x)dx)g(\mu)d\mu$	$\int_{\alpha_M}^{\theta_{B+1}}(\int_{0}^{\mu} f(x)dx)g(\mu)d\mu$
$[\theta_{B+1}, \overline{\theta}]$	$\int_{\theta_{B+1}}^{\overline{\theta}}(\int_{0}^{\mu} f(x)dx)g(\mu)d\mu$	$G(\overline{\theta}) - G(\theta_{B+1})$

indifferent between θ_B and θ_{B+1} because in both alternatives the discretionary range still includes the two subranges ($[\theta_B, \alpha_M]$ and $[\alpha_M, \theta_{B+1}]$).

It follows that the Court prefers to review θ_B rather than θ_{B+1} if and only if

$$\underbrace{G(\theta_B) - G(\underline{\theta}) + \int_{\theta_{B+1}}^{\overline{\theta}} F(\mu)g(\mu)d\mu}_{\text{SC chooses } \theta_B}$$

$$> \underbrace{G(\overline{\theta}) - G(\theta_{B+1}) + \int_{\underline{\theta}}^{\theta_B} (1 - F(\mu))g(\mu)d\mu,}_{\text{SC chooses } \theta_{B+1}} \quad (1)$$

which can be rewritten as

$$\int_{\underline{\theta}}^{\theta_B} F(\mu)g(\mu)d\mu > \int_{\theta_{B+1}}^{\overline{\theta}} (1 - F(\mu))g(\mu)d\mu \quad (2)$$

or

$$\underbrace{\frac{\int_{\underline{\theta}}^{\theta_B} F(\mu)g(\mu)d\mu}{G(\theta_B) - G(\underline{\theta})}}_{\substack{\text{Expected Pbb with which} \\ \theta \in [\underline{\theta}, \theta_B] \text{ is decided Liberal}}} \underbrace{[G(\theta_B) - G(\underline{\theta})]}_{\text{Pbb that } \theta \in [\underline{\theta}, \theta_B]}$$

$$> \underbrace{\frac{\int_{\theta_{B+1}}^{\overline{\theta}} (1 - F(\mu))g(\mu)d\mu}{G(\overline{\theta}) - G(\theta_{B+1})}}_{\substack{\text{Expected Pbb with which} \\ \theta \in [\theta_{B+1}, \overline{\theta}] \text{ is decided Conservative}}} \underbrace{[G(\overline{\theta}) - G(\theta_{B+1})]}_{\text{Pbb that } \theta \in [\theta_{B+1}, \overline{\theta}]}.$$

In words, expression (2) tell us that the Court prefers to review a case that will move the lower bound to the right of the discretion interval (force the lower courts to decide conservatively in a larger set of cases) when the distribution of the judges' ideologies is adequately skewed to the right or when the probability of future cases taking place in the interval $[\underline{\theta}, \theta_B]$ is large enough. If the opposite occurs, then the Court prefers to review a case that will move the upper bound to the left of the discretion interval.

If the probability that $\theta \in [\underline{\theta}, \theta_B]$ is 0, then expression (2) never holds. In contrast, if the probability that $\theta \in [\theta_{B+1}, \overline{\theta}]$ is 0, then expression (2) always holds. If these two probabilities are not 0, then expression (2) never holds if the judges' ideological types cluster too much to the right.[15] It would then be irrelevant whether the lower bound is $\underline{\theta}$ or θ_B, as a case that falls in that interval will be decided conservative by the lower courts anyway.[16] In contrast, for expression (2) to hold, enough future cases have to take place in the interval $[\underline{\theta}, \theta_B]$ because if that is not the case, then again it would be irrelevant whether the lower bound is $\underline{\theta}$ or θ_B and then any change of $\underline{\theta}$ will have minimum impact on the Court's payoff.

To see that it is the skewedness of the judge-type probability distribution and not the skewedness of the case-type probability distribution that determines whether (2) holds, take the case in which $f(\cdot)$ and $g(\cdot)$ are the exponential densities in the interval [0,1] in which

$$f(x) = \frac{\lambda e^{-\lambda x}}{1 - e^{-\lambda}};\, g(x) = \frac{\kappa e^{-\kappa x}}{1 - e^{-\kappa}}.$$

The parameter λ captures the probability by which a lower court ideology is liberal and the parameter κ captures the probability by which a case will be decided conservative by a random lower court. The parameters can take any real value (positive or negative). As is shown in figure 2, the sign of the parameters determines the skewness of the case and ideology types.[17] If the parameter is negative, then it is skewed to the left; the opposite occurs if the parameter is positive. In the particular case in which it takes value 0, the density becomes the uniform distribution.

Plugging the distributions in (2) implies that the Court will choose θ_B for revision if

[15] For example, the first term in the left-hand side of (2) is 0 when $F(\theta) = 0$ for all $\theta \leq \theta_B$.

[16] In more general terms, if the ideologies of the judges lean to the right, then $\int_{\underline{\theta}}^{\theta_B} F(\mu)g(\mu)d\mu$ becomes small and $\int_{\theta_{B+1}}^{\overline{\theta}} (1 - F(\mu))g(\mu)d\mu$ becomes large. Hence, (2) is less likely to hold.

[17] The skewness of the distribution $f(x)$ is $\gamma = \{[\lambda^2 e^{-\lambda}(\lambda + 3e^{-\lambda})(1 + e^{-\lambda}) + 2e^{-3\lambda}(3\lambda + 1) - 2]/[1 - \lambda^2 e^{-\lambda} - e^{-2\lambda}(1 + 2\lambda)]\} \in (-\infty, +\infty)$, which is strictly decreasing in λ.

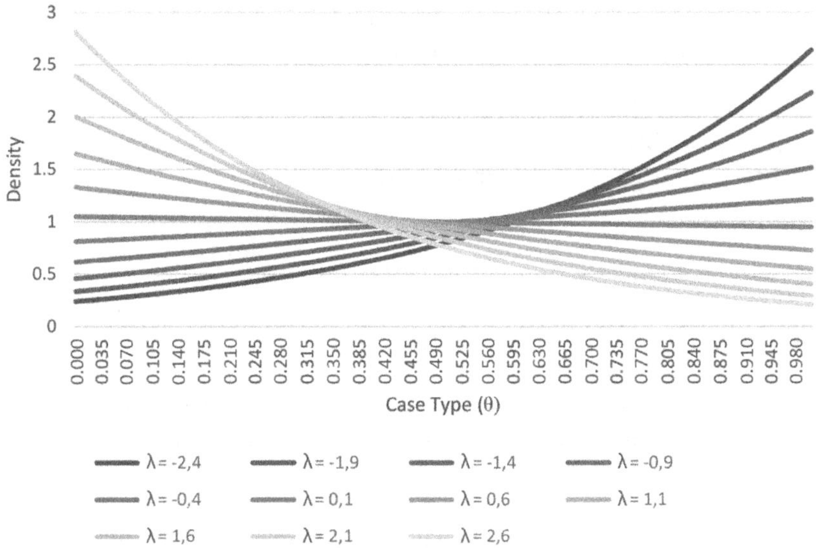

Figure 2. Illustration of the skewedness of *f(x)*

$$\frac{\kappa}{\left(1-e^{-\kappa}\right)\left(1-e^{-\lambda}\right)}\left\{\frac{\left(e^{-\kappa\theta_{B+1}}-e^{-\kappa\bar{\theta}}\right)+\left(e^{-\kappa\underline{\theta}}-e^{-\kappa\theta_M}\right)}{\kappa}-\frac{\left(e^{-(\lambda+\kappa)\underline{\theta}}-e^{-(\lambda+\kappa)\theta_B}\right)+\left(e^{-(\lambda+\kappa)\theta_{B+1}}-e^{-(\lambda+\kappa)\bar{\theta}}\right)}{(\lambda+\kappa)}\right\}\geq\frac{\left(e^{-\kappa\theta_{B+1}}-e^{-\kappa\bar{\theta}}\right)}{1-e^{-\kappa}}, \tag{3}$$

which is true for all $\lambda > \lambda^*(\kappa)$ in which $\lambda^*(\kappa) > 0$.[18] This shows that the higher the probability that the distribution of lower court ideologies leans to the left, the more likely that the Court will want to move the discretionary range to the right. The same analysis cannot be applied for κ, which means that even if the distribution of case types leans left, that does not guarantee that the Court will want to move the discretionary range to the right. As such, although the distribution of lower court ideologies determines the preferences of the Court over a case monotonically, the distribution of the cases does so nonmonotonically.

What is different when the Court is moderately liberal $(\underline{\theta} \leq \theta_i < \alpha_M < \theta_{i+1} \leq \ldots \leq \theta_B \leq \theta_{B+1})$? The analysis is a little more involved because it is not the case anymore that the Court chooses between $\{\theta_B, \theta_{B+1}\}$. It is clear that the Court prefers θ_{B+1} among all $\theta \in \overline{\Theta}$ but it is no

[18] To see this, notice that the right-hand side in (3) does not depend on λ and the left-hand side is strictly increasing in λ such that it takes value $-\infty$ when $\lambda = -\infty$ and it takes value $\{[(e^{-\kappa\theta_{B+1}} - e^{-\kappa\bar{\theta}}) + (e^{-\kappa\underline{\theta}} - e^{-\kappa\theta_B})]/(1 - e^{-\kappa})\} > [(e^{-\kappa\theta_{B+1}} - e^{-\kappa\bar{\theta}})/(1 - e^{-\kappa})]$ when $\lambda = \infty$.

longer true that θ_B is preferred among all $\theta \in \underline{\Theta}$. Because it is clear that θ_{i+1} is preferred to all $\theta \in \underline{\Theta}$, such that $\theta_{i+1} < \theta$, and θ_i is preferred to all $\theta \in \underline{\Theta}$, such that $\theta_i > \theta$, the Court first has to choose between $\{\theta_i, \theta_{i+1}\}$ and then compare it with θ_{B+1}.[19]

It is straightforward to see that the Court prefers to grant certiorari to θ_i instead to θ_{i+1} when expression (4) holds:

$$\int_{\alpha_M}^{\theta_{i+1}} F(\mu)g(\mu)d\mu > \int_{\theta_i}^{\alpha_M} F(\mu)g(\mu)d\mu. \tag{4}$$

Expression (4) makes reference to the only cases that will be decided differently by the lower courts if the Court sets the new lower bound of the discretionary range as θ_i instead of θ_{i+1}. First, in the interval $[\theta_i, \alpha_M]$, the Court prefers to have lower bound θ_{i+1} because then lower courts always resolve cases with a conservative decision, as the Court would like. Instead, if the lower bound is θ_i, then only the lower courts with ideology to the right of the case would decide the cases as the Court would like. Hence, the payoff difference in favor of bound θ_{i+1} is $\int_{\theta_i}^{\alpha_M} F(\mu)g(\mu)d\mu$. Second, in the interval $[\alpha_M, \theta_{i+1}]$, the Court prefers to have lower bound θ_i because then lower courts sometimes decide with a liberal decision, as the Court would like. Instead if the lower bound is θ_{i+1}, lower courts always decide conservative, contrary to the Court preferences. This time the payoff difference in favor of bound θ_i is $\int_{\alpha_M}^{\theta_{i+1}} F(\mu)g(\mu)d\mu$.

On one hand, if θ_i is preferred to θ_{i+1} (i.e., expression [4] holds), then next the Court has to compare the utility of revising θ_i instead of θ_{B+1}. Expression (2) is retrieved but instead of writing θ_B we have to write θ_i. That is, the Court prefers to adjust the lower bound of the discretion interval (select θ_i) instead of the upper bound (select θ_{B+1}) when

$$\int_{\underline{\theta}}^{\theta_i} F(\mu)g(\mu)d\mu > \int_{\theta_{B+1}}^{\bar{\theta}} (1 - F(\mu))g(\mu)d\mu. \tag{5}$$

On the other hand, if θ_{i+1} is preferred to θ_i (i.e., expression [4] does not hold), then the Court compares the utility of revising θ_{i+1} instead of θ_{B+1}. In that case, as we derive in the appendix (table A1), the Court chooses θ_{i+1} if

$$\int_{\underline{\theta}}^{\theta_{i+1}} F(\mu)g(\mu)d\mu - 2\int_{\alpha_M}^{\theta_{i+1}} F(\mu)g(\mu)d\mu > \int_{\theta_{B+1}}^{\bar{\theta}} (1 - F(\mu))g(\mu)d\mu. \tag{6}$$

[19] Recall our example on the speed limit. In fig. 1, possible values for $\{\theta_i, \theta_{i+1}\}$ are {21, 22}, {21,28}, {22,28}. Also evidently $\theta_{B+1} = 75$. Evidently if $\underline{\theta} < \alpha_M < \theta_1 \leq \ldots \leq \theta_B \leq \theta_{B+1}$, then the Court chooses θ_1 and has to compare that one with θ_{B+1} according to (6).

The regularity of (5) and (6) is that both are less likely to hold than (2). That allows us to conclude that a fully moderate Court is more (less) likely to revise the lower (upper) bound of the discretionary range than a moderately liberal Court. Similarly, we conclude that a moderately conservative Court is more (less) likely to revise the lower (upper) bound of the discretionary range than a fully moderate Court. This conclusion confirms the intuition that the more liberal the Court, the more attractive it is to move the upper bound to the left. However, in the corollary to come, we show that the intuition that a Court will *always* want to reduce the size of the discretionary zone as much as possible is not true.

Even more importantly, the conclusion that the Court prefers to move the lower bound (which becomes θ^*) instead of the upper bound of the discretion interval when the distribution of judges' ideologies is adequately skewed to the right or when the probability of future cases taking place in the interval $[\underline{\theta}, \theta^*]$ is large enough still holds when the Court is moderately conservative or moderately liberal.[20]

The previous discussion is summarized and formally proved in the next proposition.

Proposition 1. (i) If the Supreme Court is very liberal ($\alpha_M < \underline{\theta}$), then the Court moves the discretion interval as far left as possible by choosing to review case $\theta^* = \theta_{B+1}$. (ii) If the Supreme Court is very conservative ($\alpha_M > \overline{\theta}$), then the Court moves the discretion interval as far right as possible by choosing to review case $\theta^* = \theta_B$. (iii) If the Supreme Court is moderate ($\underline{\theta} \leq \alpha_M \leq \overline{\theta}$), then the Court restricts the discretion interval in its lower bound to θ^* if the judges' ideological distribution is adequately skewed to the right or the probability that the case type belongs to the interval $[\underline{\theta}, \theta^*]$ is large enough. Otherwise, the Court restricts the discretion interval in its upper bound.

The exact value of θ^* and the conditions that determine it are provided in the appendix, as is the proof.

Two direct corollaries follow from proposition 1.

Corollary 1 (Court does not always try to move the discretionary range closer to its own ideology). If $\alpha_M \in [\underline{\theta}, \overline{\theta}]$ and $|\alpha_M - \theta_i| < |\alpha_M - \theta_j|$ with $\theta_i, \theta_j \in \Theta$, then the Supreme Court does not necessarily prefer to grant cert to θ_i instead of to θ_j.

[20] To see that, it is enough to notice that in the left-hand side of (5) appears $\int_{\underline{\theta}}^{\theta_i} F(\mu)g(\mu)d\mu$ alone, and in (6) $\int_{\underline{\theta}}^{\theta_{i+1}} F(\mu)g(\mu)d\mu$ can be left alone in the left-hand side after $2\int_{M}^{\theta_{i+1}} F(\mu)g(\mu)d\mu$ is moved to the right-hand side.

Proof. Take the case in which both the cases and the ideologies are uniformly distributed (i.e., $f(x) = g(y) = 1$). Then (1) becomes

$$\int_{\theta_{B+1}}^{\bar{\theta}} \mu d\mu > \bar{\theta} - \theta_{B+1} - \int_{\underline{\theta}}^{\theta_B} \mu d\mu$$

or

$$(\theta_B - \underline{\theta}) > (\bar{\theta} - \theta_{B+1}) \frac{\left(1 - \frac{\bar{\theta}+\theta_{B+1}}{2}\right)}{\left(\frac{\theta_B+\underline{\theta}}{2}\right)}.$$

Then suppose that $\underline{\theta} = 0.1$; $\theta_B = 0.2$; $\alpha_M = 0.25$; $\theta_{B+1} = 0.4$; $\bar{\theta} = 0.6$. Notice that $\alpha_M - \theta_B = 0.05 < \theta_{B+1} - \alpha_M = 0.15$. However, (1) is not satisfied because the left-hand side becomes 0.1 and the right-hand side becomes 0.67. Hence, the Court prefers to review θ_{B+1}. QED

Corollary 2 (Court does not always try to reduce the size of the discretionary range). If $\alpha_M \in [\underline{\theta}, \bar{\theta}]$ and $\theta_i - \underline{\theta} < \bar{\theta} - \theta_j$ with $\theta_i, \theta_j \in \Theta$, then the Court does not necessarily prefer to grant cert to θ_j instead to θ_i.

Proof. If both the cases and the ideologies are exponentially distributed (i.e., $f(x) = [\lambda e^{-\lambda x} / (1 - e^{-\lambda})]$; $g(x) = [\kappa e^{-\kappa x} / (1 - e^{-\kappa})]$), then (1) becomes

$$\frac{\kappa}{(1 - e^{-\kappa})(1 - e^{-\lambda})} \left\{ \frac{\left(e^{-\kappa\theta_{B+1}} - e^{-\kappa\bar{\theta}}\right) + \left(e^{-\kappa\underline{\theta}} - e^{-\kappa\theta_B}\right)}{\kappa} - \frac{\left(e^{-(\lambda+\kappa)\underline{\theta}} - e^{-(\lambda+\kappa)\theta_B}\right) + \left(e^{-(\lambda+\kappa)\theta_{B+1}} - e^{-(\lambda+\kappa)\bar{\theta}}\right)}{(\lambda + \kappa)} \right\}$$

$$\geq \frac{\left(e^{-\kappa\theta_{B+1}} - e^{-\kappa\bar{\theta}}\right)}{1 - e^{-\kappa}}.$$

Then suppose that $\underline{\theta} = 0.4$; $\theta_B = 0.5$; $\theta_{B+1} = 0.6$; $\bar{\theta} = 0.8$, and $\lambda = k = 5$ (both distributions are skewed to the right). Notice that $\theta_B - \underline{\theta} = 0.1 < \bar{\theta} - \theta_{B+1} = 0.2$. Then (1) is satisfied because the left-hand side becomes 0.08 and the right-hand side becomes 0.03. Hence, the Court prefers to review θ_B even when choosing θ_{B+1} would imply reducing the discretionary range more than choosing θ_B. QED

The corollaries imply that the common intuition that the Court should always prefer to set a discretion interval that is closer to the

Court's preferences is not true. The salience of the case—that is, its relevance for shaping future expected cases given the prevalence of the lower court ideologies—defies this intuition. Even when the resulting discretion interval is not reduced by as much as it could be, the fact that many more cases will take place in one area of the doctrine implies that the Court could be more interested in making small adjustments to that area instead of making big adjustments in other areas. Alternatively, the fact that a large number of judges could make decisions that are not as the Court would like could also induce the Court to make adjustments in the doctrine in dimensions that appear to be refinements and not major shifts.

4.2. Application

This conclusion can be seen in a number of different areas of the law, and it helps explain Supreme Court behavior that may otherwise appear puzzling. We observe the Court taking multiple cases on some topics that seemingly involve minor shifts in doctrine, which has an opportunity cost in terms of taking cases in other areas that would seem to offer much more significant shifts in doctrine toward the median's ideal point.[21] Different strategies by the same Court appear in different areas of the law, and we believe the value of ideological distance minimization in the case at hand can be overwhelmed by the importance of choosing salient cases that will shape doctrine in future cases.

For instance, until recently, there was a dearth of Supreme Court cases in patent law, despite its obvious importance in affecting diverse economically significant fields from computing to pharmaceuticals. This was so extreme that scholars described the Supreme Court as "invisible," as having permanently retreated to the "peripheries of patent law" (Janis 2001, 387–88). The Supreme Court had largely delegated authority to the Federal Circuit, the specialized patent court. However, for 20 years, the Federal Circuit had taken advantage of its discretion to choose outcomes far from the Supreme Court's ideal preferences, in what scholars described as a "quiet revolution" by the lower court (Lunney 2004). Eventually, in 2005, the Supreme Court responded, increasing its review of patent cases by 2.5 times (Mandel 2016), and major shifts in doctrine followed, reversing much of that revolution.

[21] Although our main results were derived under the assumption that the Court faces cases that relate to only one legal issue, in sec. 5.2 we show how our analysis and results can be generalized to the reality in which the Court chooses among cases that relate to several legal issues.

In contrast, throughout the 20 years that the Supreme Court was largely ignoring patent law, it was taking a very high number of cases in constitutional criminal procedure every term. In just the second decade of that period, it took 8 cases on the confrontation clause, 12 on the death penalty, and 17 on ineffective assistance of counsel. A few of these cases constituted major changes in doctrine, but most involved very minor shifts. For instance, within confrontation clause doctrine, *Crawford v. Washington*, 541 U.S. 36 (2004), instituted an important change, but the following seven cases dealt with minor variations on the theme. And in its 2010 term, the Supreme Court used one of its 85 cases (*Davis v. United States*, 564 U.S. 229 [2011]) simply to dictate how to treat remnant pending cases affected by its ruling the previous year changing the search incident to arrest exception (*Arizona v. Gant*, 556 U.S. 332 [2009]).

This contrast between patent and constitutional criminal procedure may seem strange, particularly given the economic impact of patent law. However, considered in terms of doctrinal impact, the Court's choice may make more sense. With 2.8% of the adult population under some sort of correctional supervision (Glaze et al. 2015), minor slicing and dicing of very fine differences in criminal procedure could nonetheless have a significant effect on a large supply of cases. Thus sometimes the Court focuses on reducing the discretion interval as much as possible, particularly when lower courts are not trusted agents of the Supreme Court, as eventually occurred in response to the Federal Circuit. At other times, the Court appears more interested in making small adjustments of doctrine that will nonetheless have significant impact. This application compares different areas of law; in the model, we have considered the potential impact of two different cases within one given area of law. The next section considers more formally the effect of looking at cases in different areas among other extensions.

5. EXTENSIONS

5.1. If Lower Courts Are Strategic

So far we have assumed that lower courts always vote truthfully. That is, if a lower court with ideology α_L faces a case $\mu \in [\underline{\theta}, \overline{\theta}]$, then it votes liberal if $\alpha_L < \mu$ and votes conservative if $\alpha_L > \mu$. In both cases the lower court gets utility 1. If the lower court voted otherwise, then it would get utility 0. Because of this truthful behavior, we took the sets of cases $\underline{\Theta}$ and $\overline{\Theta}$ as exogenously given. However, arguably rational lower courts have incentives to decide cases strategically: because they know that later these cases could be revised by the Court and used to adjust the discretionary range, lower courts could decide cases to set $\underline{\Theta}$ and $\overline{\Theta}$ in a favorable way. Here we show that unless the expected benefits are very large (low discount rate, reduced uncertainty, or very singular shape in the distribution of cases), the incentives to vote strategically are not present and our assumption that $\underline{\Theta}$ and $\overline{\Theta}$ are exogenously given is harmless.

To see this, we adjust the basic game in a way in which there are three periods instead of two. In the first period, sequentially, each lower court i faces case μ_i and decides it with a liberal or a conservative decision. All the cases decided conservative by the lower courts still belong to $\underline{\Theta}$ (adjusting the lower bar) and all the cases decided liberal by the lower courts still belong to $\overline{\Theta}$ (adjusting the upper bar). In the second period, the Court chooses the case and in the third period the lower courts vote again. That is, the second and third periods define our original basic game where the results from proposition 1 hold. Do courts have incentives to vote untruthfully during the first period? We show that the answer is no.

Suppose that the ideology of the Court is given by $\alpha_M < \underline{\theta}$ and suppose that so far (because of the decisions made by a subset of lower courts) the sets $\underline{\Theta}$ and $\overline{\Theta}$ are given by $\underline{\Theta} = \{\theta_1, \ldots, \theta_B\}$ and $\overline{\Theta} = \{\theta_{B+1}, \ldots, \theta_N\}$ such that we know from proposition 1 that if the Court had to choose a case considering only those intervals, it will choose to revise case θ_{B+1}. If court i faces case $\mu_i \in [\underline{\theta}, \overline{\theta}]$ such that $\mu_i > \alpha_i$, then when the court truthfully votes liberal, it immediately gets utility 1 and in addition the Court grants cert to the case: $\min\{\theta_{B+1}, \mu_i\}$. Instead when the court untruthfully votes conservative, it immediately gets 0 and the Court grants cert to the case: θ_{B+1}. Then the court always votes truthfully because the utility difference between these two alternatives is $1 - \int_{\alpha_i}^{\mu_i} g(\mu) d\mu > 0$.

It is true that we are only considering two periods, but it is also true that we are not considering a discount rate, which if high would further buttress the conclusion that lower courts always vote truthfully during period 1.[22] As such we consider that there is little loss of generality in assuming that $\underline{\Theta}$ and $\overline{\Theta}$ are exogenously given.

5.2. When Cases Relate to Several Legal Issues

Our model is flexible enough to make predictions in the more realistic scenario in which the Court faces petitions for revision associated with several legal issues. Suppose that the Court faces a set of case

[22] With multiple periods, this result becomes weaker but very likely will still hold. For the result to reverse, however, the discount factor and the discretionary range would have to be very large and the case type would have to be significantly different from the lower court ideology.

$\Theta^P = \{\theta_1^P, \ldots, \theta_N^P\}$ related to patents and a set of cases $\Theta^C = \{\theta_1^C, \ldots, \theta_N^C\}$ related to criminal procedure. The ideologies of the Court in each issue are α_M^P and α_M^C, respectively. Once more, we assume that in each of these issues the Court faces a set of cases challenging the lower and the upper boundaries of the discretionary range, which is $\{\underline{\theta}^P, \overline{\theta}^P\}$ for patents and $\{\underline{\theta}^C, \overline{\theta}^C\}$ for criminal procedure. That is, $\underline{\Theta}^P = \{\theta_1^P, \ldots, \theta_B^P\}$ and $\overline{\Theta}^P = \{\theta_{B+1}^P, \ldots, \theta_N^P\}$ such that $\underline{\Theta}^P \cup \overline{\Theta}^P = \Theta^P$ and also $\underline{\Theta}^C = \{\theta_1^C, \ldots, \theta_B^C\}$ and $\overline{\Theta}^C = \{\theta_{B+1}^C, \ldots, \theta_N^C\}$ such that $\underline{\Theta}^C \cup \overline{\Theta}^C = \Theta^C$. In addition we denote by $f^P(\alpha_L) \in R^+$ and $f^C(\alpha_L) \in R^+$ the distribution of lower court ideologies regarding patents and criminal procedure, respectively, and we denote by $g^P(\mu) \in R^+$ and $f^C(\alpha_L) \in R^+$ the distribution of patent and criminal procedure cases respectively.

Then consider the case in which $\alpha_M^P < \underline{\theta}^P$ and $\alpha_M^C < \underline{\theta}^C$: we know from proposition 1 that the Court will chose between θ_{B+1}^P and θ_{B+1}^C. Although the expected benefit for the Court of changing the discretionary range for patents is $\int_{\theta_{B+1}^P}^{\overline{\theta}^P}(1 - F^P(\mu))g^P(\mu)d\mu$, the expected benefit of changing the discretionary range for criminal procedure is $\int_{\theta_{B+1}^C}^{\overline{\theta}^C}(1 - F^C(\mu))g^C(\mu)d\mu$. (Both expressions relate to cases $\theta \in [\theta_{B+1}, \overline{\theta}]$ that the Court would like to be decided liberal. Although with the old upper bound $\overline{\theta}$ only lower court judges with ideologies $\alpha_L < \theta$ will decide the case with a liberal decision, with the new upper bound θ_{B+1} all lower courts will decide the case with a liberal decision.)

It follows that the Court will grant cert to the case that revises the discretionary range associated with patent law instead of criminal procedure if

$$\int_{\theta_{B+1}^P}^{\overline{\theta}^P} (1 - F^P(\mu))g^P(\mu)d\mu > \int_{\theta_{B+1}^C}^{\overline{\theta}^C} (1 - F^C(\mu))g^C(\mu)d\mu.$$

A key assumption of this analysis is that we have assumed that the Court gets the same utility 1 when a lower court decides a case in the way it would like, regardless what legal issue is being discussed.

5.3. The Set of Cases Might Overlap

It is feasible that the set of cases that would potentially revise the lower bound of the discretionary range and the set of cases that would potentially revise the upper bound might overlap.[23] That is, $\underline{\Theta} \cap \overline{\Theta} \neq$

[23] This could arise in two quite different circumstances: first, when the law has been so developed that the discretionary range becomes negligible—Baker and Mezzetti (2012) model this as the goal of the common law; second, when the Court has developed such extensive and flexible precedent that law becomes highly indeterminate—for example, Llewellyn (1950) lists numerous and contradictory canons and countercanons that he says allow for any decision in any circumstance.

$\varnothing$, which is equivalent to $\theta_{B+1} < \theta_B$. For simplicity, we still assume that $\theta_1 < \theta_{B+1}$ and $\theta_B < \theta_N$. Then it is easy to verify that the results from proposition 1 still hold when the Court is liberal, conservative, or $\alpha_M < \theta_{B+1}$ or $\alpha_M > \theta_B$. However, the conditions that determine the Court's choice will be different when $\alpha_M \in [\theta_{B+1}, \theta_B]$. In this last case, the Court will prefer to grant cert to θ_B instead of θ_{B+1} when

$$\int_{\theta_B}^{\bar{\theta}} F(\mu)g(\mu)d\mu + G(\alpha_M) - G(\underline{\theta}) > \int_{\underline{\theta}}^{\theta_{B+1}} (1 - F(\mu))g(\mu)d\mu + G(\bar{\theta}) - G(\alpha_M). \tag{7}$$

If $G(\alpha_M) - G(\underline{\theta})$ is equal to $G(\bar{\theta}) - G(\alpha_M)$, then we would recover (2) with the roles of θ_B and θ_{B+1} interchanged. What expressions $G(\alpha_M) - G(\underline{\theta})$ and $G(\bar{\theta}) - G(\alpha_M)$ are capturing is that, unlike under the basic formulation, now α_M will lie outside the discretionary range; if θ_B is selected, the Court will be to the left of the range and if θ_{B+1} is selected, the Court will be to the right of the range. Hence, expressions $G(\alpha_M) - G(\underline{\theta})$ and $G(\bar{\theta}) - G(\alpha_M)$ are telling us that if θ_B is selected by the Court, then lower courts will tend to resolve more cases to the right of the Court, in the way the Court would like. The opposite happens if θ_{B+1} is selected by the Court.

Because now $\theta_{B+1} < \theta_B$, we cannot simply compare (2) and (7) but (7) can be re-expressed as

$$\int_{\underline{\theta}}^{\theta_{B+1}} F(\mu)g(\mu)d\mu > \int_{\theta_B}^{\bar{\theta}} (1 - F(\mu))g(\mu)d\mu + G(\theta_B) - G(\alpha_M) - [G(\alpha_M) - G(\theta_{B+1})],$$

and if we assume that θ_B and θ_{B+1} from the basic model are equal to θ_{B+1} and θ_B from this new formulation, we conclude that (7) is more likely to hold than (2) if and only if cases tend to fall more frequently in the interval $[\theta_{B+1}, \alpha_M]$ than in the interval $[\alpha_M, \theta_B]$.

5.4. A Three-Justice Court

We show here that it is harmless to assume that the ideology of the Court is exclusively represented by the ideology of its median justice α_m when the median justice is liberal or conservative, but results will depend on more than the ideology for a median who is moderate. To see that, suppose now that the Court is constituted by a liberal, a moderate, and a conservative justice with ideologies $\{\alpha_L, \alpha_M, \alpha_C\}$. The

Court uses simple majority rule to determine which case to grant cert.[24]

It is still true that if $\alpha_M < \underline{\theta}$, then the Court chooses θ_{B+1}, and if $\alpha_M > \overline{\theta}$, then the Court chooses θ_B. In order to see this is true, notice that when $\alpha_M < \underline{\theta}$, both the liberal and the moderate justices have the same preferences, and when $\alpha_M > \overline{\theta}$, both the conservative and the moderate justices have the same preferences. Because of simple majority rule, two votes are enough to determine the Court's decision.

But results as summarized in proposition 1 might not hold when $\alpha_M \in [\underline{\theta}, \overline{\theta}]$. To illustrate, we assume that the Court is fully moderate: $\theta_B < \alpha_M < \theta_{B+1}$. Then, when $\theta_B < \alpha_L < \alpha_M < \alpha_C < \theta_{B+1}$ or when $\alpha_L < \underline{\theta} < \theta_B < \alpha_M < \theta_{B+1} < \overline{\theta} < \alpha_C$, we still have that the Court chooses between $\{\theta_B, \theta_{B+1}\}$ conditional on

$$\int_{\underline{\theta}}^{\theta_B} F(\mu)g(\mu)d\mu > \int_{\theta_{B+1}}^{\overline{\theta}} (1 - F(\mu))g(\mu)d\mu$$

But in all the other order relations for $\{\alpha_L, \alpha_M, \alpha_C\}$, the conditions for proposition 1 might not hold. In particular, it might be that each justice prefers a different case. To see this, suppose that the ideologies of the justices are such that $\alpha_L < \underline{\theta} < \theta_i < \alpha_M < \theta_{i+1} < \theta_B < \theta_{B+1} < \overline{\theta} < \alpha_C$ and if it is true that $\int_{\alpha_M}^{\theta_{i+1}} F(\mu)d\mu > \int_{\theta_i}^{\alpha_M} F(\mu)g(\mu)d\mu$ and $\int_{\underline{\theta}}^{\theta_i} F(\mu)g(\mu)d\mu > \int_{\theta_{B+1}}^{\overline{\theta}} (1 - F(\mu))g(\mu)d\mu$, then we know that the liberal justice's optimal case is θ_{B+1}, the conservative justice's optimal case is θ_B, and because of proposition 1, the moderate justice's optimal case is θ_i.

In the last scenario, because cycling may occur, coalitions may become relevant.[25] The decision will depend on the details of the case selection process (order of the proposals, discussions, and votes) and in particular on the relative bargaining power of the justices.

5.5. Imperfect Prediction of Future Case Distribution

Very likely, the Court will not know the distribution of future cases perfectly.[26] However, if we relax this assumption, the bias in Court beliefs would have to be significantly large to induce the Court to make

[24] We do not include various institutional practices of the Court, such as the rule of four and the conference process, as these elements have been modeled elsewhere (e.g., Lax 2003) and a majority is ultimately the test for the outcome of the case, even if not for whether to take a case.

[25] See Kornhauser and Sager (1993) on the differences between issue votes and case decision votes.

[26] We can expect that the Court will know the current distribution of judges' ideologies and that case distributions will be similar from one term to another, an assumption built into standard tools used by the literature (e.g., Martin and Quinn 2002).

an erroneous decision (e.g., choose to revise case θ_B instead of case θ_{B+1} when, according to the true distribution of future cases, the Court should revise θ_{B+1}). The reason is that the bias has to rebalance the Court payoffs in a way in which an inequality such as (2) is reversed from the outcome obtained when the true distribution of cases is in place. If, for example, the distribution of cases leans toward the left enough to make (2) hold, then very likely a distribution less left-leaning will still make (2) hold and it will ordinarily require a drastic change to reverse (2). Next we check this more formally.

Without loss of generality, we assume that the Court believes that the distribution of cases is given by $h(u) = (1 - \varepsilon)g(u) + \varepsilon g'(u)$ in which ε is the error, $g(u)$ is the true distribution, and $g'(u)$ is a different unknown distribution.[27] We can replicate the analysis that leads us to derive (2) and rewrite it with $h(u)$ instead of $g(u)$. Rearranging terms,

$$\int_{\underline{\theta}}^{\theta_B} F(\mu)g(\mu)d\mu > \left[\begin{array}{c} \int_{\theta_{B+1}}^{\bar{\theta}} (1 - F(\mu))g(\mu)d\mu + \\ \frac{\varepsilon}{1-\varepsilon}\left(\int_{\theta_{B+1}}^{\bar{\theta}} (1 - F(\mu))g'(\mu)d\mu - \int_{\underline{\theta}}^{\theta_B} F(\mu)g'(\mu)d\mu \right) \end{array} \right]. \quad (8)$$

It follows that if (2) holds, then for (8) not to hold, ε must be large enough or else $g'(u)$ must be skewed very differently to $g(u)$. To show that, next we evaluate (8) assuming that judges' ideologies are uniformly distributed, case types are exponentially distributed, $g(u) = (\lambda e^{-\lambda\mu})/(1 - e^{-\lambda})$; $g'(u) = (\lambda' e^{-\lambda'\mu})/(1 - e^{-\lambda'})$, and $\underline{\theta} = 0{,}2$; $\theta_B = 0{,}3$; $\theta_{B+1} = 0{,}7$; $\bar{\theta} = 0{,}8$. For each pair of (λ, λ'), table 3 shows the value of ε beyond which (8) does not hold given that (2) holds or (8) does hold given that (2) does not hold. Predictions are clear: the more $g(u)$ leans to one side, the larger is the set of $g'(u)$ for which (2) and (8) always (for all values of ε which in the tables is the case $\varepsilon = 1$) hold and the larger is the error required for only (2) or (8) to hold.

The common law is primarily a system of incremental change; this claim is inherent in the model of Baker and Mezzetti (2012) and Niblett (2013) and evolutionary theories of the common law. As such, ordinarily (2) and (8) will not contradict each other because the distribution of case types at $t + 1$ should not be that different from those at t. That inertia in the type of cases will be reflected in a small ε and a similar skewedness for $g(u)$ and $g'(u)$. This is only likely not to be true when the Court makes a large enough change in the law in any one case as to present a shock to the distribution of future cases.

[27] The Court only knows $h(\mu)$.

Table 3. Values of ε beyond Which Only (2) or (8) Holds

(λ, λ')[a]	3,1	2,6	2,1	1,6	1,1	0,6	0,1	(0,4)	(0,9)	(1,4)	(1,9)	(2,4)
3,1	1	1	1	1	1	1	1	0,86	0,73	0,64	0,58	0,54
2,1	1	1	1	1	1	1	1	0,82	0,68	0,58	0,52	0,48
1,1	1	1	1	1	1	1	1	0,73	0,55	0,45	0,38	0,34
(0,9)	0,27	0,29	0,32	0,37	0,45	0,60	0,90	1	1	1	1	1
(1,4)	0,36	0,38	0,42	0,47	0,55	0,69	0,93	1	1	1	1	1
(1,9)	0,42	0,44	0,48	0,53	0,62	0,74	0,94	1	1	1	1	1
(2,4)	0,46	0,49	0,52	0,58	0,66	0,77	0,95	1	1	1	1	1

[a]Each row corresponds to a value for parameter and each column corresponds to a value for parameter. The numbers inside the table are values of associated with the two variables.

5.6. Number of Petitions for Revisions

It is easy to verify that our results in proposition 1 do not change when we increase or reduce the number of petitions for revisions (parameter N as a subindex of the set of cases). It is still the case that an extreme Court wants to move the opposite boundary of the discretionary range as close as possible to the ideology of the Court; that is, $\theta^* = \theta_{B+1}$ when the Court is liberal and $\theta^* = \theta_B$ when the Court is conservative. Also, equations (2) and (4)–(6) still determine the selections of cases made by a moderate Court.

That said, an interesting effect associated with a change in the value of parameter N is that it will affect the classification of the Court as moderately liberal, moderately conservative, or fully moderate; therefore, it will affect the probability that the Court chooses to move the upper or lower bound. To see this, suppose that $\underline{\Theta} = \{\theta_1, \theta_2\}$ and $\overline{\Theta} = \{\theta_3, \theta_4\}$ such that $\theta_2 < \alpha_M < \theta_3$. We compare that scenario to a new scenario (it could be a different year) in which the Court faces cases $\underline{\Theta} = \{\theta_1, \theta_2, \tilde{\theta}\}$; $\overline{\Theta} = \{\theta_3, \theta_4\}$ such that $\theta_2 < \alpha_M < \tilde{\theta}$ and $N = 5$. Then, whereas in the first scenario ($N = 4$) the decision of the Court is determined by equation (2), in the second scenario ($N = 5$) the decision of the Court is determined by equations (4)–(6). Evidently, it is not the increment in the number of revisions per se that changes the decision of the Court but rather it is its position vis-à-vis the discretionary range.

5.7. Confirmations and Reversals

In our basic formulation, we do not distinguish whether the Court decision is a confirmation or a reversal. Here we discuss some elements of an extension to our model, where we relax the central assumption that the Court can only alter the lower boundary, if the case it chooses is closer to that boundary, and vice versa for the upper boundary. We show that the main result still holds: the decision to confirm or reverse is determined by the ideology of the Court, with a decision that is different for extreme, moderately extreme, and moderate Courts. To more comprehensively model the confirm-reverse decision is complex, because in deciding whether to grant cert, the Court has to consider not only the future payoff associated with the adjustment in the legal doctrine (altering the discretionary range) but also the present payoff for correcting what the Court may consider an erroneous decision. This result warrants its own analysis, and in a working paper (Bustos and Jacobi 2019), we find that, contrary to intuition, the Court does not grant cert to cases with the primary objective of reversing lower court decisions. Rather, extreme Courts reverse more often than confirm decisions, moderately extreme Courts reverse and confirm decisions with equal ex ante probabilities, and moderate Courts can go both ways. We generate predictions of which cases are confirmed or reversed as a function of the Court's ideology, the set of cases petitioning for cert, and the probability distributions for future lower court cases and lower court judges' ideologies.

It also still holds that a moderate Court might choose to move the upper or the lower boundary of the discretionary range, which will centrally depend on the distributions of the lower court ideologies and case types. As a novelty, we are able to derive the exact conditions under which the Court will choose a case in order to reverse it or to confirm it. The variation stems from whether the short-term utility is not present (or negligible when compared with the expected utility in the second period): then the Court, both moderate and extreme, would only care about the ideological position of the chosen case.

Suppose that our basic two-period game is changed in the following ways. During the first period, the Court receives a set of petitions $\Theta^C = \{\theta_1^C, \dots, \theta_B^C\}$, which are cases that were decided conservative by lower courts, and a set of petitions $\Theta^L = \{\theta_1^L, \dots, \theta_B^L\}$, which are cases that were decided liberal by lower courts. We only know that $\min\{\theta_1^C, \theta_1^L\} \geq \underline{\theta}$ and $\max\{\theta_B^C, \theta_B^L\} \leq \overline{\theta}$. In the first period, the Court gets utility 1 if the revised case is decided as the Court wants.[28] In the second period, N cases distributed according to $g(u)$ as before are decided by lower courts with ideologies distributed according to $f(x)$ as before. As usual, δ is the discount factor.[29]

Although we distinguish four scenarios—namely, $\alpha_M < \underline{\theta}$; $\alpha_M \in [\underline{\theta}, \min\{\theta_1^C, \theta_1^L\}]$; $\alpha_M \in [\min\{\theta_1^C, \theta_1^L\}, \max\{\theta_1^C, \theta_1^L\}]$; $\alpha_M \in [\max\{\theta_1^C, \theta_1^L\},$

[28] That payoff only applies to the revised case. For example, if the Court reverses θ_i^C, that does not imply that all θ_j^C with $j < i$ are also reversed.

[29] We retrieve the results of our basic model if we impose that $\delta N \gg 1$.

$\min\{\theta_B^C, \theta_B^L\}]$ (we are not considering the symmetric scenarios in which the Court is conservative)—here we only discuss the scenarios in which the Court is liberal ($\alpha_M < \underline{\theta}$) and fully moderate ($\alpha_M \in [\max\{\theta_1^C, \theta_1^L\}, \min\{\theta_B^C, \theta_B^L\}]$).

When the Court is liberal and it is clear that if $\theta_1^C < \theta_1^L$, then the Court chooses to reset the upper boundary as $\theta^* = \theta_1^C$ regardless of the distribution of future cases and ideologies. Not only does the Court maximize the range of cases that the lower courts will decide liberal in the second period (no other case allows the Court to move the upper bound farther left), but also the Court gets utility 1 in the first period because it reverses a decision that was initially decided conservative. Instead if $\theta_1^L < \theta_1^C$, the Court chooses to revise and then reset the upper bound, θ_1^L instead of θ_1^C. if and only if

$$\underbrace{\delta N \int_{\theta_1^L}^{\theta_1^C} g(\mu)d\mu}_{\substack{\text{Future cases in} \\ \theta \in [\theta_1^L, \theta_1^C] \text{ are decided Liberal}}} > \underbrace{1}_{\text{Case is reversed}} + \underbrace{\delta N \int_{\theta_1^L}^{\theta_1^C} \left(\int_0^{\mu} f(x)dx \right) g(\mu)d\mu}_{\substack{\text{Some future cases in} \\ \theta \in [\theta_1^L, \theta_1^C] \text{ are decided Liberal}}} \quad (9)$$

$$\leftrightarrow \delta N \int_{\theta_1^L}^{\theta_1^C} (1 - F(\mu))g(\mu)d\mu > 1.$$

Inequality (9) implies that the Court chooses to revise (and confirm) θ_1^L instead of θ_1^C if there are a large number of lower courts with ideologies clustered to the right of θ_1^C and if those lower courts will, in the future, face a large number of cases that belong to the interval $[\theta_1^L, \theta_1^C]$.

When the Court is fully moderate, we have to distinguish the four scenarios given by the values of $\max\{\theta_1^C, \theta_1^L\}$ and $\min\{\theta_B^C, \theta_B^L\}$. The characterization will require sequential comparisons in which we would determine whether the Court prefers to revise θ_1^C or θ_1^L, then θ_B^C or θ_B^L, and then the winners of the two previous comparisons.[30] In all the scenarios, the distributions of the case types and the ideologies of the lower courts are central. In particular, we retrieve condition (2) as determining the final decision of the Court if the Court prefers to replace the lower bound and the upper bound with two confirmations (θ_1^L and θ_B^C, respectively) or two reversals (θ_1^C and θ_B^L, respectively). In that case, the Court would compare operating with intervals $[\theta_1^L, \overline{\theta}]$ and $[\underline{\theta}, \theta_B^C]$ (with two confirmations) or intervals $[\theta_1^C, \overline{\theta}]$ and $[\underline{\theta}, \theta_B^L]$ (with

[30] For example, if $\theta_1^C > \theta_1^L$, then the Court has to compare whether it prefers to set a new discretionary range $[\underline{\theta}, \theta_1^L]$ or $[\theta_1^C, \overline{\theta}]$ because clearly $[\underline{\theta}, \theta_1^L]$ dominates $[\underline{\theta}, \theta_1^C]$ and $[\theta_1^C, \overline{\theta}]$ dominates $[\theta_1^L, \overline{\theta}]$. The comparison of confirmations θ_1^C and θ_1^L will have to consider that even when lower courts decide all cases $\mu < \theta_1^C$ as the Court wants when $[\theta_1^C, \overline{\theta}]$, lower courts decide all cases $\mu > \alpha_m$ as the Court wants when $[\underline{\theta}, \theta_1^L]$.

two reversals) in which the results derived in proposition 1 for the case of a fully moderate Court hold.[31]

6. CONCLUSIONS

Most models of strategic judicial behavior assume that each justice wants to minimize the distance between his or her own ideology and the determination to be made—be it of the case outcome or of the choice of vehicle—but that approach does not account for varying salience of some cases over others. Judges report that the importance of a case is an important factor in the decision over cert (e.g., Perry 1991) and there is some supporting empirical evidence: for instance, more amicus petitions increase the likelihood of cert being granted (Black and Owens 2009). Our model suggests how importance could be assessed in terms of case salience—that is, the potential impact of the current case on future cases, which is a product of the expected distribution of future cases and the ideologies of lower court judges. The more future cases that can be anticipated to be decided in a given direction by the ruling of a potential case, the greater the significance of the current potential case.

Prior literature recognized that judges are sophisticated manipulators of their agendas, who look ahead to the merit stage when deciding whether to take a given case (e.g., Caldeira, Wright, and Zorn 1999, 550), and that the path-dependent nature of the common law renders the flow of future cases subject to prior determinations (e.g., Hathaway 2001, 129). We have brought these two elements together by considering that justices do not simply consider each case in a vacuum but weigh the relative merits of the choice among cases and by showing how a sophisticated justice will factor in the expected flow and direction of future cases when choosing among cases for certiorari.

Once case salience is considered, the choice over certiorari becomes more complicated than a simple up-down vote in each case, yet we show that nonetheless reliable patterns emerge. Choice among cases hinges on the contours of the existing doctrinal space, the ideology of the Supreme Court, the distribution of ideologies of lower court judges, the frequency of cases expected in a given area, and the interaction of these factors. Our results explain some otherwise puzzling Supreme Court behavior, such as intense focus on one area of the law at the seeming cost of other important areas.

[31] Whether we are dealing with confirmations or reversals, the Court payoff in the first period becomes irrelevant because it is the same under both choices. The same is true in the case that $\delta N \gg 1$.

This provides a concept of expected doctrinal impact that can be used by scholars going forward, in both theoretical and formal models, useful not only for models of cert but also for models of judicial decision-making over case outcomes. This has the advantage of providing a bridge between social science models of judicial utility typically focused overwhelmingly on judicial ideology and other understandings of judicial preferences that factor in amplification of the doctrinal impact of a decision.

APPENDIX

Derivation of the Values in Table 1

When $\alpha_m > \bar{\theta}$:

$$\int_0^{\underline{\theta}} 1 \cdot g(\mu)d\mu + \int_{\underline{\theta}}^{\bar{\theta}} \left(\int_0^{\mu} 0 \cdot f(x)dx + \int_{\mu}^{1} 1 \cdot f(x)dx \right) g(\mu)d\mu$$
$$+ \int_{\bar{\theta}}^{\alpha_M} 0 \cdot g(\mu)d\mu + \int_{\alpha_M}^{1} 1 \cdot g(\mu)d\mu,$$

which is

$$G(\underline{\theta}) + 1 - G(\alpha_M) + \int_{\underline{\theta}}^{\bar{\theta}} (1 - F(\mu))g(\mu)d\mu.$$

When $\alpha_M \in [\underline{\theta}, \bar{\theta}]$:

$$\int_0^{\underline{\theta}} 1 \cdot g(\mu)d\mu + \int_{\underline{\theta}}^{\alpha_M} \left(\int_0^{\mu} 0 \cdot f(x)dx + \int_{\mu}^{1} 1 \cdot f(x)dx \right) g(\mu)d\mu$$
$$+ \int_{\alpha_M}^{\bar{\theta}} \left(\int_0^{\mu} 1 \cdot f(x)dx + \int_{\mu}^{1} 0 \cdot f(x)dx \right) g(\mu)d\mu + \int_{\bar{\theta}}^{1} 1 \cdot g(\mu)d\mu,$$

which is

$$G(\underline{\theta}) + 1 - G(\bar{\theta}) + \int_{\underline{\theta}}^{\alpha_M} (1 - F(\mu))g(\mu)d\mu + \int_{\alpha_M}^{\bar{\theta}} F(\mu)g(\mu)d\mu.$$

Proof of Proposition 1. If $\alpha_M < \underline{\theta}$, then the Court faces two possibilities. The first one is that the Court restricts the upper bound of the discretion interval, which then becomes $[\underline{\theta}, \theta^*]$. Hence, the Court solves

$$\max_{\theta^*}\left\{G(\alpha_M) + 1 - G(\theta^*) + \int_{\underline{\theta}}^{\theta^*} F(\mu)g(\mu)d\mu\right\}$$

$$\text{subject to}: \underline{\theta} < \theta^* < \overline{\theta},$$

from where the first-order condition (FOC) becomes $-(1 - F(\theta^*))g(\theta^*) < 0$ when $\underline{\theta} < \theta^* < \overline{\theta}$. This implies that the objective function is decreasing when $\underline{\theta} < \theta^* < \overline{\theta}$, which implies that its maximum value in the interval takes place when $\theta^* = \underline{\theta}$. As the set of cases from which the Court chooses is discrete, the optimal solution is to choose the smallest case type from $\overline{\Theta}$, which is θ_{B+1}. The second possibility is that the Court restricts the lower bound of the discretion interval, which then becomes $[\theta^*, \overline{\theta}]$. Hence, the Court solves

$$\max_{\theta^*}\left\{G(\alpha_M) + 1 - G(\overline{\theta}) + \int_{\theta^*}^{\overline{\theta}} F(\mu)g(\mu)d\mu\right\}$$

$$\text{s.t.}: \underline{\theta} < \theta^* < \overline{\theta},$$

from where the FOC becomes $-G(\theta^*)f(\theta^*) < 0$ when $\underline{\theta} < \theta^* < \overline{\theta}$. As before, this implies that the objective function is decreasing when $\underline{\theta} < \theta^* < \overline{\theta}$, which implies once more that its maximum value in the interval takes place when $\theta^* = \underline{\theta}$. But this is equivalent to preferring no modifications in the current discretion interval (regardless of whether that is not possible because the best the Court can do is choose the smallest case type from $\underline{\Theta}$, which is θ_1). Then the Court prefers the option in which the upper bound is moved to the left. That is, $\theta^* = \theta_{B+1}$.

The solution for when $\alpha_M > \overline{\theta}$ is analogous to the solution when $\alpha_M < \underline{\theta}$. This time the solution of the maximization problem is $\theta^* = \underline{\theta}$, which implies that the Court chooses the largest case type from $\underline{\Theta}$, which is θ_B.

The solution is more cumbersome when $\alpha_M \in [\underline{\theta}, \overline{\theta}]$. Now the exact value of θ^* will depend on the following conditions:

1. If the Court is moderately liberal such that $\underline{\theta} \leq \theta_i < \alpha_M < \theta_{i+1} \leq \theta_B$, then $\theta^* = \theta_i$ if $\int_{\alpha_M}^{\theta_{i+1}} F(\mu)d\mu > \int_{\theta_i}^{\alpha_M} F(\mu)g(\mu)d\mu$ and $\int_{\underline{\theta}}^{\theta_i} F(\mu)g(\mu)d\mu > \int_{\theta_{B+1}}^{\overline{\theta}} (1 - F(\mu))g(\mu)d\mu$. But it is $\theta^* = \theta_{i+1}$ if $\int_{\alpha_M}^{\theta_{i+1}} F(\mu)d\mu < \int_{\theta_i}^{\alpha_M} F(\mu)g(\mu)d\mu$ and $\int_{\underline{\theta}}^{\theta_{i+1}} F(\mu)g(\mu)d\mu - 2\int_{\alpha_M}^{\theta_{i+1}} F(\mu)g(\mu)d\mu > \int_{\theta_{B+1}}^{\overline{\theta}} (1 - F(\mu))g(\mu)d\mu$. Otherwise $\theta^* = \theta_{B+1}$.
2. If the Court is fully moderate such that $\theta_B < \alpha_M < \theta_{B+1}$, then $\theta^* = \theta_B$ if and only if

$$\int_{\underline{\theta}}^{\theta_B} F(\mu)g(\mu)d\mu > \int_{\theta_{B+1}}^{\overline{\theta}} (1 - F(\mu))g(\mu)d\mu.$$

3. If the Court is moderately conservative such that $\theta_{B+1} \leq \theta_i < \alpha_M < \theta_{i+1} \leq \bar{\theta}$, then $\theta^* = \theta_{i+1}$ if $\int_{\theta_i}^{\alpha_M} F(\mu)d\mu > \int_{\alpha_M}^{\theta_{i+1}} F(\mu)g(\mu)d\mu$ and $\int_{\underline{\theta}}^{\theta_B} F(\mu)g(\mu)d\mu < \int_{\theta_{i+1}}^{\bar{\theta}} (1 - F(\mu))g(\mu)d\mu$. But it is $\theta^* = \theta_i$ if $\int_{\theta_i}^{\alpha_M} F(\mu)d\mu < \int_{\alpha_M}^{\theta_{i+1}} F(\mu)g(\mu)d\mu$ and $\int_{\underline{\theta}}^{\theta_B} F(\mu)g(\mu)d\mu < \int_{\alpha_M}^{\bar{\theta}} (1 - F(\mu))g(\mu)d\mu - \int_{\theta_i}^{\alpha_M} (1 - F(\mu))$. Otherwise $\theta^* = \theta_B$.

Next we explain each subcase separately. When $\alpha_M \in [\underline{\theta}, \theta_B]$ and the Court chooses to revise θ_{i+1}, such that $\underline{\theta} < \alpha_M < \theta_{i+1} < \theta_B$, then table 2 becomes table A1.

Table A1. Supreme Court Expected Payoffs

Case Interval	Expected Utility (θ_{i+1})	Expected Utility (θ_{B+1})
$[\underline{\theta}, \alpha_M]$	$G(\alpha_M) - G(\underline{\theta})$	$\int_{\underline{\theta}}^{\alpha_M} (\int_{\mu}^{1} f(x)dx)g(\mu)d\mu$
$[\alpha_M, \theta_{i+1}]$	0	$\int_{\alpha_M}^{\theta_{i+1}} (\int_{0}^{\mu} f(x)dx)g(\mu)d\mu$
$[\theta_{i+1}, \theta_{B+1}]$	$\int_{\theta_{i+1}}^{\theta_{B+1}} (\int_{0}^{\mu} f(x)dx)g(\mu)d\mu$	$\int_{\theta_{i+1}}^{\theta_{B+1}} (\int_{0}^{\mu} f(x)dx)g(\mu)d\mu$
$[\theta_{B+1}, \bar{\theta}]$	$\int_{\theta_{B+1}}^{\bar{\theta}} (\int_{0}^{\mu} f(x)dx)g(\mu)d\mu$	$G(\bar{\theta}) - G(\theta_{B+1})$

It follows that the Court prefers to review θ_i rather than θ_{B+1} if and only if

$$\underbrace{G(\alpha_M) - G(\underline{\theta}) + \int_{\theta_{B+1}}^{\bar{\theta}} F(\mu)g(\mu)d\mu}_{\text{SC chooses } \theta_i} > \tag{1$'$}$$

$$\underbrace{G(\bar{\theta}) - G(\theta_{B+1}) + \int_{\underline{\theta}}^{\alpha_M} (1 - F(\mu))g(\mu)d\mu + \int_{\alpha_M}^{\theta_{i+1}} F(\mu)g(\mu)d\mu,}_{\text{SC chooses } \theta_{B+1}}$$

which can also be rewritten as

$$\int_{\underline{\theta}}^{\alpha_M} F(\mu)g(\mu)d\mu - \int_{\alpha_M}^{\theta_{i+1}} F(\mu)g(\mu)d\mu > \int_{\theta_{B+1}}^{\bar{\theta}} (1 - F(\mu))g(\mu)d\mu. \tag{2$'$}$$

The only difference from (2) is that $\int_{\underline{\theta}}^{\theta_B} F(\mu)g(\mu)d\mu$ is now replaced by $\int_{\underline{\theta}}^{\alpha_M} F(\mu)g(\mu)d\mu - \int_{\alpha_M}^{\theta_{i+1}} F(\mu)g(\mu)d\mu < \int_{\underline{\theta}}^{\theta_B} F(\mu)g(\mu)d\mu$, which implies that (2) is more likely to be satisfied than (2)′.

When $\alpha_M \in [\theta_B, \theta_{B+1}]$, then the Court chooses to revise θ_B instead of θ_{B+1} when this inequality holds (see main text):

$$\int_{\theta_{B+1}}^{\bar{\theta}} F(\mu)g(\mu)d\mu + \int_{\underline{\theta}}^{\theta_B} F(\mu)g(\mu)d\mu > G(\bar{\theta}) - G(\theta_{B+1}).$$

When $\alpha_M \in [\theta_{B+1}, \overline{\theta}]$ and the Court chooses to revise θ_i, such that $\theta_{B+1} < \theta_i < \alpha_M < \overline{\theta}$, then table 2 becomes table A2.

Table A2. Supreme Court Expected Payoffs

Case Interval	Expected Utility (θ_M)	Expected Utility (θ_i)
$[\underline{\theta}, \theta_B]$	$G(\theta_B) - G(\underline{\theta})$	$\int_{\underline{\theta}}^{\theta_B}(\int_{\mu}^{1} f(x)dx)g(\mu)d\mu$
$[\theta_B, \theta_i]$	$\int_{\theta_B}^{\theta_i}(\int_{0}^{\mu} f(x)dx)g(\mu)d\mu$	$\int_{\theta_B}^{\theta_i}(\int_{0}^{\mu} f(x)dx)g(\mu)d\mu$
$[\theta_i, \alpha_M]$	$\int_{\theta_i}^{\alpha_M}(\int_{\mu}^{1} f(x)dx)g(\mu)d\mu$	0
$[\alpha_M, \overline{\theta}]$	$\int_{\alpha_M}^{\overline{\theta}}(\int_{0}^{\mu} f(x)dx)g(\mu)d\mu$	$G(\overline{\theta}) - G(\alpha_M)$

It follows that the Court prefers to review θ_B rather than θ_i if and only if

$$\underbrace{G(\theta_B) - G(\underline{\theta}) + \int_{\theta_i}^{\alpha_M}(1 - F(\mu))g(\mu)d\mu + \int_{\alpha_M}^{\overline{\theta}} F(\mu)g(\mu)d\mu}_{\text{SC chooses } \theta_B} > \underbrace{G(\overline{\theta}) - G(\alpha_M) + \int_{\underline{\theta}}^{\theta_B}(1 - F(\mu))g(\mu)d\mu,}_{\text{SC chooses } \theta_i} \qquad (1)''$$

which can also be rewritten as

$$\int_{\underline{\theta}}^{\theta_B} F(\mu)g(\mu)d\mu > \int_{\alpha_M}^{\overline{\theta}}(1 - F(\mu))g(\mu)d\mu - \int_{\theta_i}^{\alpha_M}(1 - F(\mu))g(\mu)d\mu. \qquad (2)''$$

The only difference with (2) is that $\int_{\theta_{B+1}}^{\overline{\theta}}(1 - F(\mu))g(\mu)d\mu$ is now replaced by $\int_{\alpha_M}^{\overline{\theta}}(1 - F(\mu))g(\mu)d\mu - \int_{\theta_i}^{\alpha_M}(1 - F(\mu))g(\mu)d\mu < \int_{\theta_{B+1}}^{\overline{\theta}}(1 - F(\mu))g(\mu)d\mu$, implying that (2)″ is more likely to be satisfied than (2).

Next we verify that the Court restricts the discretion interval in its lower bound to θ^* if the judges' ideological distribution is adequately skewed to the right *or* the probability that the case type belongs to the interval $[\underline{\theta}, \theta^*]$ is large enough. Without loss of generality, assume that the distribution of the judges' ideologies can be written as

$$F(\mu) = \begin{cases} 0 & \text{if } \mu \leq \underline{\mu} \\ \in (0,1) & \text{if } \mu \in \left(\underline{\mu}, \overline{\mu}\right). \\ 1 & \text{if } \mu \geq \overline{\mu} \end{cases}$$

Then inequality (2) always hold when $\underline{\mu} = 0$ and $\overline{\mu} = \theta_{B+1}$ (all the ideologies are to the left of θ_{B+1}) because (2) becomes

$$G(\overline{\theta}) - G(\theta_{B+1}) + \int_{\underline{\theta}}^{\theta_B} F(\mu)g(\mu)d\mu > G(\overline{\theta}) - G(\theta_{B+1}),$$

which is evidently true. On the other hand, if $\underline{\mu} = \hat{\theta}$ with $\hat{\theta} \in [\theta_{B+1}, \overline{\theta}]$ and $\overline{\mu} > \theta_{B+1}$, then the left side of the inequality becomes $\int_{\theta_{B+1}}^{\overline{\theta}} F(\mu)g(\mu)d\mu$, which is smaller than $G(\overline{\theta}) - G(\theta_{B+1})$. By continuity, for all values of $\underline{\mu} < \theta_B$ there always exists a value of $\overline{\mu}$ such that (2) holds and for all $\overline{\mu} > \theta_{B+1}$ there exists $\underline{\mu}$ such that (2) does not hold. That is, (2) always holds when the distribution of lower court ideologies is skewed enough to the right. On the other hand, (2) also holds if $[G(\theta_B) - G(\underline{\theta})] > (\{E[1 - F(\mu) \mid \mu \in (\theta_{B+1}, \overline{\theta})]\}/\{E[F(\mu) \mid \mu \in (\underline{\theta}, \theta_B)]\})[G(\overline{\theta}) - G(\theta_{B+1})]$, that is, if $[G(\theta_B) - G(\underline{\theta})]$ is large enough. Using a similar set of steps we can prove the same when $\alpha_M \in [\underline{\theta}, \theta_B]$ and $\alpha_M \in [\theta_{B+1}, \overline{\theta}]$. QED

REFERENCES

Baker, Scott, and Claudio Mezzetti. 2012. "A Theory of Rational Jurisprudence." *Journal of Political Economy* 120:513–51.

Black, Ryan C., and Ryan J. Owens. 2009. "Agenda Setting in the Supreme Court: The Collision of Policy and Jurisprudence." *Journal of Politics* 71:1062–75.

Boucher, Robert L., and Jeffrey A. Segal. 1990. "Supreme Court Justices as Strategic Decision Makers: Aggressive Grants and Defensive Denials on the Vinson Court." *Journal of Politics* 57:824–37.

Bustos, Alvaro, and Tonja Jacobi. 2015. "Communicating Judicial Retirement." *International Review of Law and Economics* 43:107–18.

Bustos, Alvaro, and Tonja Jacobi. 2019. "Reversals and Confirmations in the Choice over Cert." Working paper, Northwestern Pritzker Law School, Chicago.

Caldeira, Gregory A., John R. Wright, and Christopher J. W. Zorn. 1999. "Sophisticated Voting and Gatekeeping in the Supreme Court." *Journal of Law, Economics, and Organization* 15:549–72.

Cameron, C. M., Jeffrey A. Segal, and Donald Songer. 2000. "Strategic Auditing in a Political Hierarchy: An Informational Model of the Supreme Court's Certiorari Decisions." *American Political Science Review* 94:101–16.

Carrubba, Clifford J., and Tom S. Clark. 2012. "Rule Creation in a Political Hierarchy." *American Political Science Review* 106:622–43.

Cohen, Linda R., and Matthew L. Spitzer. 1994. "Solving the Chevron Puzzle." *Law and Contemporary Problems* 57:65–110.

Daughety, Andrew F., and Jennifer F. Reinganum. 2006. "Speaking Up: A Model of Judicial Dissent and Discretionary Review." *Supreme Court Economic Review* 14:1–41.

Epstein, Lee, Jeffrey A. Segal, and Timothy Johnson. 1996. "The Claim of Issue Creation on the US Supreme Court." *American Political Science Review* 90:845–52.

Glaze, Lauren, Danielle Kaeble, Todd Minton, and Anastasios Tsoutis. 2015. "Correctional Populations in the United States, 2014." Bulletin, Bureau of Justice Statistics, Washington, DC.

Hathaway, Oona A. 2001. "Path Dependence in the Law: The Course and Pattern of Legal Change in a Common Law System." *Iowa Law Review* 86:601–66.

Jacobi, Tonja. 2008. "The Judicial Signaling Game: How Judges Strategically Shape Their Dockets." *Supreme Court Economic Review* 16:1–38.

Jacobi, Tonja. 2009. "Competing Theories of Coalition Formation and Case Outcome Determination." *Journal of Legal Analysis* 1:411–58.

Jacobi, Tonja, and Emerson Tiller. 2007. "Legal Doctrine and Political Control." *Journal of Law, Economics, and Organization* 23:326–45.

Janis, Mark D. 2001. "Patent Law in the Age of the Invisible Supreme Court." *University of Illinois Law Review* 2001:387–420.

Kornhauser, Lewis A., and Lawrence G. Sager. 1993. "The One and the Many: Adjudication in Collegial Courts." *California Law Review* 81:1–59.

Lax, Jeffrey R. 2003. "Certiorari and Compliance in the Judicial Hierarchy: Discretion, Reputation, and the Rule of Four." *Journal of Theoretical Politics* 15:61–86.

Linzer, Peter. 1979. "The Meaning of Certiorari Denials." *Columbia Law Review* 79:1127–305.

Llewellyn, Karl. 1950. "Remarks on the Theory of Appellate Decision and the Rules or Canons about How Statutes Are to Be Construed." *Vanderbilt Law Review* 3:395–406.

Lunney, Glynn S., Jr. 2004. "Patent Law, the Federal Circuit, and the Supreme Court: A Quiet Revolution." *Supreme Court Economic Review* 11:1–80.

Mandel, Gregory N. 2016. "Congress versus the Supreme Court: Intellectual Property Conflict and Majoritarian Democracy." Unpublished manuscript, Temple Law School, Philadelphia, PA.

Martin, Andrew D., and Kevin M. Quinn. 2002. "Dynamic Ideal Point Estimation via Markov Chain Monte Carlo for the US Supreme Court, 1953–1999." *Political Analysis* 10:134–53.

McGuire, Kevin T., and Gregory A. Caldeira. 1993. "Lawyers, Organized Interests, and the Law of Obscenity: Agenda Setting in the Supreme Court." *American Political Science Review* 87:717–26.

McNollgast. 1995. "Politics and the Courts: A Positive Theory of Judicial Doctrine and the Rule of Law." *Southern California Law Review* 68:1631–83.

Niblett, Anthony. 2013. "Case-by-Case Adjudication and the Path of the Law." *Journal of Legal Studies* 42:303–30.

Owens, Ryan J., and David A Simon. 2012. "Explaining the Supreme Court's Shrinking Docket." *William and Mary Law Review* 53: 1219–85.

Perry, H. W. 1991. *Deciding to Decide: Agenda Setting in the US Supreme Court.* Cambridge, MA: Harvard University Press.

Posner, Richard A. 1993. "What Do Judges and Justices Maximize? (The Same Thing Everybody Else Does)." *Supreme Court Economic Review* 3:1–41.

Spitzer, Matthew, and Eric Talley. 2000. "Judicial Auditing." *Journal of Legal Studies* 29:649–83.

Stearns, Maxwell L., and Todd J. Zywicki. 2009. *Public Choice Concepts and Applications in Law.* St. Paul, MN: West.

Watson, Wendy W. 2006. "The US Supreme Court's in Forma Pauperis Docket: A Descriptive Analysis." *Justice System Journal* 27:47–60.

Comment on "Judicial Choice among Cases for Certiorari"

*Scott Baker**

1. INTRODUCTION

In "Judicial Choice among Cases for Certiorari," Álvaro Bustos and Tonja Jacobi develop a new model to investigate the Supreme Court's grant of certiorari. The model focuses on which case the Court should select to make new law. Should the Court hear a case that clarifies the law as much as possible? Should the Court select a case that sets the law according to the desires of the median justice? Why does the Court, on occasion, grant certiorari in a series of cases that make minor changes to the existing law and at other times make sweeping change in a single case? The prior literature on certiorari is mainly empirical, focusing on the case characteristics—like the presence of a circuit split—that predict whether the Supreme Court will hear a case (Hellman 1985; Black and Owens 2009; Beim and Rader 2015).

Bustos and Jacobi fruitfully advance the literature by asking not just whether the Supreme Court will hear a case but also what facts the Court will hunt for to develop new doctrine.

I think this an interesting and unexplored question. Described briefly later, the model is coherent and well executed. It surfaces non-obvious trade-offs faced by the Supreme Court in its selection of a case for discretionary review, trade-offs that would not be apparent without the aid of the formal analysis.

The article presents several results. I focus on two. First, the model demonstrates that, under reasonable conditions, the Court would not

* Vice Dean for Research and Faculty Development and William F. and Jessica L. Kirsch Professor of Law, Washington University in St. Louis.

Electronically published: December 23, 2019
 978-0-226-64653-4/2019/0027-0008$10.00

necessarily pick a case from the cert pool for which the median justice is indifferent between finding the conduct at issue permissible and finding the conduct impermissible. Second, it shows that the Court might not take a case that clarifies the law a great deal, even if such a case appears in the cert pool. Instead, the Court might hear a case that only makes a minor tweak to the law. And, remarkably, this is true even if the Court knows what it wants the law to be.

This comment unfolds in three parts. The next part describes the mechanics of the model. It shows how the assumptions of the model embed—correctly, in my view—jurisprudential concerns arising out of the case-or-controversy requirement, the difficulty of carving off the dicta of a case from its holding and the inability of any court to control how its opinion will be interpreted by a future court.[1]

The second part pivots to propose an alternative objective function for the lower courts. Sensibly enough, Bustos and Jacobi study lower courts composed of judges who disagree with the Supreme Court about what the law should be. I consider what might transpire with faithful lower court judges. Specifically, suppose that lower court judges tried to "read the tea leaves" in the Supreme Court precedent and resolve any new issue of law according to their best prediction about how the Supreme Court itself would do so.

This part then explores how the cert process might differ when the Supreme Court believes lower courts are faithful rather than composed of judges who disagree about what the law should be, including whether the law might converge to a standard rather than a rule.

The final part offers a short conclusion. It remarks on what models of this sort, including some I have worked on (Baker and Mezzetti 2012; Badawi and Baker 2015), fail to capture about judicial opinions and the nature of judge-made law. In so doing, I hope to provide direction for future enhancement of these models.

2. THE MECHANICS

Bustos and Jacobi set the model in case space (Kornhauser 1992a, 1992b; Lax 2011). A set of facts or cases lies on the unit interval. Cases close together on the interval share more in common than cases far apart. Each point on the interval corresponds to a different kind of conduct, where the conduct becomes increasingly problematic (e.g., in its

[1] For conflicting views on the relationship between holding and dicta, compare Goodhart (1930), "It is clear therefore, that the first rule for discovering the ratio decidendi of a case is that it must not be sought in the reasons on which the judge has based his decision," (164) with Dorf (2008), "The precedential force of an earlier case ultimately rests upon the reasons underlying the court's decision" (2059); see also Schauer (1987) and Abramowicz and Sterns (2005).

creation of negative externalities) as the number becomes larger. The role of the judiciary is to allocate the facts or cases into one of two bins: permissible conduct or impermissible conduct. The case located at 0 represents conduct that all judges believe should be permitted. The case located at 1 represents conduct that all judges believe should be impermissible.

Judicial preferences are captured by a cut point that separates permissible from impermissible conduct. Different cut points, then, capture disagreement among the courts in the hierarchy about what the law should be.

Two markers formalize the Supreme Court's legal doctrine or precedent. One marker—that will be referred to as the lower marker—says that all cases whose conduct value is less than that marker must be decided as permissible. A second marker—that will be referred to as the upper marker—says that all cases whose conduct value is greater than that marker must be decided as impermissible. In cases between the lower and upper markers, the law is uncertain. In this way, the markers constrain lower court judges but not fully: if the conduct value at issue in the case before the lower court is less than the lower marker or greater than the upper marker, the lower courts must decide according to the Supreme Court's doctrine.[2] By contrast, if the conduct value in the lower court case arises in the interval of uncertain law, lower court judges are not bound by Supreme Court precedent; in that interval the lower court faces a case of first impression.

Anticipating this behavior by the lower court, the Supreme Court decides which case in the region of uncertain law to hear; this is its certiorari decision. Specifically, how should it shrink the interval of uncertain law?

On the one hand, the Court might select a case, declare the conduct in that case permissible, and move the lower doctrinal marker to the right. On the other hand, the Court might select a case and declare the activity in that case impermissible and move the upper marker to the left.

The key assumption is that the Court cannot, in the same case, declare the conduct at issue permissible and likewise hold that closely adjacent conduct—conduct a shade to the right of the case before the Court—as impermissible. In other words, the Court cannot use the grant of certiorari in a single case to perfectly partition the fact space into one set of permissible conduct and a second set of impermissible conduct.

This assumption leads to the nonobvious results referenced in the introduction to this comment; that is, it reveals unnoticed aspects

[2] The authors, in effect, assume that a lower court will always follow Supreme Court precedent when a case arises before that lower court that is on all fours with that precedent; this assumption might be justified by thinking that lower court judges suffer a large reputational cost for flaunting a Supreme Court precedent directly on point.

about what makes a case "cert-worthy." To see why, suppose that all the lower court judges have cut points to the right of the median member of the Supreme Court, as depicted in figure 1.

The gray arrow situated directly above the horizontal line reflects the range of conduct the Supreme Court believes should be declared permissible. The black arrow situated directly above the horizontal line reflects the cases the Supreme Court prefers to find impermissible. Similarly, the gray arrow with diamond markings reflects the range of conduct all the lower courts believe should be found permissible, and the black arrow with diamond markings represents the range of conduct all the lower courts believe should be found impermissible.

The initial interval of uncertain law is captured by the curly bracket. It has two end points: the lower marker and upper marker. In deciding on which case to take for cert, the Supreme Court, in effect, must decide whether to shrink this interval by moving the lower marker to the right or moving the upper marker to the left.

With the preference conflict illustrated in figure 1, notice that the lower courts do not need a doctrinal command arising out of a specific case to do what the Supreme Court prefers them to do with respect to permissible conduct. Any conduct the Supreme Court would wish to find permissible all lower courts would find permissible if left to their own discretion (i.e., if the law remained undefined). As a result, it makes no sense for the Supreme Court to move the lower marker—that is, to grant cert in a case when that resolution case leads to a declaration that more conduct is permissible than previously stated in the precedent.

In contrast, the Supreme Court can generate more lower court compliance by shifting the upper marker to the left by defining a broader array of conduct as impermissible. Such a doctrinal command induces lower courts to issue impermissible decisions where they would have

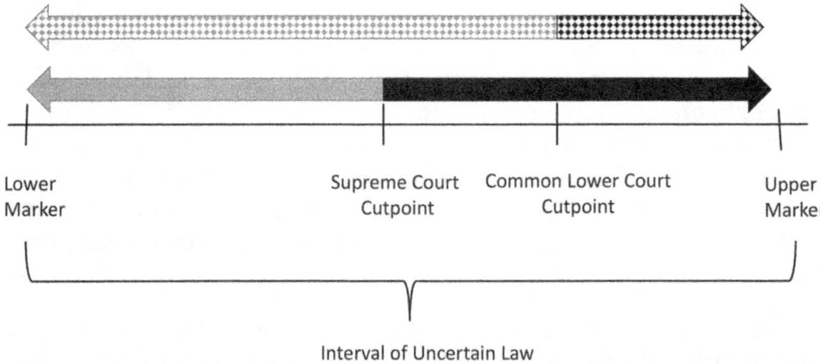

Figure 1. Judicial preferences.

otherwise not done so had the law remained undefined. Notably, the movement of the upper marker might not shrink the interval of uncertainty by very much; it could be a minor tweak to the law.

This result arises because the Supreme Court cannot credibly say that any particular case represents the most extreme conduct the Court would find permissible.

Why not? Why can't the Supreme Court announce, in effect, its ideal point—that is, announce in a single case that conduct *x* is permissible and, at the same time, conduct *x* plus a little bit more is impermissible.

I think the authors are correct that the Court cannot do this (or it is at least hard to do so) but it is interesting to explore why.

Before pursuing this question, let me put to one side the obvious answer. Scholars assert that the Supreme Court refuses to opine on cases not before it because it might make a mistake (Dorf 2000, 2008). The Court needs the facts and arguments in a case to render a well-considered judgment. That does not happen in the Bustos and Jacobi model. The Court knows what it wants. It is not trying to learn.

Of course, any opinion will decide more than the case before it. If the only change in the facts is that the plaintiff is named Smith rather than Jones, a lower court would feel bound by the Supreme Court's *Smith* decision as to the case involving Jones.

Yet as the facts between the precedent case and a subsequent case diverge—and that divergence is relevant to the ultimate policy question (e.g., the degree to which the conduct causes third-party harm)—the judicial decision in the precedent case exerts less influence on the subsequent judicial decision making.

The dwindling influence of precedent happens for three reasons. First, a lower court can more easily distinguish precedent when the facts significantly differ between the precedent case and the case at hand.

Second, lower court judges know that the Supreme Court itself does not feel bound by statements as to fact scenarios far removed from the precedent case.

Third, and perhaps most interesting, it is often the "interpreting" court, not the "writing" court, that determines the breadth or scope of a judicial decision. In other words, no matter what the Supreme Court says a case stands for at time t, it will find it hard to commit to that same reading at time $t + 1$.

3. A DOCTRINAL EXAMPLE

To flesh out these three institutional points about precedent (points that support the modeling assumption of Bustos and Jacobi), this section offers an example.

Under the First Amendment, the government cannot, absent a compelling justification and a narrowly tailored scheme, engage in viewpoint discrimination: it cannot allow the expression of views on a subject it agrees with and, at the same time, prohibit opposing views.[3] The Supreme Court has stated that this rule does not apply to so-called government speech. To see why, consider a hypothetical examined by the Supreme Court in an opinion in this area. If the government wishes to launch a campaign to encourage vaccination, it need not also launch a countercampaign detailing the argument of the antivaxxers.[4] To say otherwise would cripple the government's ability to convey a clear message to the public.

In light of this rule, it is critical to determine what is and what is not government speech. The Supreme Court cases in this area fit the model of Bustos and Jacobi. In *Pleasant Grove City v. Summum,* the Court concluded that the display of permanent monuments—that were privately donated to a park—"is best viewed as a form of government speech and is therefore not subject to scrutiny under the Free Speech Clause."[5] In terms of the model, *Summum* sets a lower marker for government speech, conduct that can be permissibly regulated without raising free speech concerns—this is speech that will be viewed as government messaging rather than as the government providing a forum for private speech.

In *Walker v. Texas Div., Sons of Confederate Veterans, Inc.*, the Court reasoned that requests for specialty license plates shared many commonalities with monuments and concluded that license plates also operated as government speech.[6] The Court recognized that monuments and license plates differ in many respects. A public park, for example, might only have capacity to hold a fixed number of permanent monuments, whereas the state could allow a very large number of privately concocted messages on specialty license plates. Given this difference, we might think of monuments as an easier case to declare as government speech rather than private speech. In terms of the model, *Walker* expanded what counted as permissible government speech beyond the statements made in the public monument case, *Summum* (i.e., it moved the lower marker to the right).

Next, in *Tam v. Matel,* the Court held that trademarks did not represent government speech. In terms of the Bustos and Jacobi model, the Court moved the upper marker to the left.[7] After so holding, the

[3] *Tam v. Matel,* 137 S.Ct. 1744 (2017), at 1757.

[4] *Walker v. Texas Div., Sons of Confederate Veterans, Inc.*, 135 S.Ct. 2239, (2015), at 2246.

[5] 555 U.S. 460 (2009), at 464.

[6] 137 S.Ct. 1744 (2015), at 2253.

[7] *Tam v. Matel,* 137 S.Ct. 1744 (2017), at 1760.

Court proceeded to find that the disparagement clause of the Lanham Act was unconstitutional viewpoint discrimination.[8]

To see the model assumption at work, consider the second case in this sequence, *Walker*. Imagine that the Court had declared, in that case, that specialty license plates were government speech and that trademarks were not government speech—the latter conclusion being, of course, the result eventually reached in the *Tam* case. Notably, the Court might need to do this to define its ideal point, that is, to set the precise marker between what is and what is not government speech, and to do so in the single opinion of *Walker*.

I submit the Court could not have done so and still comply with the norms of judicial decision making. The constitutionality of the disparagement clause of the Lanham Act was not before the Court in *Walker*. And, as a result, any statements the Court made about whether trademarks were or were not government speech would be dicta.

But maybe that is too much to ask. Perhaps the Court could have defined its ideal point another way. The *Walker* Court might have said specialty license plates represented the "most extreme" case of government speech. That is to say, any case with greater—actual or perceived—involvement by private citizens in the overall message would transform speech from "government" to "private."

The Court might have said this. And indeed Justice Alito in *Tam* characterized the *Walker* decision as "likely mark[ing] the outer bounds of the government speech doctrine."[9]

But the majority in *Walker* did not say this. It said that specialty license plates were government speech. And only later did a majority of the Court say that the license plate case was a close call.

In other words, the *Tam* Court (the interpreting court), not the *Walker* Court (the writing court), decided the facts representing the border between government speech and private speech.

Michael Dorf's work on dicta presents a number of other examples where the "interpreting" court—not the "writing" court—defined the sweep or scope of the precedent (Dorf 2008).

- In *Myers v. United States*, the Court purported to decide "whether under the Constitution the President has the exclusive power of removing *executive officers* of the United States whom he has appointed by and with the advice and consent of the Senate" (emphasis added).[10] In *Humphrey's Executor*, the Supreme Court stated "the narrow point actually decided [in *Myers*] was only that the President had power to remove a

[8] *Tam v. Matel*, 137 S.Ct. 1744 (2017), at 1765.
[9] 137 S.Ct. 1744 (2017), at 1760.
[10] 272 U.S. 52 (1926), at 106.

postmaster of the first class without the advice and consent of the Senate as required by act of Congress."[11]

- In *Roe v. Wade*, the Court referred to its "holding" as including statements about the proper constitutional evaluation of abortion restrictions based on trimester and viability.[12] In *Webster v. Reproductive Health Services*, Chief Justice Rehnquist stated that "this case therefore affords us no occasion to revisit the *holding* of *Roe*, which was that the Texas statute unconstitutionally infringed the right to an abortion derived from the Due Process Clause."[13]

Without doing a systematic survey, my instinct is that the Supreme Court in the same case does not normally say (*a*) this conduct is permissible and (*b*) other closely related conduct is impermissible or vice versa.

Maybe the justices do not because the statement about related or adjacent conduct lacks credibility. As in *Tam*, the interpreting court will decide whether or not the related conduct is impermissible.[14] Maybe the justices do not because they worry about saying that any case is a close call. Whatever the reason, Bustos and Jacobi's model rests on this assumption, which, as this section illustrates, has some grounding in actual judicial practice.

4. FAITHFUL LOWER COURT JUDGES

As noted, the Bustos and Jacobi model assumes that lower court judges prefer a different border between permissible and impermissible conduct than the median member of the Supreme Court. Lower courts follow Supreme Court doctrine if there is precedent directly on point but follow their own preferences when the law is undefined. Finally, the Supreme Court makes its selection for cert (and the subsequent establishment of new precedent) to induce the greatest amount of future compliance by the lower courts.

Rather than attempting to bend the law to their differing preferences (while complying with Supreme Court cases strictly on point), suppose that the lower courts attempted to predict how the Supreme Court might decide cases in the interval of uncertainty. They did so by looking at the available precedent—the lower and upper markers.

[11] 295 U.S. 602 (1935), at 626.

[12] 410 U.S. 113 (1973), at 165.

[13] 492 U.S. 490 (1989), at 521.

[14] Of course, this begs the question of how the Supreme Court commits itself to upholding even the most narrow reading of its prior cases.

From those cases, each lower court tried to deduce the Supreme Court's view of what the law should be, that is, the Supreme Court's preferred border between permissible and impermissible conduct.

Of course, if the lower court judges understood the Supreme Court's preferences, they would not have to look to the precedent at all. But, as I think is more likely, the lower courts might not know what the Supreme Court wants and look to the Supreme Court case law for guidance.

Suppose, as an example, that the lower marker rested at ¼ and the upper marker rested at 1. What should a lower court believe about the location of the Supreme Court's cut point or ideal point? Well, in this example, the Supreme Court has declared some activities permissible (those below ¼). It has never declared an activity impermissible. A reasonable inference, then, might be that the Supreme Court's view of the borderline case lies above ½.

In fact, assuming a uniform distribution of Supreme Court ideal points, the lower court's best prediction from these markers is that the Supreme Court's cut point is located at ⅝. In any subsequent case, a faithful lower court judge would therefore declare conduct permissible below ⅝ and declare impermissible conduct resting above ⅝.

Suppose now that the Supreme Court actually believed that the borderline case was located at ½ rather than ⅝. How could the Court signal its preference to the lower court judges via its selection of a case for discretionary review? If, say, the Court took case ¾ and declared the conduct at issue there impermissible, it would ensure that lower courts could correctly predict its view of the law from its precedent. Notably, the Supreme Court would not have to define the law for conduct resting between ¼ and ¾. Instead, it could rely on the lower courts to correctly extrapolate from the Supreme Court precedent (the lower marker of ¼ and the upper marker of ¾) its own view of the law. With lower court judges searching for Supreme Court guidance, we see the law converging to something that looks much more like a standard than a rule.

Notably, in this little example, we do not see the Court announce a standard and then take no other cases on the topic. Instead we have a standard that is tweaked and applied by the Supreme Court until lower courts have enough information culled from the Supreme Court's own application of that standard to see what the Supreme Court actually wants done in this area of law.

By contrast, under the assumptions about the preferences of lower court judges maintained in the Bustos and Jacobi model, the Supreme Court always wants to decrease the interval of uncertain law. It does so to induce greater lower court compliance with its own view of the law. Like almost all models of the evolution of law, the Bustos and

Jacobi model seems to predict a convergence to a rule rather than a standard.[15]

I think both objective functions for lower courts (faithful and not) are possible: one assumption about preferences leads to doctrine filled with rules; the alternative assumption about preferences leads to doctrine filled with standards, providing some potentially testable predictions.

5. CONCLUSION

I really like the Bustos and Jacobi article. From a plausible assumption about what courts can actually do in a case—what doctrinal commands they can commit to issue—they derive nonobvious results. These results explain patterns in the grant of certiorari that up to now have not been easily explained. In my view, the article should be commended, not critiqued. As noted earlier, this comment presents some justification for the core assumption of the model and speculates about what might transpire if lower courts had a different objective function.

I close by offering a few thoughts on the class of models of evolution of judge-made law rooted in case space. First, these models are about facts and outcomes. Courts map facts to outcome. Doctrine is laid down as markers in the fact space. Sometimes these markers constrain lower courts, as in the Bustos and Jacobi model. Other times future courts extrapolate from the markers to closely related cases, as in Baker and Mezzetti (2012).

Two aspects of judge-made law are noticeably absent from this formalization. First, in the real world judge-made law and precedent often take the form of legal tests. For example, according to the Supreme Court, the legal test for whether restrictions on commercial speech violate the First Amendment runs as follows: "At the outset, we must determine whether the expression is protected by the First Amendment. For commercial speech to come within that provision, it at least must concern lawful activity and not be misleading. Next, we ask whether the asserted governmental interest is substantial. If both inquiries yield positive answers, we must determine whether the regulation directly advances the governmental interest asserted, and whether it is not more extensive than is necessary to serve that interest."[16] How does one formalize a legal test such as this—a test that serves as a road map for future courts to follow? The result in *Central Hudson* is much

[15] An important recent exception to this trend is Cameron et al. (2019).

[16] *Central Hudson Gas & Electric Corp. v. Public Service Commission of New York*, 447 U.S. 557, 566 (1980).

broader than a conclusion linking facts to outcome: in that case, that the First Amendment prevented the Public Service Commission of New York from restricting advertising that promoted the use of electricity.[17] Further, it is more than a conclusion about closely related fact scenarios. It also provides a method of analysis for future cases.

Second, judicial decisions are coupled with reasons. A court says more than such and such conduct is permissible or impermissible. It explains why. The explanation, then, becomes important information for future courts and litigants. Following Schauer (2011), we might think that reasons allow courts to understand what makes two cases different or similar (or at least what the precedent court would view as relevant differences or similarities). In case space, future courts must look to the reasons given in the precedent opinion to decide whether case *x* is really different (e.g., located at a different place on the unit interval) than case *y*. But why does the judge writing the precedent case get to make that choice rather than the interpreting judge? Moreover, what exactly is a "reason" in a case-space model?

REFERENCES

Abramowicz, M. B., and M. L. Sterns. 2005. "Defining Dicta." *Stanford Law Review* 57:953–1094.

Badawi, A., and S. Baker. 2015. "Appellate Lawmaking in a Judicial Hierarchy." *Journal of Law and Economics* 58:139–72.

Baker, S., and C. Mezzetti. 2012. "A Theory of Rational Jurisprudence." *Journal of Political Economy* 120:513–51.

Beim, D., and K. Rader. 2015. "Evolution of Conflict in the Courts of Appeals." https://ssrn.com/abstract=2623304.

Black, R. C., and R. J. Owens. 2009. "Agenda Setting in the Supreme Court: The Collision of Policy and Jurisprudence." *Journal of Politics* 71:1062–75.

Cameron, C., L. Kornhauser, and G. Parameswara. 2019. "Stare Decisis and Judicial Log-Rolls: A Gains-from-Trade Model." *Rand Journal of Economics*. https://doi.org/10.1111/1756-2171.12288.

Dorf, M. C. 2008. "Dicta and Article III." *University of Pennsylvania Law Review* 142:1997–2069.

Goodhart, A. L. 1930. "Determining the Ratio Decidendi of a Case." *Yale Law Journal* 40:161–83.

Hellman, A. D. 1985. "Case Selection in the Burger Court: A Preliminary Inquiry." *Notre Dame Law Review* 60:947–1053.

Kornhauser, L. 1992a. "Modeling Collegial Courts. I: Path Dependence." *International Review of Law and Economics* 12:169–85.

[17] *Id.* at 572.

———. 1992b. "Modeling Collegial Courts. II: Legal Doctrine." *Journal of Law, Economics Organization* 8:441–70.
Lax, J. R. 2011. "The New Judicial Politics of Legal Doctrine." *Annual Review of Political Science* 14:131–57.
Schauer, F. 1987. "Precedent." *Stanford Law Review* 39:571–605.
———. 2011. "Precedent." https://ssrn.com/abstract=1836384.

"A Million Dollars in Free Advertising" Politics and Sex Offense Prosecution in the Wake of Duke Lacrosse

*Bryan C. McCannon**
Mark Wilson†

We explore a quasi-natural experiment to assess whether a prosecutor's political concerns affect rape's prosecution. In 2006 rape charges were filed against players on Duke University's lacrosse team. Although innocent, the student-athletes' prosecution took place during the prosecutor's primary and general election contests. We argue that this case made salient to voters across the state the concern regarding wrongful prosecution. Following a difference-in-difference strategy, we explore whether rape's prosecution varies by the prosecutor's reelection pressures and whether behavior adjusted after the media covered the scandal. We find significant changes in both the case filing levels and the use of jury trials. Fewer rape charges were filed after the Duke lacrosse case and the difference between the case filings during reelection years and nonelection years is muted. There are both fewer cases taken to trial after the scandal and an escalation in this effect during a prosecutor's reelection. The results strongly suggest that the two important margins, whether to even pursue a conviction and whether to pursue it at trial, are affected by a prosecutor's retention concerns.

* West Virginia University.
† Saint Bonaventure University. The title quote is attributed to Mike Nifong, the district attorney in North Carolina, referring to the prosecution of the Duke lacrosse players and how it will affect his reelection campaign. The quote was provided in the civil lawsuit filed by the student-athletes (civil complaint NC 07-739).

Electronically published: November 12, 2019
 978-0-226-64653-4/2019/0027-0009$10.00

1. INTRODUCTION

The prosecution of sex offenses is an especially nefarious undertaking. The crime itself is despicable. The evidence is often poor so that its prosecution can be expected to come with uncomfortably high levels of both type I and type II errors.[1] Compounding these issues, it is a salient social dilemma motivating citizens and policy makers to act.

Given this setting, we explore whether political influences distort the prosecution of rape cases. Crime's prosecution in the United States is led by local prosecutors. In the vast majority of states, these prosecutors are selected and retained using popular elections.[2] One can expect this political institution to influence behavior. It is well documented that voters are myopic holding elected officials accountable for their decisions closer to the election (or at least politicians act as if voters do so). Therefore, we investigate whether there is a systematic pattern in rape's prosecution across a prosecutor's election cycle.

To do so, we take advantage of a high-profile "shock" to prosecution. In 2006 members of the Duke University's lacrosse team were accused of rape. The case garnered national media attention and has led to an ESPN documentary and numerous books (see, e.g., Taylor and Johnson 2007; Cohan 2014; Bulger and Shelov 2016). Although the student-athletes were initially vilified by the university's faculty and media commentators, evidence eventually recognized that the student-athletes were not guilty.[3] A noteworthy feature of the case is that the head prosecutor in the district, Mike Nifong, ran in both a contested primary election and a contested general election during the period of the case's prosecution. As reported in a civil lawsuit afterward, District Attorney (DA) Nifong told his campaign manager that the case was worth a "million dollars in free advertising" for these races. It later came to light that the prosecutor had obtained evidence indicating the accused were not guilty but did not share this with the defense and instead continued to pursue a conviction. Eventually, the North Carolina attorney general took over the case and dismissed all charges. Mike Nifong was disbarred, lost a civil lawsuit, and pleaded guilty to a crime serving 1 day in jail.

We argue that this high-profile, wrongful prosecution acts as a shock to other prosecutors across the state. It improved the crime's salience and specifically highlighted the concern regarding wrongful prosecution.

[1] For a discussion, see the symposium on false allegations of rape in *Violence Against Women* (Lisak et al. 2010).

[2] Only four states appoint their local prosecutors: Connecticut, Rhode Island, New Jersey, and Alaska. Federal US attorneys are appointed as well, but only 5% of felony crimes are prosecuted in federal courts.

[3] The "Gang of 88" Duke faculty published a letter in the school newspaper within days of the charges being filed.

Thus, the case acts as an exogenous shock to rape's prosecution. Consequently, we take advantage of this quasi-natural experiment to assess whether politics influences sex offense prosecution.

Ex ante it is unclear what effect the case might have. On one hand, the extensive media coverage can be expected to bring an emphasis to the crime encouraging its prosecution. On the other hand, the case involved wrongful prosecution, which may encourage citizens and prosecutors to take heightened caution. Of course, one might hope for legal decision making to not be influenced by extralegal factors such as the retention concerns of the head prosecutor. In this case, one would expect no relationship between politics and rape's prosecution.

First, we find that case filing decisions adjust. Reelections are associated with less filing of rape and first-degree sex offenses than nonelection years. After the Duke lacrosse scandal, we observe a reduction in filing. The reelection effect, though, is muted afterward. These results do not arise for the filing of all other felonies or for reported rape incidents.

We explore alternative temporal breaks to identify whether we are capturing an overall time trend. The results cannot be explained by a downward trend in overall felony case filings or reported rape incidents. Structural break tests generate their largest test statistics close to the scandal's year. The adjustment in case filings seems to be driven by the scandal. Therefore, we conclude that we are identifying a casual impact on rape's prosecution.

Second, regarding case handling, plea bargaining decisions do not adjust. There is a slight reduction in the number of guilty pleas but not in the proportion of the caseload that results in a guilty plea. This suggests that some of the reduction in case filings after the scandal resulted in fewer pleas.

Importantly, we document substantial impacts on the decision to take a rape case to trial. Prior to the Duke lacrosse case, there had been no measurable difference in the number or proportion of cases that ended up before a jury between reelection years and nonelection years. The scandal, though, led to an overall reduction in jury trials. This effect is magnified during an incumbent's reelection season.

Our results are consistent with the hypothesis that the informational asymmetry between the voting public, which wants a skilled individual serving on its behalf, and the incumbent prosecutor, who cares not only about justice but also about keeping his or her job, is a crucial determinant in case handling decisions, as argued by Bandyopadhyay and McCannon (2015). Media coverage affects citizens' perceptions of the criminal justice system (Lim and Snyder 2015) and motivates prosecutors to act accordingly. The filing of charges and the pursuit of a conviction in a jury trial tend to elicit local media interest and, hence, the choices prosecutors make on these two margins are influenced by political concerns. With the heightened salience of wrongful rape prosecutions, prosecutors are less likely to have a case taken to trial. Enhanced distortions arise during the reelections following the scandal. Our results are also noteworthy in that they show a decrease in the number of jury trials near a prosecutor's reelection campaign, which contrasts with Bandyopadhyay and McCannon's (2014) finding of an increase in jury trial convictions for all felonies. This suggests that a prosecutor's behavior in rape cases is distinct.

To the best of our knowledge, we are the first to evaluate empirically the caseload management outcomes in North Carolina after the Duke lacrosse scandal and to identify distortions that arose. Others have studied the scandal though. It has served as a case study in public relations (Fortunato 2008), has incited debates in the academic journalism literature (Kosse 2007; Smolkin 2007), and has even been evaluated in biology research (Richman and Jonassaint 2008). Legal commentary has arisen (Entman and Gross 2008; Elder 2009), but a rigorous analysis of the data has not been undertaken before now.

We primarily contribute to the literature studying rape's prosecution. A number of other important dimensions to the dilemma have been addressed previously. For example, the relationship between the accused and the victim has been explored (Spears and Spohn 1997). Spears and Spohn (1996) consider the connection between the accused's race and the victim's race in the outcomes of sexual assault cases. Spohn and Holleran (2001) show that charging decisions are conditioned by the personal relationship between the victim and the accused. The prosecutor's role has been studied previously as well. Spohn, Beichner, and Davis-Frenzel (2001) evaluate observational data and interviews to assess the drivers to the decision to charge in sexual assault cases. They argue that the charging decisions primarily reflect the prosecutor's assessment of the likelihood of conviction. To the best of our knowledge, we are the first to explore political influences.

We also contribute to the growing literature evaluating how political concerns affect prosecutor decision making. Early theoretical analysis emphasized the election mechanism's ability to incentivize prosecutorial effort (Gordon and Huber 2002). The asymmetric information problem between the incumbent and the poorly informed voting public can be expected to lead to distortions in the decision to go to trial during the election season (Bandyopadhyay and McCannon 2015). Bandyopadhyay and McCannon (2014) show the proportion of convictions that come from trials increases when a prosecutor is running for reelection. Prosecutor reelections have been shown to correlate with case dismissals (Dyke 2007), success of appeals (McCannon 2013), and incarceration (Nadel, Scaggs, and Bales 2017). We differ from this work in that we focus on one particular crime that can be expected to generate substantial media attention rather than all felonies, as they study, and take advantage of a quasi-natural experiment.[4]

2. THE DUKE LACROSSE CASE

On April 27, 2005, Mike Nifong was appointed as the interim DA in Durham County, North Carolina, the home of Duke University. He filled the vacancy left by his former boss who was appointed to a judge position. In spring 2006 he ran in a contested primary election, winning it on May 2, and in fall 2006 he won a contested general election. During this period of political competition, a crime was reported.

On March 13, 2006, members of the Duke University's lacrosse party held a party. A woman told police that after she was hired to perform at the party she was assaulted by three student-athletes. By March 28 the players were suspended and by April 5 the team's coach was fired and the lacrosse season was canceled. On April 18 the three student-athletes were arrested for rape, first-degree sex offense, and kidnapping.

Over the course of the spring and summer the crime was investigated. On April 10 (prior to the filing of charges) the North Carolina crime lab failed to find DNA evidence supporting the guilt of those accused of the assault. On May 12 a private DNA lab hired by DA Nifong again was unable to connect the student-athletes to the crime. The results from this test were withheld from the defense. By June 8 a witness present told prosecutors that there had not been an attack. It was not until October that anyone from the DA's office interviewed the accuser. After DA Nifong won the general election, the case was transferred to the attorney general's office, which proceeded to drop the charges on December 22.

The public outrage led to noteworthy follow-up events. On December 28 the North Carolina bar filed ethics violations against Mike Nifong. By June 16, 2007, he was disbarred and by September 7 Mike Nifong was convicted and served 1 day in jail.

It is important for the identification strategy that this event made salient the importance of rape and its prosecution. To provide suggestive evidence that the case had widespread interest, figure 1 considers Google searches for "rape" by those in North Carolina. The data are

[4] One can also place our work in the literature on career concerns of prosecutors such as the effect of salaries on turnover (Boylan 2004), the influence of private market opportunities on jury trials (Boylan and Long 2005), and the decision of subordinates within the prosecutor's office to challenge the incumbent (McCannon and Pruitt 2018). Retention concerns studied here are just one dimension of the career concerns affecting prosecutors' behavior.

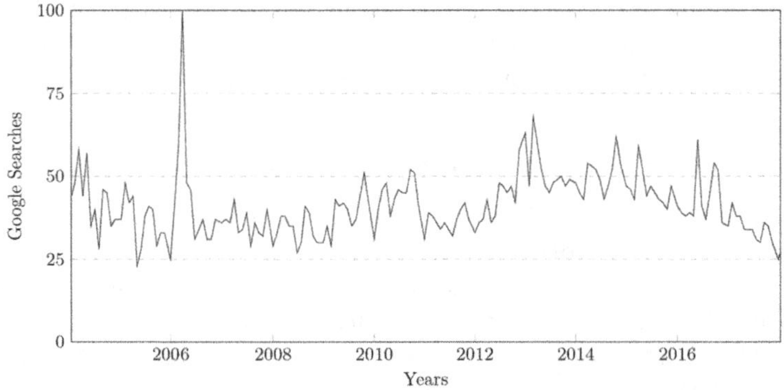

Figure 1. Searches in North Carolina for "rape." Number of searches for "rape" from those in North Carolina normalized by the peak month. Data collected in April 2018 from Google Trends.

normalized by the peak observation in the date range, which is (not coincidentally) April 2006.

Interest in the crime, while consistently searched, peaks during the scandal. We argue, though, that this effect rippled across the state affecting prosecutors not involved in the particular case. Thus, figure 2 compares searches by those in the Raleigh/Durham area (the case's location) with the two other heavily populated regions of the state, namely, the Greensboro/Winston-Salem area and the Charlotte area.

Searching is correlated across regions of the state. The correlation coefficient between searches in Raleigh/Durham and Greensboro/Winston-Salem and Charlotte is .35 and .56, respectively. Importantly, the frequency of rape's interest peaks in all three regions at the time period of the Duke lacrosse case. Therefore, we can be confident that the

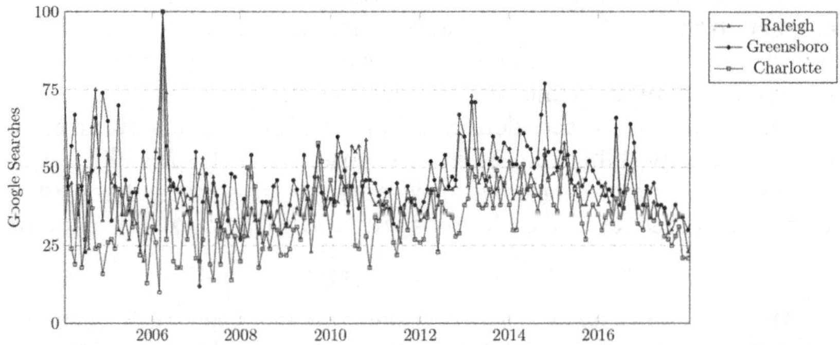

Figure 2. Searches in regions of North Carolina. Number of searches for "rape" from those in North Carolina normalized by the peak month. Data collected in April 2018 from Google Trends

salience of the case affected citizens across the state. Similar trends occur in other regions of the state as well. We ask whether this trend affected decisions made in reported rapes in areas of the state other than Durham County in events unrelated to the Duke lacrosse scandal. In other words, did the salience of wrongful prosecution by one DA in the state have a spillover effect on citizens in other counties in the state holding their prosecutors more accountable for prosecution decisions made?

3. DATA

To appreciate the intersection of politics and sex offense prosecution, we collect data from North Carolina. DAs in the state serve 4-year terms. They compete in popular elections without term limits. Elections are held in even-numbered years and are staggered across the state.

North Carolina's 100 counties are organized into prosecutorial districts. There has been a slight expansion in the number of these districts over time as North Carolina's population has grown. By 2017, the 39 districts existing in the 1990s had grown to 44 districts. Heavily populated counties are their own districts. Rural counties tend to be consolidated.[5]

3.1. Caseload Data

To evaluate case handling, we use data from the North Carolina Administrative Office of the Courts, which provides annual caseload processing data at the district level (North Carolina Judicial Branch 2019). The reports provide the number of cases filed, dismissed, disposed, and left pending at the year's end. Regarding cases disposed, the report identifies how many went to a jury trial and resulted in a guilty plea.[6]

The report groups crimes into categories. The one of interest here is "rape and first-degree sex offenses." These include the most egregious sex crimes. Throughout the rest of the article, we refer to crimes within this category as "rape" for ease of exposition. There is also a separate

[5] See Detotto and McCannon (2019) for an analysis of the impact of prosecutor office consolidation.

[6] The report disentangles pleading as charged from pleading to lesser offenses, which we do not analyze here. Also the report does not separate (for all years studied here) acquittals from convictions at trial. There is also an "other" category, which would include numerous additional outcomes such as dismissal due to speedy trial concerns, deferred prosecution, and transfers to juvenile court. Thus, outcomes do not sum up to the caseload. The four outcome variables presented in table 1 account for 97.7% of the caseload for rape cases and 96.6% for all felonies. Finally, North Carolina does not allow nonjury bench trials for felonies.

Table 1. Descriptive Statistics

	μ	σ	Minimum	Median	Maximum
Rape:					
Filed	36.6	48.9	0	27	258
Pending (from previous year)	40.4	40.6	0	28	363
Dismissed	17.5	23.1	0	10	252
Guilty plea	15.3	13.7	0	11	110
Jury trial	3.1	4.1	0	2	28
Pending (end of year)	40.3	41.3	0	28	389
All felonies:					
Filed	2,511.1	1,812.4	470	1,997	11,678
Pending (from previous year)	1,821.2	1,466.2	113	1,468	9,972
Dismissed	907.8	880.0	66	665	6,314
Guilty plea	1,543.5	1,043.2	263	1,276	6,508
Jury trial	50.2	45.3	0	37	352
Pending (end of year)	1,684.3	1,349.4	114	1,315	9,660

Note: $N = 755$ (1999–2000 through 2016–17).

category for "other sex offenses," which includes nonrape, lower-level sex offenses, violations of the sex offender registry, and other post-release restrictions.[7] We record the caseload flows for all felonies as well.

The data are reported for fiscal years (July 1 through June 30). Availability begins in 1999–2000, and we collected data through the 2016–17 year ($N = 755$). Table 1 presents descriptive statistics.

Overall, the backlog of unresolved felony cases is shrinking in North Carolina. The percentage change in the number of cases left pending at the beginning of the year to the end of the year is −7.5%. For sex offenses, there is almost no change in the backlog.

Regarding case disposal, one may expect that the decision to pursue a sex offense case is different. The proportion of the caseload that is dismissed is similar for all felonies and rape cases (21.0% versus 22.7%). Mode of conviction, though, differs. For those filed charges where a conviction is pursued, only 1.16% of all felony cases are resolved via

[7] For the past few years in our data, the crimes are not aggregated but instead are reported for each crime code.

a jury trial. This percentage bounces up to 4.03% for rape. Along those same lines, 35.6% of the caseload of all felonies in a year results in a guilty plea. For rape cases it is 19.9%. Thus, there are substantial differences in prosecution decisions in rape cases compared with other felonies. The research question, though, is whether there is systematic temporal variation in rape case handling coinciding with the election cycle.

3.2. Election Data

Election data are collected from the North Carolina Board of Elections. Elections for DA occur in even-numbered years and are staggered so that 11.4% of prosecutors were up for election in 2016 and 88.6% in 2014.

For each prosecutor election, we record whether the seat was contested and whether it involved an incumbent seeking reelection. We consider both primary and general elections. Because our caseload data cover fiscal years, we choose to denote the election year as the fiscal year that leads up to the election, that is, the one that ends on June 30 of the election year. This would, then, include the campaign filing period (i.e., entry), the primary election, and much of the general election campaigning. Applying the election to the following fiscal year would include 8 months of the postelection period. Table 2 provides information on the election characteristics.

Relative to other offices, such as legislative seats, prosecutor elections are different. For a comparison, the 2016 House of Representatives elections were contested 94.3% of the time and involved an incumbent running for reelection 88.3% of the time. Thus, there is more variation in whether an incumbent prosecutor runs for reelection and whether he or she is challenged. See Wright (2009, 2014) for a discussion of the relative infrequency of contested prosecutor elections and Gordon, Huber, and Landa (2007) and McCannon and Pruitt

Table 2. Election Variables

Description	Variable	Sample (%)	Elections (%)
Observations where an election is occurring	Election	23.07	100
Observations where a contest is occurring	Contest	7.86	34.09
Observations where an incumbent is running for reelection	Reelection	15.86	68.75

Note: $N = 755$ (1999–2000 through 2016–17).

(2018) for game-theoretic investigations of the decision to contest an incumbent prosecutor.

4. RESULTS

The research question of interest here is whether there is a systematic pattern to rape's prosecution. We divide the analysis into the decision to file charges and the prosecution method, given that the decision to prosecute has been made.

4.1. Case Filings

Because one can reasonably expect both the perpetration and reporting of the crime to be unrelated to the retention concerns of the elected prosecutor, evaluating systematic patterns to filings can be expected to be driven primarily by the political concerns of those within the office.

Figure 3 compares the sample's partition into district-years before and after the Duke lacrosse scandal. The sample mean and the 95% confidence intervals are depicted.

As one can see, there is a noticeable reduction in case filings after the Duke lacrosse case. The mean reduces by 30.4%. Statistical tests confirm the distinction in the distribution functions. This finding is consistent with the hypothesis that prosecutors respond to voters concerned with wrongful prosecution.

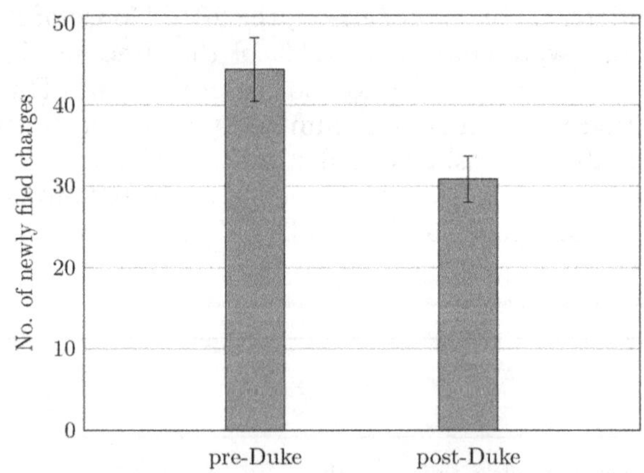

Figure 3. Rape case filing before and after the Duke Lacrosse scandal. Each column depicts the subsample mean ($n = 320$ and $n = 435$, respectively). A difference-in-means t-test (allowing for unequal variances) has $|t| = 5.50$ ($p < .001$). A Wilcoxon rank sum test has $|z| = 7.55$ ($p < .001$).

We can also ask whether there is a pattern to case filings that coincides with the election cycle. Figure 4 considers subsamples based on whether the observation arises during the election season.

There is a slight election effect. When an incumbent is running for reelection, there is little change in case filings overall (approximately a 1% reduction). After the Duke lacrosse scandal, though, there is a noticeable drop. In the postscandal period, reelections are associated with almost a 2% reduction in rape case filings. However, the confidence interval is quite wide. Taken together, the figures provide (weak) suggestive evidence supporting the hypothesis that politics influences case filing decisions.

The suggested reelection effect does not arise for other felony crimes. Although not depicted here, there is a slight increase in case filings during reelection years relative to the nonelection periods. The differences are all statistically indistinguishable. The distinction between filing decisions in rape cases and all other felonies can be illustrated further by considering their time trends.

For both time series the number of case filings is normalized by the 2006–7 value. For rape cases, a level decrease exists. The maximum observed after 2006 is less than the minimum value arising prior to 2006. The overall number of felony cases filed is flat over the time period. Thus, the pattern observed for rape's prosecution does not arise for other crimes.

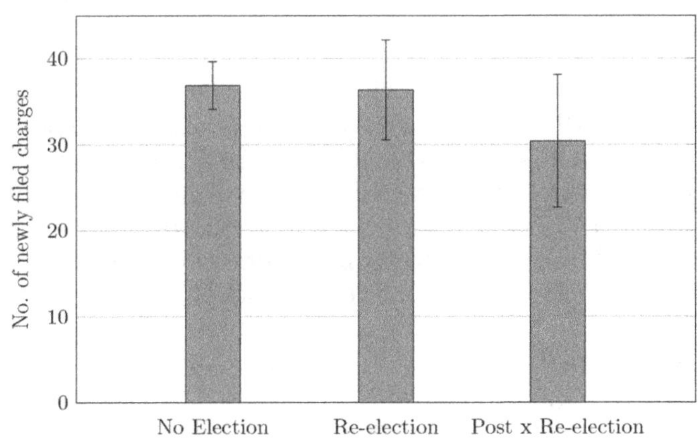

Figure 4. Rape case filings and the election cycle. Each column depicts the subsample mean (n = 581, n = 119, and n = 61, respectively). A difference-in-means t-test (allowing for unequal variances) for no election and election has $|t| = 0.43$ ($p = .67$); reelection and no reelection has $|t| = 0.09$ ($p = .93$); and post × reelection and no reelection has $|t| = 1.66$ ($p = .10$).

Table 3. Rape Case Filings

	(1)	(2)	(3)	(4)
Reelection	−.0008	. . .	−.0012	−.0028*
	(.0009)	. . .	(.0009)	(.0011)
Post	. . .	−.0054**	−.0055**	−.0059**
	. . .	(.0009)	(.0009)	(.0010)
Post × reelection	. . .	. . .	. . .	.0029+
	. . .	. . .	. . .	(.0018)
District fixed effects	✓	✓	✓	✓
R^2	.251	.307	.309	.312
AIC	−4,940	−5,001	−4,999	−5,000

Note: Dependent variable = number of filed rape charges relative to total number of filed felony charges; $\mu = 0.18$, $\sigma = 0.015$. Each specification, except (2), includes an indicator variable for whether there is a vacant seat. Standard errors presented in parentheses are clustered at the district level. $N = 755$. AIC = Akaike information criterion.
$^+p < .10$.
$^*p < .05$.
$^{**}p < .01$.

Turning to regression analysis, table 3 presents results from a fixed-effects estimation exploring the temporal changes in the pursuit of rape convictions across North Carolina. Prosecutorial district fixed effects allow for the time-invariant characteristics of different areas of the state to be accounted for.[8] The dependent variable is the number of rape charges filed normalized by the total number of felony cases filed. Standard errors are clustered at the district level to account for within-district variation differing from between-district volatility.

The column 1 of table 3 suggests reelections are associated with a reduction in filings, relative to the total number of felonies, compared with the nonelection season. This effect, though, is small and statistically insignificant. In columns 2 and 3 the postscandal period is differentiated from the prescandal period. A sizable reduction is identified, consistent with figure 3. The estimated effect is a 36% reduction from the mean. The final column conducts a difference-in-difference estimation allowing for the difference between the reelection season and the nonelection season to be separated by the shock to prosecution. The reduction in filings after the Duke lacrosse case is slightly muted

[8] Although not presented here, if socioeconomic characteristics are introduced, the main results are unaffected.

during reelection season. Prior to this event, a significant election effect exists. Reelections were associated with fewer convictions being pursued. The difference between the reelection season and nonelection years is reduced after the scandal.

One interpretation of these results is that after the scandal, which highlighted the problem of wrongful prosecution, prosecutors avoided filing charges and pursuing a conviction, at least at the margin. Prior to the scandal, they only systematically avoided case filings near the election period.

One can be concerned that the change in case filings is not due to prosecutors altering their decision making but simply is an artifact of the underlying perpetuation of the crime. Of course, reliable data on the occurrence of these crimes do not exist. However, data on the number of reported incidents are available from the North Carolina State Bureau of Investigation. One way to be confident that our results are not simply reflecting occurrence of the underlying crime is to replace the number of filed rape cases with reported rapes in the specifications presented in table 3. Although not presented here, a relationship between prosecutors' reelection cycles and rape incidents does not exist, as to be expected. For example, in the fourth column the coefficients on reelection and post × reelection are both highly statistically insignificant.

There is, though, a downward trend in reported rapes. Figure 5 depicts graphically the time series. This trend raises the concern that the postperiod effect identified previously is driven not by the scandal's shock but by fewer crimes being committed. To illustrate, the post-scandal years have 20.8% fewer reported rapes per district than in the pre-Duke period. Rape case filings, though, are influenced to a

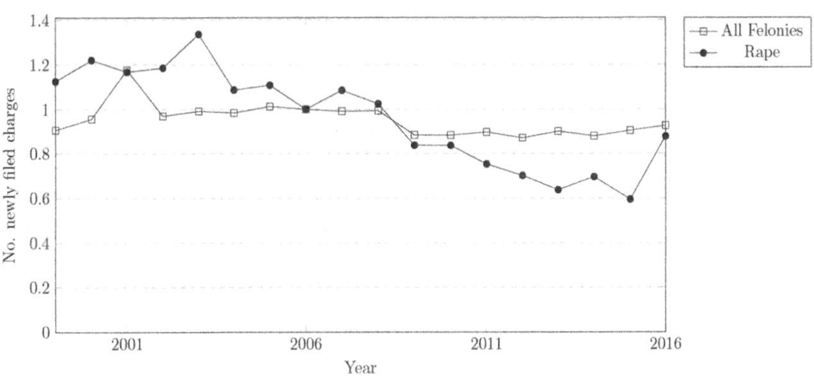

Figure 5. Case filings over time. Mean number of newly filed cases in each year normalized by the 2006–7 value.

Table 4. Chow Tests for Break in Case Filings

Year of Structural Break	Chow Test *F*-Statistic
2000–2001	1.68
2001–2	1.72
2002–3	2.55
2003–4	3.13
2004–5	3.01
2005–6	4.06
2006–7	3.36
2007–8	3.19
2008–9	3.35
2009–10	3.66
2010–11	3.20
2011–12	2.56
2012–13	2.30
2013–14	1.53
2014–15	1.34

Note: Results using an ordinary least squares regression with the number of filed rape charges (relative to all felony charges filed) as the dependent variable. Along with constant district fixed effects and a control for vacancy, a prosecutor's reelection year is the explanatory variable. Thus, the $F(3,749)$ statistics are reported.

greater extent with a decrease of 30.6%.[9] Nevertheless, we address this concern in two ways.

First, we detrend the data by including a time trend in the primary specification of table 3, column 4. Doing so, the main results persist in that reelections prior to the Duke lacrosse case have a negative and statistically significant relationship with filings and the difference-in-difference coefficient also retains its positive sign and statistical significance. The magnitude of the post coefficient remains negative but reduces substantially in magnitude. Therefore, the main result is not indicative of only a downward trend in the crime's prevalence.

[9] Interestingly, while reported total felony crimes dropped by 27.2%, case filings dropped by only 8.8%. Thus, while other crimes saw only slight reductions in prosecutions, the prosecution of rape was overly reduced.

Second, we conduct a series of Chow tests to assess the existence of structural, temporal breaks in the data. We conduct a Chow test not only for the year of the Duke lacrosse scandal but for other years as well. If a break in the data is detected near the time of the scandal, and the magnitude of the test statistic diminishes as the year of the tested break is farther from the actual year of the scandal, then we can be more confident that the postscandal control is not capturing a downward time trend. Table 4 presents the test statistics.

Structural break tests generate the greatest test statistics in the years close to the scandal and diminish as we move farther from that date. This result provides additional evidence that it is the scandal that is altering case filing decisions.

4.2. Case Handling

Now consider how the cases are disposed when convictions are pursued. First, we evaluate plea bargaining. Figure 6 compares the number of guilty pleas across the election cycle and on either side of the scandal.

The first three columns suggest a negligible impact of retention pressures on plea bargaining. A slight drop after the scandal is observed in the reelection effect but is statistically indistinguishable from the prescandal election years. The last two columns indicate that there is a change in the total number of guilty pleas after 2006. It is unclear whether the modest post × reelection decrease is, in fact, due to retention concerns directly or is capturing a downward trend.

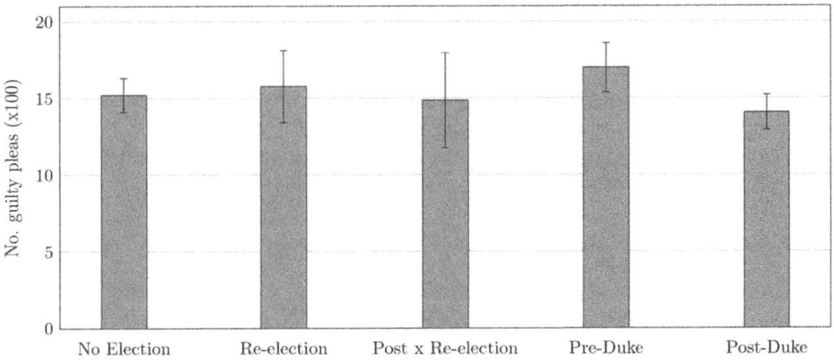

Figure 6. Plea bargaining and the election cycle. Each column depicts the subsample mean (n = 581, n = 119, and n = 61, respectively). A difference-in-means t-test (allowing for unequal variances) for no election and election has $|t|$ = 0.32 (p = .76); reelection and no reelection has $|t|$ = 0.42 (p = .671); post × reelection and no reelection has $|t|$ = 0.29 (p = .77); and pre-Duke versus post-Duke has $|t|$ = 2.79 (p < .01).

Table 5. Plea Bargaining Rape Cases

	(1)	(2)	(3)	(4)
Reelection	.6266	. . .	.4848	.2029
	(.9962)	. . .	(.4908)	(1.7662)
Post	. . .	-1.7530*	-1.7093*	-1.7970+
	. . .	(.8529)	(.8473)	(.0470)
Post × reelection	. . .	. . .	. . .	.5385
	. . .	. . .	. . .	(2.3807)
District fixed effects	✓	✓	✓	✓
R^2	.539	.562	.562	.562
AIC	5,485	5,478	5,481	5,483
	(1)	(2)	(3)	(4)
Reelection	.0091	. . .	.0093	.0041
	(.0121)	. . .	(.120)	(.0170)
Post	. . .	.0015	.0022	.0005
	. . .	(.0137)	(.0137)	(.0133)
Post × reelection	. . .	. . .	. . .	.0099
	. . .	. . .	. . .	(.0264)
District fixed effects	✓	✓	✓	✓
R^2	.353	.352	.353	.354
AIC	-1,170	-1,171	-1,168	-1,166

Note: Dependent variable = number of rape cases resulting in plea (top panel); μ = 15.29, σ = 13.74. Dependent variable = number of rape cases resulting in plea relative to rape caseload (bottom panel); μ = 0.228, σ = 0.139. Each specification, except (2), includes an indicator variable for whether there is a vacant seat up for election. Standard errors presented in parentheses are clustered at the district level. N = 755. AIC = Akaike information criterion.

$^+p < .10$.

$^*p < .05$.

Table 5 provides fixed-effects estimates to explore the impact of election pressure on guilty pleas. The top panel considers the total number of guilty pleas, whereas the bottom panel uses the number of guilty pleas relative to the rape caseload as the dependent variable. District fixed effects allow us to control for time-invariant characteristics.[10] Clustered standard errors are presented.

[10] Again, if socioeconomic controls are included, the main results are unaffected.

For the most part, there is neither a reelection effect nor a scandal effect on plea bargaining. The total number of guilty pleas reduces after 2006–7, but the proportion of the rape caseload is unaffected. Thus, the reduction in case filings documented in the previous subsection results in fewer pleas.

Although not presented here, similar findings arise if case dismissals are considered. The total number of cases dismissed reduces after 2006–7, coinciding with the reduction in rape cases filed, but measurable reelection effects do not exist. Taken together case handling for these two important outcome variables is not sensitive to the political concerns of the DAs.

We turn to the final outcome variable of interest—namely, whether a case goes to a jury trial. Figure 7 reproduces figure 6 for jury trials.

A decrease in jury trials exists when comparing reelection years with those observations outside of the reelection season. The confidence interval is too wide to make a conclusive claim. After 2006–7, though, a sizable reduction occurs. Very few rape cases are taken to trial during a prosecutor's reelection season after the Duke lacrosse case. Considering the final two columns, a level effect occurs as well. Not only does the shock of the case reduce a prosecutor's willingness to take a rape case to trial, but also the additional concern of a reelection season dramatically reduces it.

Table 6 verifies these observations in fixed-effects models. Again, standard errors are clustered at the district level.

Consistent with figure 7, the difference between the reelection season and the nonelection years grows in both level and proportion of the rape caseload. Fewer jury trials occur after 2006–7 and the reduction

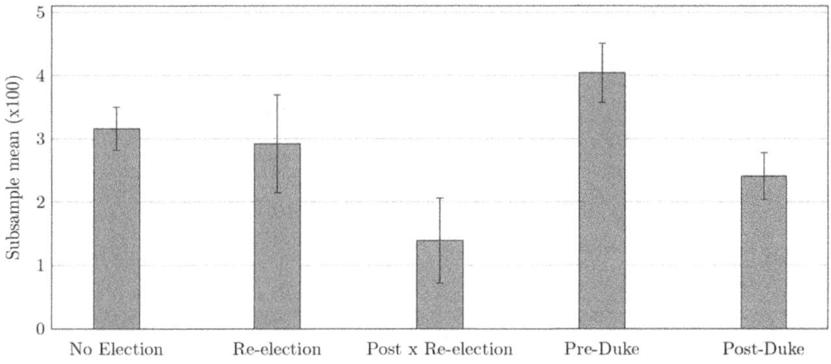

Figure 7. Jury trials and the election cycle. Each column depicts the subsample mean ($n = 581$, $n = 119$, and $n = 61$, respectively). A difference-in-means t-test (allowing for unequal variances) for no election and election has $|t| = 0.74$ ($p = .46$); reelection and no reelection has $|t| = 0.50$ ($p = .62$); post × reelection and no reelection has $|t| = 5.06$ ($p < .001$); and pre-Duke versus post-Duke has $|t| = 5.40$ ($p <. 001$).

Table 6. Rape Cases at Trial

	(1)	(2)	(3)	(4)
Reelection	–.2392	. . .	–.3451	.5098
	(.3195)	. . .	(.3151)	(.5552)
Post	. . .	–1.2584**	–1.2766**	–1.0107**
	. . .	(.3220)	(.3201)	(.3642)
Post × reelection	. . .	. . .	. . .	–1.6329*
	. . .	. . .	. . .	(.7575)
District fixed effects	✓	✓	✓	✓
R^2	.295	.3151	.316	.321
AIC	4,012	3,988	3,991	3,988
	(1)	(2)	(3)	(4)
Reelection	–.0069	. . .	–.0083	.0021
	(.0059)	. . .	(.0058)	(.0087)
Post	. . .	–.0165**	–.0169**	–.0136*
	. . .	(.0048)	(.0047)	(.0055)
Post × reelection	. . .	. . .	. . .	–.0198+
	. . .	. . .	. . .	(.0102)
District fixed effects	✓	✓	✓	✓
R^2	.157	.172	.176	.180
AIC	–2,315	–2,332	–2,331	–2,332

Note: Dependent variable = number of rape cases resulting in a jury trial (top panel); μ = 3.10, σ = 4.10. Dependent variable = number of rape cases resulting in jury trial relative to rape caseload (bottom panel); μ = 0.044, σ = 0.057. Each specification, except (2), includes an indicator variable for whether there is a vacant seat. Standard errors presented in parentheses are clustered at the district level. N = 755. AIC = Akaike information criterion.

$^+p < .10$.

$^*p < .05$.

$^{**}p < .01$.

is escalated during prosecutors' reelections. Overall, there is a 41% reduction in jury trials after the scandal. Compared with reelection years prior to the case, the number of jury trials during incumbent prosecutor reelections after the Duke lacrosse scandal reduces by almost 53%. Likewise, the proportion of the rape caseload that goes to trial reduces by 45%. Thus, the magnitude of the effects is substantial.

Therefore, unlike plea bargaining and case dismissals, jury trials reduce in prevalence not only because fewer cases are being filed but also because a smaller proportion of the caseload is taken to trial. The significant event led to avoidance of trials, especially during prosecutors' reelections.

5. CONCLUSION

We use the 2006 Duke lacrosse scandal to evaluate the impact of reelection pressures on prosecutors' handling of sex offenses. Prior research has shown that case handling is influenced by the election cycle, but sex offenses have not been analyzed previously. This is an important omission as violence against women is an important social problem and, with the poor evidence that is common, it is fraught with concerns over type I and type II errors. As the scandal received nationwide attention, voter salience on wrongful convictions can be expected to be heightened across the state. Therefore, we explore how this case "shocked" rape's prosecution and whether the effect interacted with prosecutor reelections to influence case handling.

We find important distortions in the handling of rape cases. After the scandal, fewer cases were filed. Prior to the scandal, prosecutors only systematically avoided case filings near the election period. Regarding the handling of those cases filed, we find a strong effect on the number and proportion of rape cases that go to trial. Fewer cases were taken to trial after the scandal, and the decrease is escalated for reelection periods in the period after the scandal. Therefore, the exogenous shock to rape's prosecution led to fewer case filings and less use of jury trials. These distortions are enhanced during a reelection year.

It is important to emphasize the relationship between the findings here and those of Bandyopadhyay and McCannon (2014). They too consider the relationship between prosecutor reelections and case handling. They find that elections are associated with more convictions arising from jury trials being taken to trial. They consider all felonies, whereas we only consider rape and first-degree sex offenses here. Therefore, the election's distortionary effects move in opposite directions. Presumably, a prosecutor is interested in both looking "tough on crime" and avoiding wrongful prosecutions. Although many felonies allow a prosecutor to achieve the former by prosecuting cases at trial, rape cases provide a heightened opportunity to being exposed as wrong.

The work also points to the importance of citizen accountability for decisions made by prosecutors. Presumably, when voter salience is enhanced, prosecutors respond. Therefore, this provides an avenue for improvements in the criminal justice system. Public choice distortions are important to consider and document. Our work further highlights their importance in the legal system.

REFERENCES

Bandyopadhyay, Siddhartha, and Bryan C. McCannon. 2014. "The Effect of the Election of Prosecutors on Criminal Trials." *Public Choice* 161:141–56.

———. 2015. "Prosecutorial Retention: Signaling by Trial." *Journal of Public Economic Theory* 17:219–56.

Boylan, Richard T. 2004. "Salaries, Turnover, and Performance in the Federal Criminal Justice System." *Journal of Law and Economics* 47:75–92.

Boylan, Richard T., and Cheryl X. Long. 2005. "Salaries, Plea Rates, and the Career Objectives of Federal Prosecutors." *Journal of Law and Economics* 48:627–51.

Bulger, Jay, and Joshua Shelov. 2016. "We Are." *ESPN Films*.

Cohan, William D. 2014. *The Price of Silence: The Duke Lacrosse Scandal, the Power of the Elite, and the Corruption of Our Great Universities*. New York: Scribner.

Detotto, Claudio, and Bryan C. McCannon. 2019. "The Consolidation of Prosecutor's Offices." *Journal of Law and Courts* (Forthcoming).

Dyke, Andrew. 2007. "Electoral Cycles in the Administration of Criminal Justice." *Public Choice* 133:417–37.

Elder, David A. 2009. "A Libel Law Analysis of Media Abuses in Reporting on the Duke Lacrosse Fabricated Rape Charges." *Vanderbilt Journal of Entertainment and Technology Law* 11:99–178.

Entman, Robert M., and Kimberly A. Gross. 2008. "Race to Judgment: Stereotyping Media and Criminal Defendants." *Law and Contemporary Problems* 71:93–133.

Fortunato, John A. 2008. "Restoring a Reputation: The Duke University Lacrosse Scandal." *Public Relations Review* 34:116–23.

Gordon, Sanford C., and Gregory A. Huber. 2002. "Citizen Oversight and Electoral Incentives of Criminal Prosecutors." *American Journal of Political Science* 46:334–51.

Gordon, Sanford C., Gregory A. Huber, and Dimitri Landa. 2007. "Challenger Entry and Voter Learning." *American Political Science Review* 101:303–20.

Kosse, Susan Hanley. 2007. "Race, Riches and Reporters—Do Race and Class Impact Media Rape Narratives? An Analysis of the Duke Lacrosse Case." *Southern Illinois University Law Journal* 31:243–73.

Lim, Claire S. H., and James M. Snyder Jr. 2015. "Is More Information Always Better? Party Cues and Candidate Quality in US Judicial Elections." *Journal of Public Economics* 128:107–23.

Lisak, David, Lori Gardiner, Sarah Nicksa, and Ashley Cote. 2010. "False Allegations of Sexual Assault: An Analysis of Ten Years of Reported Cases." *Violence against Women* 16:1318–34.

McCannon, Bryan C. 2013. "Prosecutor Elections, Mistakes, and Appeals." *Journal of Empirical Legal Studies* 10:696–714.

McCannon, Bryan C., and Joylynn Pruitt. 2018. "Taking on the Boss: Informative Contests in Prosecutor Elections." *Journal of Public Economic Theory* 20:657–71.

Nadel, Melissa R., Samuel J. A. Scaggs, and William D. Bales. 2017. "Politics in Punishment: The Effect of the State Attorney Election Cycle on Conviction and Sentencing Outcomes in Florida." *American Journal of Criminal Justice* 42:845–62.

North Carolina Judicial Branch. 2019. "Civil Overall Caseload Activity Report." https://www.nccourts.gov/documents/publications/civil-overall-caseload-activity-report.

Richman, Laura S., and Charles Jonassaint. 2008. "The Effects of Race-Related Stress on Cortisol Reactivity in the Laboratory: Implications of the Duke Lacrosse Scandal." *Annals of Behavioral Medicine* 35:105–10.

Smolkin, Rachel. 2007. "Justice Delayed." *American Journalism Review* 29:1–16.

Spears, Jeffrey W., and Cassia C. Spohn. 1996. "The Effect of Offender and Victim Characteristics on Sexual Assault Case Processing Decisions." *Justice Quarterly* 13:649–79.

———. 1997. "The Effect of Evidence Factors and Victim Characteristics on Prosecutors' Charging Decisions in Sexual Assault Cases." *Justice Quarterly* 14:501–24.

Spohn, Cassia, Dawn Beichner, and Erika Davis-Frenzel. 2001. "Prosecutorial Justifications for Sexual Assault Case Rejection: Guarding the 'Gateway to Justice.'" *Social Problems* 5:206–35.

Spohn, Cassia, and David Holleran. 2001. "Prosecuting Sexual Assault: A Comparison of Charging Decisions in Sexual Assault Cases Involving Strangers, Acquaintances, and Intimate Partners." *Justice Quarterly* 18:651–88.

Taylor, Stuart, Jr., and K. C. Johnson. 2007. *Until Proven Innocent: Political Correctness and the Shameful Injustices of the Duke Lacrosse Rape Case*. New York: St. Martin's.

Wright, Ronald F. 2009. "How Prosecutor Elections Fail Us." *Ohio State Journal of Criminal Law* 6:581–610.

———. 2014. "Beyond Prosecutor Elections." *SMU Law Review* 67: 593–615.

Comment on "'A Million Dollars in Free Advertising': Politics and Sex Offense Prosecution in the Wake of Duke Lacrosse"

*Adi Leibovitch**

Prosecutors play a central role in how cases proceed and are resolved in the criminal justice system. They command a wide degree of discretion over the question of indictment, the charged offenses, and the terms of plea bargains. Yet the study of prosecutorial decision making has been hampered by lack of data and by the problem of endogeneity between the behavior of prosecutors and the institutional and local environments in which they operate. In quest of exogenous sources of legal variation, the passage of sentencing reforms has been helpful in exploring the extent of prosecutorial discretion. For example, empirical studies of prosecutors' response to the legislation of three-strikes laws or mandatory minimum sentences have demonstrated how prosecutors exercise discretion to increase sentences (Kessler and Piehl 1998) or to effectively circumvent the mandatory statutory requirements through altering the conviction charges (Engen and Steen 2000; Bjerk 2005). Whether prosecutors use their power benevolently or strategically, however, is a different question. In particular, prosecutors may be driven by reelection pressure and other career advancement opportunities in choosing which cases to prosecute (Glaeser, Kessler, and Piehl 2000) and in pursuing more trials (Boylan and Long 2005; Bandyopadhyay and McCannon 2014) and longer sentences (Boylan 2005).

Such political incentives are at the heart of "'A Million Dollars in Free Advertising': Politics and Sex Offense Prosecution in the Wake of Duke Lacrosse." McCannon and Wilson (2019, in this issue) propose

* Assistant professor, Hebrew University of Jerusalem Faculty of Law.

Electronically published: December 12, 2019
 978-0-226-64653-4/2019/0027-0010$10.00

that the publicized wrongful prosecution of the members of Duke University's lacrosse team with charges of rape—allegedly driven by the district attorney's political ambitions while facing contested elections—could serve as a quasi-natural experiment to further the study of the impact of political incentives on prosecutors' decision making. McCannon and Wilson's approach is novel in using the Duke lacrosse case, not as a source of legal change stemming from the content of a decision in the case but for the media attention it garnered. This inventive move enables the authors to identify a plausibly exogenous shock to the extent of public scrutiny over prosecutorial conduct and to employ it to study the possible role of public opinion in curtailing or inducing prosecutorial hawkish behavior. By comparing differences in the number of serious sex offenses charged and in the disposition of such cases through trials or plea bargains, before and after the unraveling of the scandal in 2006, the authors aim to test the impact of the extensive media coverage of the case on the exercise of prosecutorial discretion, both in general and in particular when prosecutors face reelection.

The North Carolina data, however, allow the authors to observe only the cases that end in a criminal disposition but not the universe of cases to which prosecutors apply their discretion. In light of the limitations of the data, it is important to have not only a theory of how public attention could affect the decisions of prosecutors but also a theoretical framework of the potential mechanisms for the influence of public attention on cases throughout the different stages of the criminal justice system—from the initial criminal behavior to the final disposition—and on the magnitude of the effect attributable specifically to prosecutorial discretion.

The Duke lacrosse scandal could have affected prosecutorial incentives and behavior in two opposite ways. District Attorney Nifong's statement to his campaign manager, as captured in the article's title, that the case is worth "a million dollars in free advertising" suggests a positive incentive for prosecutors to pursue similarly high-profile cases in light of the heightened media attention to rape prosecutions. Alternatively, the public outcry sparked by the wrongful prosecution could have generated a chilling effect, warning off prosecutors from misconduct and from the bad press associated with it. Under either theory, however, the existence of an effect depends crucially on the availability of a large enough number of cases amendable to a different decision following the change to prosecutorial incentives. The media-seeking motivation could have changed prosecutors' charging decisions only to the extent that prosecutors were largely unaware of such a consideration before and only if, once informed, they had enough available cases that they had been otherwise reluctant to charge but could nevertheless credibly file post 2006. With regard to a possible chilling effect, it should be noted that the Duke lacrosse case involved the district attorney withholding exculpatory evidence from the defense. The unraveling of the scandal may have thus discouraged prosecutors from knowingly charging innocent defendants (or from withholding exculpatory evidence), but it is unclear why it would have discouraged them from bringing charges in cases that were evidentiary sound. The article does not directly address these assumptions and, consequently, the extent that findings on this margin rely on a presumption of the prevalence of prosecutorial misconduct.

The two aforementioned hypotheses further assume that prosecutors continue to make their decisions based on a relatively stable stream of cases and similar availability of resources. The data, however, span a period of 18 years from 1999 to 2017, during which time many factors could have contributed to changes in the underlying composition of cases from which prosecutors decide, including changes in offending rates and reporting. Furthermore, both a change to prosecutorial charging policy and the media coverage of the Duke lacrosse case (as well as of other cases and legislation)[1] could have also altered the behavior of potential perpetrators and victims as well. McCannon and Wilson (2019) seek to address these concerns by constructing the dependent variable as the number of filed rape charges relative to the number of filed felony charges and interpreting the negative coefficient as evidence of a relative reduction in the prosecution of sex offenses specifically. Using felonies as a benchmark presumes that the crime and reporting trends of different types of offenses are similar enough for one to serve as a comparison group for another. The period of study, however, has seen a downward trend in the reporting of sex offenses in the United States in general and in North Carolina in particular.[2] Using the ratio of filings to complaints in rape cases as a dependent variable could have better taken into account changes in the composition of cases available to prosecutors.[3]

[1] McCannon and Wilson (2019) focus on the Duke lacrosse case, but during the period of study other high-profile rape cases garnered media attention as well, including the Kobe Bryant prosecution in 2003 and the vacating of the convictions of the Central Park Five in 2002. Increased public awareness to the accumulating backlogs in the processing and testing of DNA evidence in sexual assault cases was also at the backdrop of the passage of the Debbie Smith Act and the DNA Sexual Assault Justice Act of 2004. The multiplicity of prominent cases and legislation involving sex offenses in close temporal proximity complicates the ability to isolate the impact of any one event in particular.

[2] https://crime-data-explorer.fr.cloud.gov/explorer/state/north-carolina/crime.

[3] In addition, sex offense prosecutions are often laborious. If prosecutors reasonably operate under resource constraints, then a reduction in rape prosecutions could potentially allow prosecutors to devote more resources to other felonies and vice versa, and the use of felonies as the denominator may exacerbate any differences.

In addition, the negative trend documented in the article does not seem to differ across years whether or not prosecutors ran for reelection. The findings of a decline in the charging of sex offenses over the last decade is interesting and valuable in and of itself, especially in light of the severity of these crimes and their prominence in the public discourse. There is a question though about the proposed political mechanism in the aftermath of the Duke lacrosse case.[4] McCannon and Wilson's interpretation of the results is that before 2006 prosecutors were less likely to file rape charges in reelection years, whereas after 2006 the reelection effect is muted and prosecutors are less likely to file rape cases in general. The first finding—that previously prosecutors pursued less rape cases in reelection years—runs counter to the district attorney's action in the Duke lacrosse case (and to the presumption underlying the chilling effect hypothesis that this may have been a more widespread phenomenon). The second finding—that after 2006 prosecutors became less likely to file rape cases in general but no more so in years when they face reelection—does not lend preference to political incentives as the underlying cause among potential explanations.

McCannon and Wilson (2019) also present results regarding the different ways that cases are disposed following the decision to press charges. As the authors acknowledge, the analysis is impeded by the inability to observe acquittals in the data, but they conjecture that the smaller proportion of cases disposed in jury trials post 2006 might serve as an indication that prosecutors file cases that are more evidentiary sound. This part of the analysis further emphasizes the challenge to the study of prosecutors, where not only is the universe from which prosecutors are selecting the cases to bring to court unknown, but the bargaining dynamics are also unobserved. One can only speculate about the reasons why less cases end with a jury trial. If defendants are the ones who prefer to avoid trials, would that be because cases are more evidentiary sound or perhaps because defendants have become increasingly suspicious of prosecutors and of how they might conduct such trials? Alternatively, perhaps prosecutors are less inclined to

[1] Note that the majority of prosecutors need not be concerned about retention: in about a third of the elections in the sample the incumbent prosecutor did not run for reelection and in another third the incumbent prosecutor run uncontested. One may plausibly expect heightened political pressure to be associated with contested reelections specifically and, although both an incumbent and a challenger's decision to run for election may not be exogenous, it would have been interesting to see those results. Prosecutors' likelihood of running for reelection may also be correlated with exogenous factors, such as age or the availability of other lucrative employment opportunities (Boylan and Long 2005). Utilizing such variation could have been useful to scrutinize the robustness of the findings and of the proposed political channel specifically.

pursue trials and are willing to offer more favorable plea bargains to defendants—because they worry about the heightened scrutiny that might accompany a publicized trial, because they are concerned that the salience of wrongful prosecutions might make jurors less likely to convict, or because they have less resources to devote to litigation?

Some of those hypotheses could, at least initially, be probed by looking at changes to the average sentences in cases that end in plea bargains as an indication of the relative attractiveness of plea bargains and trials. It seems, however, that the data lend at least some support to resource constraints as one possible explanation. Following 2006, a smaller proportion of sex offense cases were disposed through trials, but a similar proportion of cases were resolved with guilty pleas, and a similar proportion of cases were dismissed. Ostensibly, the change in the proportion of cases ending in trial is countered by an increase in the proportion of cases that remain pending by the end of the year. More pending cases can impose a greater toll on prosecutors' resources (or reflect resource constraints of the prosecutors' offices or of the courts) leading them to resolve less cases, and less trials, per year. This also highlights more generally the dynamic equilibrium underlying prosecutors' decisions and the challenges it poses to the study of prosecutorial behavior throughout the chain of criminal justice.

REFERENCES

Bandyopadhyay, Siddhartha, and Bryan C. McCannon. 2014. "The Effect of the Election of Prosecutors on Criminal Trials." *Public Choice* 161 (1–2): 141–56.

Bjerk, David. 2005. "Making the Crime Fit the Penalty: The Role of Prosecutorial Discretion under Mandatory Minimum Sentencing." *Journal of Law and Economics* 48 (2): 591–625.

Boylan, Richard T. 2005. "What Do Prosecutors Maximize? Evidence from the Careers of US Attorneys." *American Law and Economics Review* 7 (2): 379–402.

Boylan, Richard T., and Cheryl X. Long. 2005. "Salaries, Plea Rates, and the Career Objectives of Federal Prosecutors." *Journal of Law and Economics* 48 (2): 627–51.

Engen, Rodney L., and Sara Steen. 2000. "The Power to Punish: Discretion and Sentencing Reform in the War on Drugs." *American Journal of Sociology* 105 (5): 1357–95.

Glaeser, Edward L., Daniel P. Kessler, and Anne Morrison Piehl. 2000. "What Do Prosecutors Maximize? An Analysis of the Federalization of Drug Crimes." *American Law and Economics Review* 2 (2): 259–90.

Kessler, Daniel P., and Anne Morrison Piehl. 1998. The Role of Discretion in the Criminal Justice System." *Journal of Law, Economics, and Organization* 14 (2): 256–76.

McCannon, Bryan C., and Mark Wilson. 2019. "'A Million Dollars in Free Advertising': Politics and Sex Offense Prosecution in the Wake of Duke Lacrosse." *Supreme Court Economic Review* 27 (1): 1–6.

Accuracy in Public Law Enforcement under Political Competition

*Marie Obidzinski**

The article investigates the impact of political competition on the level of accuracy in law enforcement. The model looks at the potential distortions implied by political competition relative to the Beckerian benchmark, where a benevolent social planner decides on the resources allocated to accuracy. I show that an elected law enforcer may promote a lower level of accuracy (for crimes inducing moderate harm) or a higher level of accuracy (for crimes inducing extensive harm) than the socially optimal level. Potential extensions are discussed in the last section.

1. INTRODUCTION

Political competition affects public law enforcement policies. The impact has been empirically identified notably by Levitt (1997), who shows that the number of police officers per capita significantly increases during gubernatorial and mayoral election years in the United States. In other words, political competition appears to influence the resources allocated to law enforcement. The present contribution sheds light on the impact of political competition on accuracy in the determination of liability, that is, on the relationship between the election of the law enforcer and errors in the process of law enforcement.

* Associate Professor of Economics, Paris II Panthéon-Assas University, CRED (TEPP). I am very grateful to Yves Oytana, to an anonymous referee, and to the participants of the Supreme Court Economic Review Research Roundtable for insightful comments and suggestions. Any remaining errors or omissions are, of course, my own.

Electronically published: November 21, 2019
 978-0-226-64653-4/2019/0027-0011$10.00

Legal errors refer here to the conviction of individuals who have not committed a crime (type I errors) and to the exoneration of individuals who did actually commit a crime (type II errors).

Two contributions provide some empirical evidence that elections, or more broadly the degree of democracy, may affect accuracy in public law enforcement. First, McCannon (2013) showed that prosecutors' elections in the United States have an impact on legal errors. Theoretically, prosecutors' reelection aims at encouraging accountability. McCannon investigated data on decisions of appeal and showed that, if the initial conviction occurs in the 6 months prior to reelection, the likelihood of the court of appeal upholding the original decision decreases significantly. The author therefore considers that the accountability of prosecutors via elections is not necessarily a good solution, as it generates errors.[1] Second, Lin (2007) empirically showed that democracy coincides with a lower incidence of major crimes but with more frequent petty crimes and that this phenomenon can be explained mainly by deterrence. Lin measures deterrence by taking into account the length of prison sentences, clearance rates, and prisoners per crime rate.[2] Differences in clearance rates between "high" and "low" democracy are the following: for homicide and serious assault, the clearance rate is higher in high democracy. The opposite is true for petty crimes such as burglary and car theft. Note that the clearance rate is a general measure covering both detection and conviction. It is not a direct measure of errors (false negative).[3]

A few theoretical contributions have amended the classical public law enforcement model in the manner of Becker (1968; see Garoupa 1997; Polinsky and Shavell 2000) to take into account the public law enforcers' private benefits and their consequences on sanctions and detection. For instance, Garoupa and Klerman (2002) develop a rent-seeking model of public law enforcement.[4] Another set of papers focuses on the procedural or constitutional constraints to limit the rent-seeking behavior of public law enforcers (Friedman 1999; Wickelgren 2003; Hylton and Khanna 2007). Among others, the presumption of innocence, the high standard of proof in criminal law, and the prohibition of corporal punishment are good examples of such protections.

[1] Note that the subject is related but noticeably different because I focus on electoral platforms rather than on incentives provided by reelection.

[2] The "level" of democracy is calculated by Lin (2007) by using the political liberty index from the Comparative Freedom Survey.

[3] Furthermore, I do not wish to directly compare accuracy in autocratic and democratic countries. Garoupa and Klerman (2002) develop a rent-seeking model of public law enforcement that may represent the case of a rent-seeking autocratic government.

[4] A larger set of articles considers corruption (e.g., Becker and Stigler 1974; Bowles 2000; Garoupa and Klerman 2004).

Law enforcers may also be considered as agents choosing strategically their level of effort. Dharmapala, Garoupa, and McAdams (2016) develop an agency model where public law enforcers have intrinsic preferences for punishment. Individuals with punitive preferences self-select into law enforcement jobs, which may have as a consequence excessive zeal in searching, seizing, and punishing suspects. A related contribution is Garoupa (2017), where the prosecutor may distort evidence produced in court. In Obidzinski and Oytana (2019), law enforcers choose their investigative effort under alternative rules of procedure.[5] More broadly, some contributions have highlighted the trade-offs faced by prosecutors, who may be stuck between personal and career concerns (Gordon and Huber 2009).

In this article, I focus on the motivations produced by political competition and their consequences in terms of electoral platforms and law enforcement policies.[6] To better understand the relationship between political competition and errors, I develop a theoretical model based on both Kaplow and Shavell (1994) and Langlais and Obidzinski (2017). Kaplow and Shavell formally introduce accuracy in a standard law enforcement model. They investigate how accuracy affects the optimal level of both the sanction and the probability of detection. They show that the maximum feasible sanction is also optimal and that accuracy and enforcement effort are alternative ways (substitutes) of increasing deterrence. The present article differs from Kaplow and Shavell in introducing political competition in the manner of Downs (1957).[7] However, the same definition of accuracy is used. The model developed by Langlais and Obidzinski introduces an electoral process in a standard law enforcement model to identify the impact of elections on the optimal sanctions and enforcement efforts. Here, I extend the analysis by focusing on accuracy.

The results suggest that the electoral process generates two types of distortions. Political competition leads to a low level of accuracy (lower than the socially optimal level) for crimes implying moderate harm and to a high level of accuracy (higher than the socially optimal level) for crimes implying substantial harm. Consequently, the electoral process seems to be associated with more errors (false negative and false positive) than with a benevolent social planner for moderate crimes, whereas the reverse is true for more the serious crimes.

The article is organized as follows. Section 2 sets out the general framework and introduces the benchmark. Section 3 develops the

[5] Obidzinski and Oytana (2019) focus the presumption of innocence versus the presumption of guilt.

[6] See also Mungan (2017) for an investigation of the consequences of disenfranchisement laws which prohibit convicted felons of voting.

[7] Further, I assume that the level of detection is given.

model of law enforcement under electoral competition. Section 4 offers concluding comments.

2. ACCURACY AND SOCIAL WELFARE

2.1. The Framework

Let us consider a public law enforcement framework in the manner of Becker (1968). The model builds on the work of Kaplow and Shavell (1994) and Langlais and Obidzinski (2017). Risk-neutral individuals decide whether or not to commit an offense. If an individual commits an offense, he or she will obtain benefit b. The gains from b are distributed according to a uniform probability density function with support [0, 1]. In the event of detection and conviction, the exogenous monetary fine involves no social cost (it is a simple transfer between offender and society). Each crime imposes an external cost $h > 0$ on society.

An individual who has committed the offense may erroneously escape the sanction with probability $q(k) \geqslant 0$. An innocent person may be convicted with probability $r(k) \geqslant 0$. Both errors depend on the level of accuracy k invested in criminal procedures and investigations with $k \in [0,1]$. More precisely, I assume that the first derivatives of both error functions with respect to accuracy effort are negative: $(\partial q)/(\partial k) < 0$ and $(\partial r)/(\partial k) < 0$, and that the second derivatives are positive: $(\partial^2 q)/(\partial^2 k) > 0$ and $(\partial^2 r)/(\partial^2 k) > 0$.

Enforcement effort is reflected by p, which might be seen as the probability of control (monitoring probability). For instance, p captures the probability that a taxpayer may be audited. The accuracy level, on the contrary, reflects the intensity and the quality of investigations given that there is an audit.

Accuracy is costly. The overall law enforcement cost is denoted $c(k)$.[8] The first and the second derivatives are positive: $(\partial c)/(\partial k) > 0$, $(\partial^2 c)/(\partial^2 k) \geq 0$. The cost is covered by taxes t paid by every citizen and fines s paid by convicted individuals (truly guilty or false positive). Only budget-balanced policies are considered:

$$c(k) = t + (1 - \bar{b}(k))(1 - q(k))ps + \bar{b}(k)r(k)ps. \qquad (1)$$

The threshold benefit $\bar{b}$ is endogenously determined in a later section. The proportion of individuals who abide by the law equals $\bar{b}$ as benefits are uniformly distributed. Conversely, the proportion of

[8] Increasing the monitoring probability is also costly. Therefore, the enforcement costs depend on both detection and accuracy. However, I assume that p is given for simplicity reasons and focus on the level of accuracy k.

individuals who commit crimes equals $1 - \bar{b}$. In what follows, I assume for the sake of simplicity that both the monetary fine s (with $s > 0$) and the level of enforcement p are given (with $0 < p < 1$).

The timing of the game is the following: at stage 0, nature defines the type of citizens (the benefits b they get from crime not directly observable by the law enforcer); at stage 1 the law enforcer chooses the observable level of accuracy k; at stage 2 the individuals decide whether or not to commit a crime and, finally, at stage 3 the law is enforced.

2.2. The Decision to Commit an Offense

Individuals decide whether or not to commit an offense by comparing their utility level in both cases. The utility of a citizen who considers the opportunity of abiding by the law is written as

$$u_a = w - t - (1 - \bar{b})h - r(k)ps,$$

with w the utility of reservation, t the tax paid by each citizen, and $(1 - \bar{b})h$ the external harm, which depends on the proportion of offenders in the population $1 - \bar{b}$ (endogenously determined later). The term $r(k)ps$ represents the expected punishment cost of law-abiding citizens, given the probability of being convicted by mistake $r(k)$.

Let us now denote the utility of a citizen who considers the opportunity of committing a crime:

$$u_c = w - t - (1 - \bar{b})h + b - (1 - q(k))ps,$$

with $(1 - q(k))ps$ the expected fine, given the probability of being exonerated by mistake $1-q(k)$ and b the benefit from crime.

The deterrence threshold is given by

$$\bar{b}(k) = (1 - q(k) - r(k))ps.$$

Errors dilute deterrence by reducing the expected utility of abiding by the law (by producing an expected sanction) and by increasing the expected utility from committing the crime (by reducing the expected sanction).

Consequently, deterrence increases with accuracy:[9]

$$\frac{\partial \bar{b}(k)}{\partial k} = -\left(\frac{\partial q(k)}{\partial k} + \frac{\partial r(k)}{\partial k}\right)ps > 0.$$

[9] With $\partial^2 \bar{b}(k)/\partial^2 k = -\{[\partial^2 q(k)/\partial^2 k] + [\partial^2 r(k)/\partial^2 k]\}ps < 0$. Note that $(\partial \bar{b})/(\partial p) = [1 - q(k) - r(k)]s > 0$ and $\partial^2 \bar{b}/\partial p \partial k = -\{[\partial q(k)/\partial k] + [\partial r(k)/\partial k]s\} > 0$, which means that increasing p has a larger marginal effect on deterrence when the level of accuracy is higher. Note also that $\partial \bar{b}(k)/\partial s = [1 - q(k) - r(k)]p > 0$ as long as $1 > q(k) + r(k)$.

Given the deterrence threshold and the impact of accuracy on deterrence, let us now determine the optimal level of accuracy to define the benchmark.

2.3. The Optimal Level of Accuracy (the Benchmark)

The social welfare function is defined as the sum of the utility of the individuals:

$$W = \int_0^{\bar{b}(k)} u_a db + \int_{\bar{b}(k)}^1 u_c db. \tag{2}$$

Substituting the expressions of u_a and u_c in (2) obtains

$$W = w - t + \int_{\bar{b}(k)}^1 (b - h)db - (1 - \bar{b}(k))(1 - q(k))ps - \bar{b}(k)r(k)ps.$$

Recall the budgetary constraint (1):

$$c(k) = t + (1 - \bar{b}(k))(1 - q(k))ps + \bar{b}(k)r(k)ps.$$

Introducing the budgetary constraint gets

$$W = w + \int_{\bar{b}(k)}^1 (b - h)db - c(k).$$

The optimal level of accuracy k^* (interior solution) is implicitly defined by

$$\frac{\partial \bar{b}(k)}{\partial k}(h - \bar{b}(k)) = \frac{\partial c(k)}{\partial k}. \tag{3}$$

On the left-hand side of the equation, the term $[\partial \bar{b}(k)/\partial k][h - \bar{b}(k)]$ represents the marginal benefit of increasing accuracy. More accuracy increases the proportion of law-abiding citizens (by $[\partial \bar{b}(k)]/\partial k > 0$), thereby diminishing the net harm $h - \bar{b}$. The term on the right-hand side represents the marginal cost of increasing accuracy. There is under-deterrence ($h > \bar{b}$) because $\partial c(k)/\partial k > 0$ by assumption.[10]

Let us specify the conditions for an interior solution. Note that $(\partial W/\partial k)|_{k=0} > 0$ if and only if

$$h > \frac{\frac{\partial c(k)}{\partial k}\big|_{k=0}}{\frac{\partial \bar{b}(k)}{\partial k}\big|_{k=0}} + \bar{b}(0) \equiv h_0.$$

[10] Let us consider the second-order condition $\partial^2 W/\partial k^2 = \{[\partial^2 \bar{b}(k)/\partial k^2](h - \bar{b})\} - \{[\partial \bar{b}(k)/\partial k][\partial \bar{b}(k)/\partial k]\} - \partial^2 c(k)/\partial k^2$, where k^* is a maximum if $\partial^2 W / \partial k^2 < 0$. This condition is satisfied because $\partial \bar{b}/\partial k > 0, \partial^2 \bar{b}/\partial k^2 < 0, \partial^2 c(k) / \partial k^2 \geq 0$, and $h > \bar{b}$ at equilibrium.

Also, $(\partial W/\partial k)|_{k=1} < 0$ if and only if

$$h < \frac{\frac{\partial c(k)}{\partial k}|_{k=1}}{\frac{\partial \bar{b}(k)}{\partial k}|_{k=1}} + \bar{b}(1) \equiv h_1$$

with $h_0 < h_1$. Consequently, the optimal level of accuracy is such that $0 < k^* < 1$ for every h between $[h_0, h_1]$. When $h < h_0$, the optimal level of accuracy is 0. On the contrary, when $h > h_1$, the optimal degree of accuracy equals 1.[11]

3. ACCURACY AND POLITICAL COMPETITION

In this section, the case of an elected public law enforcer is considered in the line of Langlais and Obidzinski (2017). To do so, political competition in the manner of Downs (1957) is introduced. Assume there are two candidates competing for election. The winning candidate will get an exogenous rent $V > 0$. To that purpose, each candidate proposes an electoral platform consisting of a degree of accuracy k, which maximizes the candidate's probability of winning. This probability depends on the share of votes obtained. Citizens vote for the platform providing them the highest level of utility.[12] The timing of the game is partially modified in the sense that at stage 1, candidates announce their electoral platform, and at stage 2, elections take place. At stage 3, the elected candidate implements his or her platform (i.e., the level of accuracy).[13] At stage 4, individuals decide whether or not to commit a crime, and finally at stage 5, the law is enforced.

Let us consider stage 2 (citizens' best policies) first and then stage 1 (candidates' platform choice) to solve the game backward.

3.1. The Best Level of Accuracy for the Citizens

Citizens vote for a candidate whose electoral platform consists of a certain degree of accuracy k in criminal procedures. Citizens vote consistently by taking into account their future decisions whether or not to comply. Let us consider the best policies successively for those who will abide by the law and those who will not.

[11] Furthermore, note that $\partial\bar{b}(k)/\partial k > 0$, $\partial^2\bar{b}(k)/\partial^2 k < 0$, and $\partial^2 c(k)/\partial^2 k \geqslant 0$. Therefore, $h_1 > h_0$.

[12] When both platforms provide the same level of utility, citizens pick a name randomly.

[13] Electoral promises are binding and enforceable as usual in models of preelection politics (Persson and Tabellini 2000).

3.1.1. The Best Policy for Those Who Will Comply. Let us denote k_a^* the level of accuracy that maximizes the utility of individuals abiding by the law. Recall that the utility of law-abiding citizens is written as

$$u_a(k) = w - t - (1 - \bar{b}(k))h - pr(k)s. \tag{4}$$

The budgetary constraint (1) is inserted into (4), and (4) is derived with respect to k:

$$\begin{aligned}\frac{\partial u_a(k)}{\partial k} = \frac{\partial \bar{b}(k)}{\partial k}h + (1 - \bar{b}(k))\left(-\frac{\partial q(k)}{\partial k} - \frac{\partial r(k)}{\partial k}\right)ps \\ - \frac{\partial \bar{b}(k)}{\partial k}(1 - q(k) - r(k))ps - \frac{\partial c(k)}{\partial k}.\end{aligned}$$

Thus, the first-order condition (FOC) that defines the interior solution is written

$$\frac{\partial \bar{b}(k)}{\partial k}(h - \bar{b}(k)) + \frac{\partial \bar{b}(k)}{\partial k}(1 - \bar{b}(k)) = \frac{\partial c(k)}{\partial k}. \tag{5}$$

First, an increase in accuracy reduces the proportion of offenders and, consequently, the net expected harm by $[\partial\bar{b}(k)/\partial k][h - \bar{b}(k)]$. Second, higher accuracy positively impacts the expected fines collected from offenders $[\partial\bar{b}(k)/\partial k][1 - \bar{b}(k)]$. More accuracy (1) increases the probability of fining offenders (contributing positively to the budget dedicated to investigations) and (2) decreases the likelihood of imposing a fine on compliant individuals. This second effect corresponds to a transfer between the innocent citizen (who sees the probability of receiving a fine by mistake decrease) and the society (which sees the amount of fines recovered decrease). Third, increasing accuracy imposes additional cost $\partial c(k)/\partial k$. By comparison with the FOC (3) defining the socially optimal level of accuracy k^*, the marginal benefit $[\partial\bar{b}(k)/\partial k][1 - \bar{b}(k)]$ consists of an additional effect.[14]

Let us specify the conditions for an interior solution. Note that $[\partial u_a(k)/\partial k]|_{k=0} > 0$ if and only if

$$h > \frac{\frac{\partial c(k)}{\partial k}\big|_{k=0}}{\frac{\partial \bar{b}(k)}{\partial k}\big|_{k=0}} + \bar{b}(0) - 1 - \bar{b}(0) \equiv h_0^a.$$

[14] Note that $[\partial\bar{b}(k)/\partial k][1 - \bar{b}(k)]$ represents the net effect of a decrease in the expected fine imposed on law-abiding citizens, a reduction in the revenue from fines because of this lower probability of fining the innocent, and a rise in the expected fine imposed on offenders.

Note that $h_0^a = h_0 - (1 - \bar{b}(0))$. Also, $(\partial W / \partial k)|_{k=1} < 0$ if and only if

$$h < \frac{\frac{\partial c(k)}{\partial k}|_{k=1}}{\frac{\partial \bar{b}(k)}{\partial k}|_{k=1}} + \bar{b}(1) - (1 - \bar{b}(1)) \equiv h_1^a.$$

Note that $h_1^a = h_1 - (1 - \bar{b}(1))$. To sum up, the threshold values on h are ordered as follows: $h_0^a < h_0 \leq h_1^a \leq h_1$ or $h_0^a < h_1^a \leq h_0 \leq h_1$.

Proposition 1. Compliant citizens vote for a level of accuracy k_a^*, which is higher than or equal to the optimal level of accuracy k^*.

Proof. See the proof in the appendix.

More precisely, both the optimal level of accuracy and the level that maximizes the utility of those who decide to abide by the law are 0 $(k^* = k_a^* = 0)$ when the level of harm is sufficiently low $(h \leq h_0^a$, with $h_0^a < h_0)$.[15] The level of accuracy that maximizes the utility of those who decide to abide by the law is higher than the optimal level of accuracy $(k_a^* > k^*)$ when $h_0^a < h < h_1$. When $h_1 \leq h$, both levels of accuracy equal 1 $(k_a^* = k^* = 1)$.

By comparison with the optimal level of accuracy k^*, the level k_a^* that maximizes the utility of law-abiding citizens is higher because law-abiding citizens retrieve an additional marginal benefit of increasing the level of accuracy. Indeed, more accuracy increases the probability of fining offenders, and consequently more accuracy raises offenders' expected contribution to the budget dedicated to investigations.[16]

3.1.2. The Best Policy for Those Who Will Commit Crimes. Let us now consider the case of offenders. Recall that the utility of a citizen who considers committing a crime is written as

$$u_c(k) = w - t - (1 - \bar{b}(k))h + b - p(1 - q(k))s. \quad (6)$$

Let us define k_c^* as the level of accuracy that maximizes the utility of individuals contemplating committing a crime:

$$\frac{\partial u_c(k)}{\partial k} = (h - \bar{b}(k))ps\left(-\frac{\partial q(k)}{\partial k} - \frac{\partial r(k)}{\partial k}\right) - \frac{\partial c(k)}{\partial k} - \bar{b}(k)ps\left(-\frac{\partial q(k)}{\partial k} - \frac{\partial r(k)}{\partial k}\right)$$

[15] Note that $h_0^a = h_0 - (1 - \bar{b}(0))$.

[16] Let us recall budget constraint (1): $c(k) = t + (1 - \bar{b}(k))(1 - q(k))ps + \bar{b}(k)r(k)ps$.

That is, the FOC that defines the interior solution k_c^* is written as

$$\frac{\partial \bar{b}(k)}{\partial k}(h - \bar{b}(k)) = \frac{\partial c(k)}{\partial k} + \bar{b}(k)\frac{\partial \bar{b}(k)}{\partial k}. \quad (7)$$

As for the individuals who abide by the law, an increase in accuracy reduces the proportion of offenders and, consequently, the net expected harm by $[\partial \bar{b}(k)/\partial k][h - \bar{b}(k)]$. Furthermore, increasing accuracy imposes marginal cost $\partial c(k)/\partial k$. In addition, the expected fines perceived from those who abide by the law decrease.[17]

Let us specify the conditions for an interior solution. Note that $[\partial u_a(k)/\partial k]|_{k=0} > 0$ if and only if

$$h > \frac{\frac{\partial c(k)}{\partial k}|_{k=0}}{\frac{\partial \bar{b}(k)}{\partial k}|_{k=0}} + \bar{b}(0) + \bar{b}(0) \equiv h_0^c .$$

Note that $h_0^c = h_0 + \bar{b}(0)$. Also, $\frac{\partial W}{\partial k}|_{k=1} < 0$ if and only if

$$h < \frac{\frac{\partial c(k)}{\partial k}|_{k=1}}{\frac{\partial \bar{b}(k)}{\partial k}|_{k=1}} + \bar{b}(1) + \bar{b}(1) \equiv h_1^c .$$

Note that $h_1^c = h_1 + \bar{b}(1)$. To sum up, the threshold values on h are ordered as follows: $h_0 < h_0^c < h_1 < h_1^c$ and $h_0 < h_1 \leq h_0^c < h_1^c$.

> **Proposition 2.** Offenders vote for a policy k_c^*, which is lower than or equal to the optimal level of accuracy k^*.
>
> ***Proof.*** See the proof in the appendix.

More precisely, both the optimal level of accuracy k^* and the level that maximizes the utility of those who will commit the crime k_c^* are 0 ($k^* = k_c^* = 0$) when the level of harm is sufficiently low ($h \leq h_0$). When $h_0 < h < h_1^c$ (with $h_1^c = h_1 + \bar{b}(1)$), then $k_c^* < k^* < 1$. When $h > h_1^c$, both levels of accuracy equal 1 ($k_c^* = k^* = 1$).

By comparison with the optimal level of accuracy k^*, the level k_c^* that maximizes the utility of offenders is lower because offenders retrieve an additional marginal cost of increasing the level of accuracy. More accuracy raises the expected fine on offenders (which is compensated by the revenue from these fines, because fines are pure transfers) but decreases the probability of fining the innocent.

[17] Again, $\bar{b}(\partial \bar{b}/\partial k)$ represents a net effect. Increasing accuracy raises the expected fine on offenders (which is compensated by the revenue from these fines, as fines are pure transfers) but decreases the probability of fining the innocent.

To sum up, from proposition 1 and proposition 2, it is straightforward to see that

$$k_c^* \leq k^* \leq k_a^*.$$

3.2. The Voting Equilibrium

Let us now consider electoral competition (stage 1). Recall that the electoral platform only consists in a certain degree of accuracy k in criminal procedures. The candidate wins the election if his or her platform obtains the highest share of the vote. Both candidates will announce the same electoral platform.[18] If one platform obtains a higher share than another hypothetical platform, then the candidate with the less successful platform will choose the other platform. Consequently, the candidates will have a 50% chance of winning.

In the remainder of the model, the following assumption (denoted assumption 1) holds: $\bar{b}(0) < 1/2 < \bar{b}(1)$. According to this assumption, the proportion of individuals abiding by the law is lower than half of the population when the level of accuracy is 0. Conversely, the proportion of individuals abiding by the law is higher than half of the population when the level of accuracy equals 1. If the hypothesis does not hold, it means that either there exists a majority of individuals abiding by the law (if $1/2 < \bar{b}(0)$), even with the lowest possible level of accuracy, or a majority of offenders (if $1/2 < 1 - \bar{b}(1)$), even with the highest possible level of accuracy. In such cases, the majority can never be overturned, and the implemented policy will reflect either the preferences of law-abiding citizens (if $1/2 < \bar{b}(0)$) or the preferences of offenders (if $1/2 < 1 - \bar{b}(1)$).[19]

The results are evaluated according to the level of harm. Let us first begin with the most usual case involving medium and extensive harm when $h_0^a < h < h_1^c$.

Proposition 3. Assume that $h_0^a < h < h_1^c$. When $h < \hat{h}$, the unique political equilibrium is such that both candidates announce $k = k_c^*(h)$ with $k_c^*(h) < k^*(h)$. On the contrary, when $h > \hat{h}$, the unique equilibrium is such that both candidates announce $k = k_a^*(h)$ with $k^*(h) < k_a^*(h)$. If $h = \hat{h}$, the candidates announce either both $k_a^*(\hat{h})$ or both $k_c^*(\hat{h})$, or one $k_a^*(\hat{h})$ and the other $k_c^*(\hat{h})$, with $k_c^*(\hat{h}) < k^*(\hat{h}) < k_a^*(\hat{h})$.

[18] Except when $h = \hat{h}$. See proposition 3 and n. 20.

[19] In reality, such cases are quite plausible. It means that the level of accuracy does not modify the majority. Such cases are not the core of this model because I focus on situations where the level of accuracy affects the majority. However, they are not in contradiction with the empirical results. For instance, the clearance rate for homicide is high in democracy, reflecting the preferences of the majority: law-abiding citizens.

Proof. See the proof in the appendix.

Distortions because of the political competition appear for medium or extensive levels of harm when $h_0^a < h < h_1^c$. Distortions go toward opposite directions according to the level of harm. In the case of crimes producing medium harm $(h_0^a < h < \hat{h})$, elections lead to lower degrees of accuracy than the optimal one, as $k_c^*(\hat{h}) < k^*$. As a consequence, the probabilities of type I and type II errors are higher than with a "benevolent social planner." The deterrence threshold $\bar{b}(k_c^*)$ is lower than the optimal one $\bar{b}(k^*)$, and more citizens decide to commit a crime. On the contrary, in the case of crimes producing extensive harm $(\hat{h} < h < h_1^c)$, elections lead to a higher level of accuracy than the optimal one k^*. As a consequence, the probabilities of type I and type II errors are lower than under the socially optimal level of accuracy. The deterrence threshold $\bar{b}(k_a^*)$ is higher than the optimal one $\bar{b}(k^*)$, and fewer citizens decide to commit a crime. If $h = \hat{h}$, then any combination of platforms where each candidate announces either $k_a^*(\hat{h})$ or $k_c^*(\hat{h})$ is an equilibrium.[20]

Proposition 4. If $h \leq h_0^a$, both candidates propose $k^* = 0$. If $h \geq h_1^c$, both candidates propose $k^* = 1$.

Proof. The proof is straightforward. When $h < h_0^a$, the best policy of law-abiding citizens is $k_a^* = 0$, whereas the best policy of offenders is $k_c^* = 0$. Consequently, both candidates choose to propose $k = 0$. Conversely, when $h > h_1^c$, both candidates propose $k_a^* = k_c^* = 1$. QED

Let us now be more specific about what happens at the boundaries. To start, assume that $h \leq h_0^a$. Then $k_a^* = k_c^* = 0$. Both candidates announce the socially optimal level of accuracy $k^* = 0$. Now assume that $h \geq h_1^c$. Then $k_a^* = k_c^* = 1$. Both candidates announce the optimal level of accuracy $k^* = 1$. Therefore, for extreme levels of harm (high or low), the political process produces no distortion.

If assumption 1 is not satisfied, the game is much simpler because both candidates propose the political platform preferred by the majority, whatever the level of harm induced by the offense. For instance, if offenders form the majority for any level of accuracy $(\bar{b}(1) < 1/2)$, both candidates propose $k_c^*(h)$. Conversely, if law abiders form the majority for any level of accuracy $(1/2 < \bar{b}(0))$, both candidates propose $k_a^*(h)$. The level of accuracy at the voting equilibrium would respectively be either under or above the optimal one.

[20] In this particular case, the candidates do not necessarily propose the same platform.

4. CONCLUDING REMARKS

In this article, I focus on the impact of electoral competition on accuracy in determining liability. In doing so, I provide an extension of the work of Langlais and Obidzinski (2017), whose contribution focuses on the impact of electoral competition on the resources spent on detection in a framework with no legal error. Here I look at the quality of investigations emerging at the political equilibrium. The level of accuracy determines the probability of type I errors (convicting an innocent person) and type II errors (exonerating a guilty person).

The level of detection indirectly affects law-abiding citizens through the budgetary constraint and the external harm (by deterring offenses). Similarly, accuracy indirectly affects law-abiding citizens through the budgetary constraint and the external harm. In addition, accuracy directly impacts law-abiding citizens' utility through type I errors. Furthermore, when conviction errors occur, the expected fine paid both by truly guilty and innocent is positive. Therefore, both offenders and law-abiding citizens contribute to finance accuracy through the fines paid. Citizens who anticipate not abiding by the law may wish to decrease the level of accuracy to favor false positive errors (and to escape conviction via a type II error). On the contrary, citizens who anticipate complying may favor a higher level of accuracy to decrease type I errors and to raise the expected fine faced by offenders. Recall that the sanction here is a pure transfer from one citizen to the law enforcement budget.

The voting equilibrium depends on the level of harm induced by the offense with everything else remaining equal. I show that an elected law enforcer may promote a lower level of accuracy (for the crime inducing medium harm) or a higher level of accuracy (for the crime inducing large harm) by comparison with the socially optimal level. Taking errors into account, I obtain results consistent with Langlais and Obidzinski (2017). Furthermore, the results appear to be in line with the results obtained by Lin (2007) regarding the level of democracy and clearance rates. In countries with a higher degree of democracy, clearance rates are lower for petty crimes, such as car theft or burglary, by comparison with "low democracy" countries. The opposite is true for very serious crimes such as homicide or serious assault.[21]

Many extensions may be worth developing. Here, to focus on accuracy and for clarity of the exposition, I assume that the fine is given as well as the monitoring probability. It could be interesting to develop the trade-off when considering different law-enforcement tools.

[21] As noted in the introduction, cautious should be used in interpreting clearance rates because they are not a direct measure of errors.

Intuitively, both the optimal (costless) fine and the fine resulting from the electoral process are the maximum ones that are feasible, as in Kaplow and Shavell (1994) and Langlais and Obidzinski (2017).[22] Even so, the trade-off between enforcement effort and accuracy might be worth investigating. Both tools increase deterrence.[23] Enforcement efforts increase the probability of sanction of both compliant citizens and offenders for a given level of accuracy and thus error. Accuracy lowers the probability of sanction of individuals who did not commit an offense but increases the probability of sanction for those who did. Therefore, both tools have different impacts and elections might reflect more complex trade-offs.

In addition, looking at the impact of political competition on accuracy with privately and socially costly sanctions such as imprisonment would make sense. Contrary to monetary sanctions, nonmonetary sanctions do not contribute to the law enforcement budget. Imprisonment is costly for the society. Therefore, taxes would have to finance both accuracy in investigations and imprisonment. For a given sanction of imprisonment, law-abiding citizens would prefer a higher degree of accuracy to reduce their probability of being wrongfully convicted. On the contrary, law offenders would prefer a lower degree of accuracy to reduce their probability of being convicted. Therefore, the impact of political competition on accuracy with imprisonment is likely to be similar to the impact of political competition on accuracy with fines.

Note also that the law enforcer may affect legal errors through the standard of proof. The standard of proof is the minimum degree of certainty the judge or jury has to reach to convict a defendant, such as "beyond any reasonable doubt."[24] A higher standard of proof goes with a lower probability of false positives at the expense of a higher probability of false negatives. Therefore, the mechanism differs from accuracy, as a higher degree of accuracy reduces the occurrence of both types of error. It is worth observing, however, that the standard of proof is generally set in the Constitution and is not directly subject to electoral competition. Consequently, the standard is supposed to be isolated from political influence and may work as a constraint on public law enforcers (Friedman 1999).

[22] This conjecture does not hold if the assumption is that additional cost is associated with type I error, such as the cost of a miscarriage of justice (Miceli 1991).

[23] An additional hypothesis should be made regarding the cost function. Kaplow and Shavell (1994) assume that the cross derivative of the cost function with detection (p) and accuracy (k) is positive. That is, the higher the probability of detection, the higher is the marginal cost of an increase in accuracy.

[24] Kaplow (2012) explains the differences between the concepts of accuracy and burden of proof.

APPENDIX

Proof of Proposition 1

The conditions for an interior solution are written as $(\partial u_a/\partial k)|_{k=0}>0$ if and only if $h > \{[\partial c(k)/\partial k]|_{k=0}\}/[(\partial \bar{b}/\partial k)|_{k=0}] + \bar{b}(0) - [1 - \bar{b}(0)] \equiv h_0^a$ with $h_0^a = h_0 - (1 - \bar{b}(0))$. Thus, if $h \leq h_0^a$, $k_a^* = 0$. Also, $(\partial u_a/\partial k)|_{k=1} <$ 0 iff $h < \{[\partial c(k)/\partial k]|_{k=1}\}/(\partial \bar{b}/\partial k)|_{k=1} + \bar{b}(1) - [1 - \bar{b}(1)] \equiv h_1^a$ with $-(1 - \bar{b}) < 0$ and $k = 1$. Note that $h_1^a = h_1 - (1 - \bar{b}(1))$. Thus, if $h \geq h_1^a$, $k_a^* = 1$. Because $\partial \bar{b}(k)/\partial k > 0$, $\partial^2 \bar{b}(k)/\partial k^2 < 0$ and because $\partial^2 c(k)/\partial k^2 \geq 0$, then $h_0^a < h_1^a$.

Furthermore, note that $h_0^a < h_0$ because $1 - \bar{b}(0) > 0$. Also, $h_1^a \leq h_1$ because $1 - \bar{b}(1) \geq 0$. Two subcases should be considered: $h_0^a < h_0 \leq h_1^a \leq h_1$ and $h_0^a < h_1^a \leq h_0 \leq h_1$.

Let us consider first the case where $h_0^a < h_0 \leq h_1^a \leq h_1$. The following results are obtained: when $h \leq h_0^a$, $k_a^* = k^* = 0$. When $h_0^a < h \leq h_0$, k_a^* is the solution of (5) and $k_a^* \in (0, 1)$, whereas $k^* = 0$. When $h_0 < h < h_1^a$, k_a^* is the solution of (5) and $k_a^* \in (0, 1)$, whereas k^* is the solution of (3) and $k^* \in (0,1)$. The marginal benefit in (5) is written $[\partial \bar{b}(k)/\partial k][h - \bar{b}(k)] + [\partial \bar{b}(k)/\partial k][1 - \bar{b}(k)]$, whereas in (3) it is written $[\partial \bar{b}(k)/\partial k][h - \bar{b}(k)]$, the marginal cost being written c_k in both cases. Because $[\partial \bar{b}(k)/\partial k][1 - \bar{b}(k)] > 0$, raising k implies an additional marginal benefit to compliant citizens by comparison with the benevolent law enforcer benchmark. Consequently, $k_a^* > k^*$ when $h_0 < h < h_1^a$. When $h_1^a \leq h < h_1$, $k_a^* = 1$, whereas k^* is the solution of (3) and $k^* \in (0,1)$. When $h_1 < h$, $k_a^* = k^* = 1$.

Let us now consider the case where $h_0^a < h_1^a \leq h_0 \leq h_1$. When $h \leq h_0^a$, $k_a^* = k^* = 0$. When $h_0^a < h < h_1^a$, k_a^* is the solution of (5) and $k_a^* \in (0, 1)$, whereas $k^* = 0$. When $h_1^a \leq h < h_1$, $k_a^* = 1$, whereas k^* is the solution of (3) and $k^* \in (0,1)$. When $h_1 \leq h$, $k_a^* = k^* = 1$.

To conclude, k_a^* is always higher than or equal to k^*.

Proof of Proposition 2

Recall the conditions for an interior solution: $(\partial u_c/\partial k)|_{k=0} > 0$ iff $h > \{[\partial c(k)/\partial k]|_{k=0}\}/(\partial \bar{b}/\partial k)|_{k=0}\} + 2\bar{b}(0) \equiv h_0^c$ with $h_0^c = h_0 + \bar{b}(0)$. Also $(\partial u_c/\partial k)|_{k=1} < 0$ iff $h < \{[\partial c(k)/\partial k]|_{k=1}\}/(\partial \bar{b}/\partial k)|_{k=1} + 2\bar{b}(1) \equiv h_1^c$ with $h_1^c = h_1 + \bar{b}(1)$. Two subcases should be considered: $h_0 < h_0^c < h_1 < h_1^c$ and $h_0 < h_1 \leq h_0^c < h_1^c$.

Let us consider first the case where: $h_0 < h_0^c < h_1 < h_1^c$. The following results are obtained: When $h \leq h_0$, $k_c^* = k^* = 0$. When $h_0 < h \leq h_0^c$, $k_c^* = 0$ and k^* is the solution of (3) and $k^* \in (0,1)$. When $h_0^c < h < h_1$, k_c^* is the solution of (7) and $k_c^* \in (0, 1)$, whereas k^* is the solution of (3) and $k^* \in (0,1)$.

The marginal benefit in (7) is written $[\partial\bar{b}(k)/\partial k][h - \bar{b}(k)]$ as those in (3). The marginal cost is written $\partial c(k)/\partial k$ in (3) and $\partial c(k)/\partial k + \bar{b}(k)[\partial\bar{b}(k)/\partial k]$ in (7). Because $\bar{b}(k)[\partial\bar{b}(k)/\partial k] > 0$ for any $k^* \in (0,1)$, raising k implies an additional marginal cost to offenders by comparison with the benevolent law enforcer benchmark. Consequently, $k_c^* < k^*$ when $h_0^c < h < h_1$. When $h_1 \leq h < h_1^c$, $k^* = 1$, whereas k_c^* is the solution of (7) and $k_c^* \in (0, 1)$. When $h_1^c < h$, $k_c^* = k^* = 1$.

Let us now consider the case where $h_0 < h_1 \leq h_0^c < h_1^c$. When $h \leq h_0$, $k_c^* = k^* = 0$. When $h_0 < h < h_1$, k^* is the solution of (3) and $k^* \in (0,1)$, whereas $k_c^* = 0$. When $h_1 \leq h < h_0^c$ $k^* = 1$, whereas k_c^* is the solution of (7) and $k^* \in (0,1)$. When $h_0^c \leq h$, $k_c^* = k^* = 1$. To conclude, k_c^* is always lower than or equal to k^*.

Proof of Proposition 3

Assume that $h_0^a < h < h_1^c$. Let us recall the best level of accuracy for the law-abiding citizen is

$$k_a^*(h) = \begin{cases} 0 \text{ if } h \leq h_0^a \\ 1 \text{ if } h \geq h_1^a \\ \text{else, implicit solution of (4)} \end{cases}$$

The best level of accuracy for the offender is

$$k_c^*(h) = \begin{cases} 0 \text{ if } h \leq h_0^c \\ 1 \text{ if } h \geq h_1^c \\ \text{else, implicit solution of (6)} \end{cases}$$

Note that $k_a^*(h)$ is constant for $h \leq h_0^a$ and $h \geq h_1^a$. Let us consider the case where $h_0^a \leq h \leq h_1^a$.

Based on the implicit function theorem,

$$sign\left(\frac{\partial k_a^*}{\partial h}\right) = sign\left(\frac{\partial\bar{b}(k)}{\partial k}\right).$$

Thus, $\partial k_a^*/\partial h > 0$. The function k_a^* is increasing with h, for any $h \in [h_0^a, h_1^a]$. Because $\partial\bar{b}(k)/\partial k > 0$, it can be deduced that $\bar{b}[k_a^*(h)]$ is increasing with h. Conversely, it can similarly be shown that $\bar{b}[k_c^*(h)]$ is increasing with h.

Each candidate proposes the platform (consisting in the level of accuracy) that receives the largest share of votes. The proportion of individuals who vote for $k_a^*(h)$ equals $\bar{b}[k_a^*(h)]$, whereas the proportion of individuals who vote for $k_c^*(h)$ equals $1 - \bar{b}[k_c^*(h)]$. The platform k_a^* (respectively, k_c^*) obtains the largest share of the vote if $\bar{b}[k_a^*(h)] > (<) 1 - \bar{b}[k_c^*(h)]$.

Note that $\lim_{h \to h_0^a} \bar{b}[k_a^*(h)] = \lim_{h \to h_0^a} \bar{b}[k_c^*(h)] = \bar{b}(0)$. So, the platform k_c^* obtains the largest share of the vote if

$$\bar{b}(0) < 1 - \bar{b}(0) \langle = \rangle \bar{b}(0) < \frac{1}{2}. \tag{8}$$

Following the same reasoning, the platform k_a^* obtains the largest share of the vote if

$$\bar{b}(1) > 1 - \bar{b}(1) \langle = \rangle \bar{b}(1) > \frac{1}{2}. \tag{9}$$

Under assumption 1, both conditions (8) and (9) are satisfied and there exists a unique value of $h = \hat{h}$ with $\hat{h} \in (h_0^a, h_1^c)$ such that $\bar{b}(k_a^*(h)) = 1 - \bar{b}(k_c^*(h))$. Therefore, if $h_0^a < h < \hat{h}$, both candidates propose $k_c^*(h)$, with $0 < k_c^*(h) < 1$. If $\hat{h} < h < h_1^c$, both candidates propose $k_c^*(h)$, with $0 < k_a^*(h) < 1$.

REFERENCES

Becker, Gary S. 1968. "Crime and Punishment: An Economic Approach." *Journal of Political Economy* 76:169–217.

Becker, Gary S., and G. J. Stigler. 1974. "Law Enforcement, Malfeasance, and Compensation of Enforcers." *Journal of Legal Studies* 3:1–18.

Bowles, R. 2000. "Corruption." In *Encyclopedia of Law and Economics*, edited by B. Bouckaert and G. D. Geest, 460–91. Cheltenham: Edward Elgar.

Dharmapala, Dhammika, Nuno Garoupa, and Richard H. McAdams. 2016. "Punitive Police? Agency Costs, Law Enforcement, and Criminal Procedure." *Journal of Legal Studies* 45:105–41.

Downs, Anthony. 1957. *An Economic Theory of Democracy*. New York: Harper & Row.

Friedman, David. 1999. "Why Not Hang Them All: The Virtues of Inefficient Punishment." *Journal of Political Economy* 107:259–69.

Garoupa, Nuno. 1997. "The Theory of Optimal Law Enforcement." *Journal of Economic Surveys*, 11:267–95.

———. 2017. "Explaining the Standard of Proof in Criminal Law: A New Insight." *Supreme Court Economic Review* 25 (1): 111–22.

Garoupa, Nuno, and Daniel Klerman. 2002. "Optimal Law Enforcement with a Rent-Seeking Government." *American Law and Economics Review* 4 (1): 116–40.

———. 2004. "Corruption and the Optimal Use of Nonmonetary Sanctions." *International Review of Law and Economics* 24 (2): 219–25.

Gordon, Sanford C., and Gregory A. Huber. 2009. "The Political Economy of Prosecution." *Annual Review of Law and Social Science* 5: 135–56.

Hylton, Keith N., and Vikramaditya Khanna. 2007. "A Public Choice Theory of Criminal Procedure." *Supreme Court Economic Review* 15:61–118.

Kaplow, Louis. 2012. "Burden of Proof." *Yale Law Journal* 121:738–861.

Kaplow, Louis, and Steven Shavell. 1994. "Accuracy in the Determination of Liability." *Journal of Law and Economics* 37 (1): 1–15.

Langlais, Éric, and Marie Obidzinski. 2017. "Law Enforcement with a Democratic Government." *American Law and Economics Review* 19 (1): 162–201.

Levitt, Steven D. 1997. "Using Electoral Cycles in Police Hiring to Estimate the Effect of Police on Crime." *American Economic Review* 87 (June): 270–90.

Lin, Ming-Jen. 2007. "Does Democracy Increase Crime? The Evidence from International Data." *Journal of Comparative Economics* 35 (3): 467–83.

McCannon, Bryan C. 2013. "Prosecutor Elections, Mistakes, and Appeals." *Journal of Empirical Legal Studies* 10 (4): 696–714.

Miceli, Thomas. 1991. "Optimal Criminal Procedure: Fairness and Deterrence." *International Review of Law and Economics* 11 (1): 3–10.

Mungan, Murat C. 2017. "Over-Incarceration and Disenfranchisement." *Public Choice* 172 (3–4): 377–95.

Obidzinski, Marie, and Yves Oytana. 2019. "Presumption of Innocence and Deterrence." *Journal of Institutional and Theoretical Economics* (Forthcoming).

Persson, Torsten, and Guido Tabellini. 2000. *Political Economics: Explaining Public Policy*. Cambridge, MA: MIT Press.

Polinsky, A. M., and Steven Shavell. 2000. "The Economic Theory of Public Enforcement of Law." *Journal of Economic Literature* 38 (1): 45–76.

Wickelgren, Abraham L. 2003. "Justifying Imprisonment: On the Optimality of Excessively Costly Punishment." *American Law and Economics Review* 5 (2): 377–411.

Comment on "Accuracy in Public Law Enforcement under Political Competition"

*Francesco Parisi**

1. INTRODUCTION

Marie Obidzinski's (2019) article analyzes from a theoretical perspective the effects of political competition on the accuracy of law enforcement and criminal justice. The existing literature, both theoretical and empirical, is rich and the author provides a valuable contribution by developing an economic model to explain the empirical findings of Lin (2007) and McCannon (2013). The model generates novel insights, showing that political competition does not foster optimal enforcement and accuracy in criminal justice and that distortions are generated by political competition relative to Becker's (1968) optimality benchmark by a benevolent social planner. The model shows that when law enforcement actors operate under the pressures of political competition, they engage in lower than optimal levels of enforcement and accuracy for smaller crimes and higher than optimal levels of enforcement and accuracy for larger crimes.

2. THEORY AND EVIDENCE

In conventional law and economics, theory papers are often self-standing. Economic models of tort law, contract law, and even criminal law are built upon stylized assumptions on the preferences and rationality of the parties. Results are derived on the basis of such assumptions. Propositions are formulated, but they are not aimed at

* Oppenheimer Wolff and Donnelly Professor of Law, University of Minnesota School of Law, and Professor of Economics, University of Bologna, Department of Economics.

Electronically published: December 4, 2019

explaining existing empirical findings or at fostering empirical tests. Articles at the intersection of political economics and law and economics on the contrary exhibit a greater interaction between theory and empirical evidence. This happens in either of two ways. Some articles develop theory models to explain empirical findings presented in the existing literature. Other articles are empirical in nature and provide valuable testing of existing theoretical models. The article by Obidzinski (2019) falls in the first of the two groups, developing a novel theoretical model to explain the empirical findings of Lin (2007) and McCannon (2013) who respectively noted that deterrence for major crimes and reversal rates of criminal convictions on appeal decreased with democratic pressure and political competition.

In addition to providing a plausible theoretical explanation for the empirical literature, Obidzinski's model offers numerous novel insights and conjectures on the workings of elected actors of the criminal justice system under political competition. In the following, I suggest that her article should also serve as a springboard for future empirical research to test some of the additional theoretical results of her model.

Let me begin my substantive comment by focusing on the core assumption of her model. This assumption requires that "the proportion of individuals abiding by the law is lower than half of the population when the level of accuracy is 0 [and that] the proportion of individuals abiding by the law is higher than half of the population when the level of accuracy equals 1" (Obidzinski 2019, in this issue). This assumption is at the same time critical and questionable for the results of the model.

The author cites no evidence to support this assumption. The reader naturally thinks of counterhypotheticals. There are probably many social settings in which the majority of citizens are likely to be law-abiding even with low levels of law enforcement and/or accuracy. The vast literature on lawmaking and norm internalization (Carbonara, Parisi, and von Wangenheim 2008), expressive law (Cooter 1998), and focal-point theory of law (McAdams 2000) provides ample foundations for such counterhypotheticals. There could also be other social settings with opposite dynamics in which we could observe a majority of law offenders even with high levels of enforcement and accuracy. The literature on the backlash effect of legal enforcement (Depoorter, Parisi, and Svanneste 2005) and countervailing norms (Carbonara, Parisi, and von Wangenheim 2012) provides numerous examples in which human behavior could lead to such counterhypotheticals. In both situations considered earlier, the core assumption of Obidzinski (2019) would not hold, and the main results cited in her article, as motivated to explain the findings of Lin (2007) and McCannon (2013), would implode.

Obidzinski's (2019) article could indeed be enriched by relaxing the initial assumption and more transparently unveiling the additional results of the model when the two counterhypothetical scenarios are considered. What would be the political equilibrium generated by political competition when a majority of the population is law-abiding even with low levels of enforcement and accuracy? And what would be the political equilibrium generated by political competition when the majority of the population might be offenders even with high levels of enforcement and accuracy? These extensions of the model would likely generate results that do not support the empirical findings of Lin (2007) and McCannon (2013) and would entail the need to engage in empirical testing of Obidzinski's model in social environments characterized by different proportions of law abiders and law offenders.

3. OTHER CONSIDERATIONS

As it is often the case, the results of a theory article hinge on a stylized model that explicitly or implicitly assumes away several elements of reality. In the following, I point to some of the elements that I think should be considered in future work on this subject to develop a more complete understanding of the behavior of elected actors of the criminal justice system under political competition.

Time Lag: Type I versus Type II Errors

A time lag occurs between the initial conviction of a criminal and a possible reversal on appeal. If political elections happen between these two moments, political players would get the immediate payoff from the criminal convictions (for both small crimes and big crimes) and only partially internalize the future cost of possible future reversals on appeals.

Ceteris paribus, this should lead to a drift toward more type I errors (false convictions) shortly before elections. This should further lead to an asymmetric enforcement and accuracy with a changing ratio of type I and type II errors under political competition. McCannon's (2013) data do not provide enough information to test this hypothesis because (false) acquittals are not generally appealed and type II errors are therefore not measurable in the manner of McCannon (2013).

Deterrence—Time Elasticity of Offenders' Reaction

The model implicitly assumes that all criminals react to changes in enforcement and accuracy in the same way and with the same speed. But this may not be the case. The model and the underlying narrative seem to overlook the different time elasticities of offenders' reaction. Small and large criminals may react differently to changes in enforcement and accuracy. For example, it may be the case that small offenders adjust more rapidly to changes in enforcement and/or accuracy. This may be because of the greater opportunities they have to revert back to noncriminal living. Likewise, it may be the case that violent criminals and other big offenders have a slower speed of adjustment to changes in enforcement and/or accuracy. If that is the case, the effect of accuracy on deterrence will not be uniform across types of crimes, and accuracy and deterrence will no longer be necessarily correlated as Obidzinski's electoral model requires.

Opening the Enforcement Box: Who Is the Producer of Accuracy?

Who are the criminal process actors who are influenced by political competition? The previous empirical literature looks at various players in the criminal justice system, ranging from the role of police (Levitt 1997) and prosecutors (McCannon 2013) to judges (Lin 2007).

Obidzinski's model does not openly explain how accuracy in criminal justice is effectively produced. Overturning a decision on appeal is detrimental for the reputation of the prosecutor as well as the trial judge who issued the decision, as it sends a negative signal of quality that may compromise future elections. The increase in accuracy under political competition may thus be driven by reputational reasons that are independent from the law-abiding proportions of the electorate. Relevant criminal justice players may invest greater resources to avoid negative signals in high-visibility cases under political competition. Hence, accuracy increases for big crimes or more sensitive crimes relative to small crimes, as shown respectively by McCannon (2013, 2019).

The model could also be extended to consider the natural trade-offs between quality and quantity in law enforcement. Greater levels of accuracy in criminal justice come at a cost. In the short term, if constraints in the criminal justice system (e.g., workforce size) are exogenously set, greater quality can only be achieved at the expense of lower quantity. This may likely materialize as a trade-off between accuracy and filing rates as observed by McCannon (2019), who showed a reduction in the volume of filings prior to elections for rape cases.

Given that trade-off—namely, accuracy versus filing rates—greater accuracy may not necessarily lead to greater deterrence, as Obidzinski's (2019) model assumes. The driving force of Obidzinski's model of elected criminal justice actors targeting the voter's preference for greater deterrence would no longer explain the rise in accuracy under political competition.

4. MODEL VERSUS REALITY—MOVING FORWARD

Journal editors and reviewers of law and economic articles occasionally have easy decisions to make when evaluating submissions. They occasionally come across submissions with (maybe, beautiful) models in the search for a legal application. Those submissions are easy rejections, as there is nothing that can be learned from those virtuous technical exercises. In other instances, they come across submissions with (maybe, less beautiful) models that explain a legal reality. There is something that can be learned from those articles. The article by Marie Obidzinski (2019) falls in the latter category as the development of an elegant model that provides a valuable building block toward understanding the changes triggered by political competition on the criminal justice system.

As suggested by my comments, the model is stylized and the assumptions are restrictive, and as such the article cannot provide a definitive explanation of the evidence discussed by Lin (2007) and McCannon (2013). There are alternative theories and models that can explain those same empirical findings. But that is often the case. More often than not, there is more than one plausible theoretical explanation of a single factual reality. Obidzinski's (2019) theoretical model provides a plausible explanation of the empirical evidence at hand, but further theoretical extensions and empirical research should be encouraged to foster a deeper understanding of this important building block in the political economy of criminal justice.

REFERENCES

Becker, Gary S. 1968. "Crime and Punishment: An Economic Approach." *Journal of Political Economy* 76:169–217.

Carbonara, Emanuela, Francesco Parisi, and Georg von Wangenheim. 2008. "Lawmakers as Norm Entrepreneurs." *Review of Law and Economics* 4:779–99.

———. 2012. "Unjust Laws and Illegal Norms." *International Review of Law and Economics* 32:285–99.

Cooter, Robert D. 1998. "Expressive Law and Economics." *Journal of Legal Studies* 27:585–608.

Depoorter, B., F. Parisi, and S. Svanneste. 2005. "Problems with the Enforcement of Copyright Law: Is There a Social Norm Backlash?" *International Journal of the Economics of Business* 12:361–69.

Levitt, Steven D. 1997. "Using Electoral Cycle in Police Hiring to Estimate the Effect of Police on Crime." *American Economic Review* 87 (June): 270–90.

Lin, Ming-Jen. 2007. "Does Democracy Increase Crime? The Evidence from International Data." *Journal of Comparative Economics* 35 (3): 467–83.

McAdams, Richard H. 2000. "A Focal Point Theory of Expressive Law." *Virginia Law Review* 86:1649–729.

McCannon, Bryan C. 2013. "Prosecutor Elections, Mistakes, and Appeals." *Journal of Empirical Legal Studies* 10 (4): 696–714.

———. 2019. "'A Million Dollars in Free Advertising': Politics and Sex Offense Prosecution in the Wake of Duke Lacrosse." *Supreme Court Economic Review* 27:167–88.

Obidzinski, Marie. 2019. "Accuracy in Public Law Enforcement under Political Competition." *Supreme Court Economic Review* 27: 195–212.